10/82

2|⁰⁰

1⁵⁰

7⁵⁰

The Family in Past Time

Garland Reference Library of Social Science (Vol. 32)

The Family in Past Time
A Guide to the Literature

James Wallace Milden

Garland Publishing, Inc., New York & London

1977

Copyright © 1977
by James Wallace Milden

All Rights Reserved

Library of Congress Cataloging in Publication Data

Milden, James Wallace.
  The family in past time.

  (Garland reference library of social science ; v. 32)
  Includes index.
  1. Family research--Historiography--Bibliography.
I. Title.
Z5118.F2M54   [HQ503]   016.907'2   76-24767
ISBN 0-8240-9910-9

Contents

Preface

This book is the product of a personal and scholarly interest in family history and of the recognition that the field is at present in dire need of bibliographical control. While the term "family history" is frequently associated with genealogy and heraldry, its use in this volume refers not to studies of individual or influential families, but to the growing body of literature dealing with the social history of the family and the family life of ordinary people in past time. Sparked by the belief that the family is important to the understanding of past social behavior, historians, sociologists, and other social scientists have recently begun to re-examine the history of the family. This renewed interest has been accompanied by an outpouring of literature in family history. The need to systematize and provide quick access to these materials has now become imperative.

The intent of this volume is to provide students, scholars, genealogists, and librarians with a comprehensive, accurate, and current sourcebook to the secondary and theoretical literature in historical family studies. The scope is worldwide, although time and space limitations have restricted the bibliography to English-language citations. With few notable exceptions, the entries included were written prior to December 31, 1975. In addition to books and articles, the bibliography contains unpublished papers and theses. For quick reference, these citations are annotated and arranged geographically, chronologically, and topically. Within each subcategory entries are listed alphabetically by author and include bibliographical data. An author index provides an additional access point to the literature.

This guide also has several noteworthy features. For the nonspecialist, the introductory essay presents a brief overview of family history, its significance and development as a scholarly endeavor, and areas of needed research. It is designed to acquaint the general reader with the organization and

PREFACE

parameters of the field. The first chapter, of interest to both specialist and nonspecialist, lists entries whose inter-disciplinary, methodological, or theoretical approach is important to the history of the family. For those interested in writing their family history or using family biographies as a teaching strategy, the final chapter on family history projects will prove a useful guide to the source materials. Also included in this section are basic reference sources for genealogical research.

Many debts were incurred in the compilation of this bibliography. I am especially grateful to Sally Franklin and Connie Coy for their assistance in the preparation of the manuscript. This book would have been impossible without the help and cooperation of Diane Cotter and the Interlibrary Loan staff at the University of Wisconsin-Milwaukee Library. To them I express my sincere gratitude. I owe my greatest debt to my wife, Rosalie Jean, whose criticism, understanding, and love were invaluable in the completion of this project.

An Introduction to Family History

Family history was reborn in the 1960s. Apart from several studies written by early twentieth-century sociologists tracing the progressive evolution of the family as an institution, a handful of popular accounts, and individual genealogies of eminent or powerful families, scholars have generally ignored the family in history, its interaction with the social order, and its transformation through time. But the 1960s witnessed an unprecedented upsurge of interest in the history of the family. Academic circles have now recognized family studies as a significant mode of historical, psychological, and sociological inquiry. Not only have courses dealing with family history sprung up on many college campuses, but on the popular level as well genealogy has become one of the nation's most-pursued hobbies, and publications dealing with the history of the family have multiplied severalfold during the past decade. While the recent burgeoning of family history cannot be denied, the reasons for this activity remain less clear.

I

Interest in family history is, of course, as old as man himself. From time immemorial man has pondered his origins, his place in history, and his family heritage. What distinguishes the recent resurgence of family history is the changed character of its practitioners and their perspective of the family in past time. Whereas family history formerly remained in the hands of genealogists who spent countless hours in musty archives diligently researching the ancestral origins of wealthy or influential families, the contemporary thrust stems from social scientists—primarily historians, demographers, and sociologists—who are investigating the subject in growing proportions and with increasingly sophisticated research tools. As social scientists have moved into the field, the emphasis has shifted from the reconstitution of a single family to the demographic analysis of a multitude of families over time, from tracing a family backward in time to analyzing the changing individual and family life cycle through time. This is not to imply that our dogged genealogist has been cast aside. Rather, social scientists have mined the rich sources of genealogy in an attempt to understand the dynamics of family life among all segments of society in past time.

To achieve their goals, these social scientists have brought to family history theories, models, and methodologies from several disciplines as well as techniques in quantitative and computerized data analysis. The latter has resulted in ever larger and more complex studies of the family in history and has permitted the use of new and potentially rich source materials such as vital statistics and census schedules. Rather than reconstructing the history of one family, family historians now attempt to recreate the collective biography of all families of a given ethnic or economic group or in a particular community. This shift in perspective from the individual to the many, from the unique to the normative, has altered significantly the character of historical family studies. The revival of family history in the sixties thus marked a trend towards both complexity and generality. It marked a renewed interest in the family life of the common people and a conviction that demographic configurations ultimately shape the course of history itself.

Not all recent scholars have approached family history through quantitative techniques. Others—notably cultural historians—have maintained that values and beliefs concerning family life in the past are as important as family structure and fertility differentials. These individuals have begun to investigate popular materials such as child-rearing or marriage manuals, best-selling novels, and even domestic architecture, searching for clues about the concerns and convictions of the masses. Also rejecting the quantitative mode is another group of scholars—the psychohistorians—who have thus far played a relatively minor role in family history. These individuals underscore the relationship between child-rearing and cultural values, between personality change and alterations in family structure, and advocate approaching the family as a psychological experience. Despite their dissimilarities in methodology, however, the cultural historians, the psychohistorians, and the quantifiers all agree that the family's role in history has long been neglected.

Why did historians and other social scientists of the 1960s suddenly become attracted to family history? There are several reasons—all interrelated. The greatest impetus came from a reorientation within the historical profession itself, that is, the growing inclusion by historians of groups traditionally forgotten or ignored. This rediscovery of the common people and minorities laid the underpinnings for what has now been termed the "new social history," of which family history is but one important branch. The younger historians of the 1960s, imbued with the egalitarian and grass-roots sentiments of the decade, became increasingly dissatisfied with history defined as the study of great events and past politics. To this younger generation, history assumed a wider dimension and encompassed a broader spectrum of experiences. It was now defined as the examination of all people in past time and their everyday life, aspirations, and frustrations. This concept of history implied going beyond the social experiences of the articulate, male elite and re-examining history "from the bottom up." This shift in viewpoint fostered an interest in the history of women, children, Blacks, the poor, ethnics, and, most important for our purposes, the family.

Yet studying the history of groups formerly obliterated by traditional historiography necessitated new techniques of historical analysis, techniques that not only addressed themselves to the new questions posed by historians, but that also lent themselves to the analysis of an entirely different set of historical records. Many historians thus drew upon a technique first introduced in the profession in the late nineteenth century: quantitative analysis. The reliance on a statistical approach was not a revitalization of scientific history but a recognition that the problems and questions inherent in the new source materials—be they census schedules, parish records, or records of vital events—could best be answered by quantification. Other historians, displeased with quantitative analysis, sought their answers in psychological or anthropological models. All

INTRODUCTION

wished to make history more "scientific" and to restore its former camaraderie with the social sciences.

The search by historians for sociological and psychological modes of explanation and the stress placed on a behavioral approach to historical analysis heralded the acceptance by the historical profession of interdisciplinary inquiry. Since family history is inescapably interdisciplinary, this acceptance was necessary before the field could make significant advances. The developing fields of psychohistory, historical demography, historical sociology, and historical anthropology stimulated new interest in the history of the family and provided exciting and suggestive approaches to family studies research. Further prompting came with the willingness of large grant-giving institutions and agencies to finance both interdisciplinary-oriented research and large-scale social history projects that purportedly promised to "scientize" history. Many of these projects—the Philadelphia Social History Project at the University of Pennsylvania and the Canadian Social History Project at the Ontario Institute for Studies in Education are the best known—were directly concerned with family structure and composition, family and individual life cycles, and residential patterns. Equally important was their intention to describe the family life and social behavior of common people, not the literate elite.

The youth movements and the renascence of new feminism in the sixties also created an interest in family history by demonstrating that adolescents and women are historical forces with distinctive histories and experiences apart from, yet intertwined with, those of adult or male society. Accompanying the growing concern with sex roles and woman's historical position in the economic and social structure was a re-examination of the historical role of the family in the traditional subordination of women. Although such analyses have occasionally sparked repudiations of traditional familial living arrangements, their importance lies in their recognition that many of the ills plaguing contemporary family life have deep historical roots and that identifying and explaining the source of such ills is an important first step towards their solution.

Historians' embracing of social science techniques, the

growing acceptance of interdisciplinary studies, and the desire of historians to write the history of all segments of the population have made family history a respectable historical endeavor. Family studies has been further legitimated by academic conferences, a newsletter and a recent scholarly journal, workshops and summer institutes, and the promising Anonymous Families History Project. Together with the proliferation of books and articles, these programs and projects have provided a forum for and facilitated information flow and exchange among scholars in the field. But family history has not been restricted to scholarly or genealogical circles; it has penetrated educational systems at several levels. Students, from secondary school through graduate school, have become involved in the field through participation in family history projects where they write family biographies and examine the relationships among their families, social forces, and cultural change. And the use of family biographies as a teaching strategy and as a means of approaching grass-roots history has accelerated considerably in recent years. As a result of this expanded activity, family history has now been accorded an unprecedented importance and esteem by academics as well as the general public.

II

Family history, as currently practiced, suffers from several serious shortcomings. One major problem has been the uncritical acceptance of grand theories of familial change or the modification of existing theories without questioning assumptions or examining historical evidence. Until recently, for example, many individuals involved in family history assumed that the family had undergone significant structural changes over time, that it had evolved from the pre-industrial, extended family of three generations in one household to the two-generational nuclear form characteristic of most industrialized societies. Concurrent with this assumption was the belief that the extended family generated closer intergenerational relationships and was thus more personally satisfying than its nucleated descendant. The family through time, according to this theory, begins as an integrated social institution, but undergoes the process of disintegration and differentiation. And invariably this erosion of familial cohesiveness is linked to modernization.

While the theme of order giving way to disorder makes dramatic reading, its basis in social reality is highly questionable. For one thing, European historians have already shown that the nuclear family has been the predominant familial form in Western Civilization from at least the sixteenth century, although their findings may be somewhat exaggerated due to their failure to consider family life cycle. Furthermore, to envisage the family as a dependent variable that responds to socio-economic oscillations but has no creative ability of its own is to oversimplify grossly the family's role in society. That the family deeply colors its members' belief systems and perceptions of reality and may in fact have prepared the ground psychologically for the advent of modernization are as-yet-unresolved matters requiring serious investigation. Family change may in fact be highly independent of larger social forces or economic transitions. And finally, to posit a theory of family change based exclusively on a structural-functional approach eschews a more fundamental issue: the influence of family life on personality formation. As psychiatrist Ronald D. Laing has suggested, the family is an emotional and psychological unit that may or may not coincide with legal or social definitions of the family. Individuals are born into a family and create their own families, but during their life cycle the form of the family may vary significantly because of birth, death, marriage, or other socio-economic variables. The family is thus a constantly shifting experience for its members. Exactly how the family has shaped its members' personalities over time is a thorny but paramount question in family studies.

Another problem area of family history is the absence of comparative analysis, although serious attempts are now underway to rectify this problem. Failure to make cross-cultural comparisons has led several historians to arrive at sweeping interpretations later proven incorrect with comparable data—historian Bernard Bailyn's application of structural differentiation theory to the colonial American family provides an excellent example. A comparative perspective is essential before we can differentiate clearly between the features of an American and a Chinese family, an urban and a rural family, or between families of different economic levels. Comparative studies also demand standardized definitions and methodologies, needs addressed only recently by scholars. Until these problems are resolved, generalizing about family history in even the smallest geographical or social unit will be exceedingly difficult. Comparative analysis is important, too, to determine the representativeness of the many micro-studies currently comprising the bulk of family studies research.

Other problems in family history arise when scholars apply to historical situations modes of explanation derived from the social sciences. Since the avowed intent of these disciplines is the study of present rather than past conditions, applying their theories to historical circumstances immediately raises questions of validity and relevance. This is especially true of modernization theory—originally used by sociologists to describe the evolution of underdeveloped countries and now enjoying a vogue among family scholars. But the reliance on social science models has also been family history's most innovative and noteworthy contribution to historical knowledge.

From sociology family scholars have borrowed the model of structural differentiation, a model that has remained essentially unchanged since the turn of the century. Concerned with structural adaptability, this theory maintains that as a society develops, its social structure and institutions become more complex and specialized. Consequently, the functions of these older institutions are assumed by newer, specialized ones. In the case of the family, social development has produced a shift from a multifunctional, integrated familial structure (usually referred to as the "traditional" or "pre-industrial" family) to a nucleated structure which is socially isolated and has surrendered formerly held functions—economic, educational, and so on—to newly created social institutions and agencies. Many aspects of this theory, however, are debatable, including the existence of the family as traditionally defined, the belief that the modern family is isolated in terms of kin relations, and the positing of a causal relationship between the family and economic transformations. Also implied in the structural differentiation model is the equation of structural change with family disorganization. But the family's influence in society and its control over its members may be unrelated to structural shifts.

Although structural differentiation has serious problems as a mode of explanation in family history, other sociological contributions have had immense value. This is particularly true of the family life cycle approach. Analyzing the family in terms of life cycle or a series of developing stages has been a part of sociological theory since the 1950s but did not command the attention of family historians until the 1970s. The concept of family life cycle offers a developmental or dynamic model of domestic life that supplements the snap-shot technique of cross-sectional analysis. Yet despite its obvious importance, little research has been completed to document changes in family cycle through time.

Examining the family as process is related closely to the techniques developed by historical demographers to analyze the demographic experience of a group or generation through its life cycle. It was this reliance on longitudinal or cohort analysis that signaled both the break of demographic history from traditional demography and the convergence of demography and family history. Under the leadership of French demographer Louis Henry, demographic historians began to compile and link demographic statistics by individual families for successive generations. Taken collectively, such data have made it possible to "reconstitute" the family experiences of common people. Besides family reconstitution, historical demographers have used aggregate analysis—the examination of the vital statistics of a particular community over time—to discern historical trends in fertility, mortality, age at marriage, pre-marital conceptions, and birth control. Both family reconstitution and aggregate analysis have added an important new dimension—the demographic perspective— to historical family studies.

Family historians have turned to the theories and models of psychology and anthropology markedly less than to those of sociology and demography. The reason for this lies, in large measure, in the abstractness and presentism of psychological theory and in the difficulty involved in linking family, personality patterns, and cultural configurations over time. The developmental model of psychologist Erik H. Erikson—a model that presumes that psychic development accompanies physical and mental maturation—is the approach most employed in psychologically oriented family studies. But Lloyd deMause's recent advocacy of a "psychogenic" theory of history, which posits ever closer parent-child relationships and improvements in child care with time, promises to make a significant contribution to the history of childhood and the family. Family historians also need to examine the psychological implications of privacy and the use of space within the household; how the concepts of childhood and aging are related to family experience; how the family shapes individual behavior, sex roles, and work patterns; and how the family acts upon and is acted upon by its culture. Here the anthropological stress on comparative analysis and on the linkage between child nurture and culture may prove useful.

Despite their enormous contribution to historical family studies, the social sciences have not solved family history's most pressing problem: periodization. We know that the family has undergone change, albeit exceedingly slowly, but categorizing and explaining that change have proven to be formidable tasks. The periodization model presently receiving the greatest attention from family historians, and the one used to organize this bibliography, is the theory of demographic transition. According to this hypothesis, pre-industrial populations experienced slow population growth because of high birth and mortality rates. With the onset of industrialization, the death rate fell for a number of reasons while fertility remained high. As economic growth continued, the birth rate dropped, and the rate of population growth subsequently declined to its former low level. This theory thus posits an interaction between economic resources and demographic behavior. Although coming under sharp criticism in recent years, and rightly so, the theory of demographic transition provides family history with a convenient framework upon which to test hypotheses and to build a coherent body of knowledge. This structure will doubtless be drastically modified as evidence is collected and synthesized, but its formulation marks a significant beginning towards an understanding of the sequence and patterns of the family in past time.

III

For the student who wishes up-to-date information about conferences, books, methodological problems, and current research in the field, the *Family in Historical Perspective: An International Newsletter* (1972-) is an excellent starting point. Beginning in September 1976, this newsletter will be replaced with the *Journal of Family History*, a periodical with a decidedly sociological bent towards family history. The *History of Childhood Quarterly* (1973-), on the other hand, contains articles and reviews concerned with the psychological dimension of family studies. Methodological and theoretical discussions are also found in the *Historical Methods Newsletter* (1967-), a serial devoted to the application of social science techniques to historical analysis, and in the British publication *Local Population Studies* (1968-), a periodical concerned with demographic history and problems encountered in the population analysis of communities and parishes in England. Another useful guide to recent books and articles in family history is *Population Index* (1935-), although this indexing service contains entries with a primarily demographic emphasis. Several journals have also devoted entire issues to the history of the family and these are listed in the bibliography below.

Other serious attempts have been made to define, organize, and structure the field. Under the able guidance of Richard Jensen, the Family and Community History Program at the Newberry Library in Chicago offers an intensive summer training program in demographic history, census analysis, and quantitative techniques. At Princeton University, the subject of the Shelby Cullom Davis Center for Historical Studies for 1976-1978 is the history of the family, and the Center plans to offer several seminars to researchers in the field. Another active program in family history is sponsored by Clark University and the American Antiquarian Society; it consists of research seminars, post-doctoral fellowships, and conferences and colloquia. To promote an interdisciplinary approach to historical family studies, Boston State College has established a Center of Family Studies. This Center is presently collecting manuscripts, paintings, and artifacts dealing with family life in America and England.

Much of the American interest in family history stems from an earlier French and English preoccupation with the subject. In England, the program and activities of the Cambridge Group for the Study of Population and Social Structure have been instrumental in the promotion of family reconstitution and aggregate analysis of English parishes prior to the mid-nineteenth century. One of the Group's principal concerns has been family structure, particularly the prevalence of nuclear families in pre-industrial societies. The French, however, were the real pioneers in historical demography. The French demographer Louis Henry and his followers originated and perfected the techniques of family reconstitution and have already reconstructed the demographic experience of numerous French villages prior to industrialization. These techniques have in turn been adopted by scholars worldwide.

As our discussion has indicated, the future of family history looks promising and prosperous. With the publication of this bibliographical guide, the past accomplishments, present trends, and future needs of the field should become readily discernible. Organizing and providing ready access to the literature of any new field, particularly an interdisciplinary one such as family history, are indeed formidable tasks, but are necessary for the legitimation and development of that field. This reference guide will, I hope, mark a milestone in the historical study of the family and help to stimulate further activity and research in the field.

CHAPTER I:

METHODOLOGY AND THEORY

GENERAL

1. ARMENS, Sven M. Archetypes of the Family in Literature.
    Seattle: Univ. of Washington Press, 1966.
    Examines literary depictions of the parent-child relation-
    ship, especially the conflict between patriarchal demands
    and matriarchal nurture.

2. AXELSON, Leland J. "Promise or Illusion: The Future of
    Family Studies." The Family Coordinator, 24 (1975),
    3-6.
    Explores the present state of family studies, its rela-
    tionship to traditional disciplines, and offers suggestions
    for its development in the future.

3. BARDIS, Panos D. "Synopsis and Evaluation of Theories
    Concerning Family Evolution." Social Science, 38 (1963),
    42-52.
    Summarizes the varying theories of family evolution es-
    poused by early social scientists, and dismisses unilinear
    evolutionary theories as deficient and unproven hypotheses.

4. BULLOUGH, Vern L. "Sex History: A Virgin Field." Journal
    of Sex Research, 8 (1972), 101-16.
    Deals with the failure of historians to do research on the
    sexual behavior of man, and cites examples of bad existing
    histories of sexuality.

5. BURGESS, Ernest, et. al. The Family: From Institution
    to Companionship. 3rd ed. New York: American Book Co.,
    1963.
    Argues that the family has been in transition from an in-
    stitutional to a companionship form, a result of urban-
    ization, mobility, individualism, and changing family life
    cycle.

6. BURNHAM, John C. "American Historians and the Subject of
    Sex." Societas, 2 (1972), 307-16.
    Observes that few historians have examined sexual matters
    and that existing studies are fragmentary and incomplete.
    Advocates new studies incorporating sex into cultural his-
    tory.

7. CERNY, Vera, et. al. "International Development in Family
    Theory: A Continuance of the Initial Pilgrim's Progress."
    Journal of Marriage and the Family, 36 (1974), 169-84.
    Assesses family literature published internationally be-
    tween 1962 and 1970 in an attempt to measure future devel-
    opments and trends in family theory.

8.   CHRISTENSEN, Harold T.   "Development of the Family Field of
     Study." Handbook of Marriage and the Family. Ed. Harold
     T. Christensen. Chicago: Rand McNally, 1964, pp. 3-32.
     Reviews the development and orientations of family research
     from the mid-19th century to the present, emphasizing the
     growing acceptance of a scientific viewpoint, and notes
     areas for future research.

9.   CREMIN, Lawrence.   "The Family as Educator: Some Comments
     on the Recent Historiography." Teachers College Record,
     76 (1974), 251-65.
     Examines the family as a subject of historical investigation
     and, noting that few scholars have addressed the family in
     terms of education, suggests ways to approach the family as
     educator.

10. ENGELS, Frederick.   The Origin of the Family, Private Prop-
     erty and the State. 1884; rpt. New York: International
     Publishers, 1972.
     Illustrates the historical materialistic theory of social
     development borrowed from anthropologist Lewis H. Morgan.
     A good introduction to a Marxist interpretation of family
     history.

11. GOODE, William Josiah.   "The Theory and Measurement of Fam-
     ily Change." Indicators of Social Change: Concepts and
     Measurements. Ed. Eleanor Bernert Sheldon and Wilbert
     E. Moore. New York: Russell Sage Foundation, 1968, pp.
     295-348.
     Discusses theories of family change, types of problems in
     family change, the units observed, the uses of historical
     data, and trends in family change analysis.

12. GOODE, William Josiah.   World Revolution and Family Patterns.
     Glencoe, Ill.: Free Press, 1963.
     Contends that most family systems of the world are moving
     toward a conjugal system and that no family system may be
     called nuclear.

13. GOODY, John Rankin.   "The Evolution of the Family." House-
     hold and Family in Past Time. Ed. Peter Laslett and
     Richard Wall. Cambridge: Cambridge Univ. Press, 1972,
     pp. 103-24.
     Discusses the issues involved in dealing with family change,
     places these issues in a comparative framework, and concludes
     that the farm family in preindustrial societies needs more
     attention.

14. HAMMEL, Eugene A., and Peter LASLETT.   "Comparing Household
     Structure Over Time and Between Cultures." Comparative
     Studies in Society and History, 16 (1974), 73-109.
     Discusses ways of recording and analyzing household structure
     in past time to make comparative analysis possible, with
     emphasis on social anthropological methods of recording kin
     relations and computerized coding and analysis.

2

15. HAREVEN, Tamara K. "Evolution of Studies of the Social History of the Family." Paper delivered at the Society for the Study of Social Problems, New York, August 1973.

16. HAREVEN, Tamara K. "The History of the Family as an Interdisciplinary Field." Journal of Interdisciplinary History, 2 (1971), 399-414.
Observes that family history is an interdisciplinary field which draws on the models and methodologies of demography, sociology, anthropology, and psychology. Argues that the fundamental issue of family history is the interaction between the family and social change.

17. HAREVEN, Tamara K. "Introduction: The Historical Study of the Family in Urban Society." Journal of Urban History, 1 (1975), 259-67.
Argues that urban historians have ignored the relationship between social and spatial mobility, economic behavior, education, and the family; nor have they adopted a comparative perspective to determine the distinctiveness of urban patterns.

18. HAYS, Samuel P. "History and the Changing University Curriculum." History Teacher, 8 (1974), 64-72.
Advocates the development of a history curriculum based on shared patterns of experience and values of people in history and changes in different life-settings over time. One such approach is the history of the family.

19. HILL, Reuben, and Donald A. HANSEN. "The Identification of Conceptual Frameworks Utilized in Family Study." Marriage and Family Living, 22 (1960), 299-311.
Identifies the competing approaches--interactional, structural-functional, situational, institutional, and developmental--to family study and discusses the problems inherent in each.

20. JEFFREY, Kirk. "Varieties of Family History." The American Archivist, 38 (1975), 521-32.
Discusses the trends in family history research, and interprets the broad schools of thought in American family history, notably the differences and similarities between the cultural and quantitative family historians.

21. JENSEN, Richard. "Archives and Ancestors: The Study of the American Family." Paper delivered at the Society of American Archivists, San Francisco, December 1973.
Examines the demands that family history will place on America's archives, especially in the areas of data storage, retrieval, and linkage, and calls for close cooperation between genealogists, archivists, and family historians.

22. JENSEN, Richard. "Quantitative American Studies: The State of the Art." American Quarterly, 26 (1974), 225-40.
Surveys excellently the trends, problems, and major studies

in quantitative history as well as comments on the future
prospects of quantitative American Studies.

23. LASCH, Christopher. "The Family and History." New York
    Review of Books, November 13, 1975, pp. 33-8; November
    27, 1975, pp. 37-42; December 11, 1975, pp. 50-4.
    Offers a perceptive, and at times scathing critique of the
    assumptions and methodology of recent studies in family
    history. Argues that family historians should begin with
    the relationship between the family and the psychic devas-
    tation of modern society.

24. LASLETT, Peter. "Historical and Regional Variations in
    Great Britain." Quantitative Ecological Analysis in
    the Social Sciences. Ed. Mattei Dogan and Stein Rokkan.
    Cambridge: M.I.T. Press, 1969, pp. 507-18.
    Discusses the program of the Cambridge Group, the research
    techniques used and variables studied, and the future di-
    rection and activities of the Cambridge Group.

25. LASLETT, Peter. "The History of Population and Social
    Structure." International Social Science Journal, 17
    (1965), 582-94.
    Discusses parish registers, census materials, and problems
    of demographic analysis and reconstruction of social struc-
    ture currently engaged in by the Cambridge Group. Notes
    that the nuclear family is not a product of modernization.

26. MODELL, John. "Economic Dimensions of Household Organ-
    ization." Paper delivered at the American Studies
    Association, San Francisco, October 1973.
    Emphasizes the close connection between the family and
    economic matters, and speculates how "environing condi-
    tions" have historically affected various aspects of fam-
    ily economics such as income, consumption, wealth, and
    non-pecuinary functions.

27. MOGEY, J. M. "Contribution of Frederic Le Play to Family
    Research." Marriage and Family Living, 17 (1955),
    310-15.
    Examines Le Play's background and his desire as a social
    reformer to restore harmony to society by returning to the
    patriarchal family.

28. OPLER, Marvin K. "History of the Family as a Social and
    Cultural Institution." The Family in Contemporary
    Society. Ed. Iago Galdston. New York: International
    Univ. Press, 1958, pp. 23-38.
    Argues that the family and its relationships are the pro-
    duct of its social and cultural context and thus are flex-
    ible, not rigidly defined.

29. RUSSO, David J. Families and Communities: A New View of
    American History. Nashville: American Association for
    State and Local History, 1974.

4

Argues that instead of maintaining a national perspective, historians should use as their organizing principle the study of the individual, the family, and the levels of communities they have lived in.

30. SAVETH, Edward Norman. "The Problems of American Family History." _American Quarterly_, 21 (1969), 311-29.
Reviews the state of family history in the mid-1960s. Discusses problems of sources, theory formulation, periodization, subjectivism, quantification, and family-society interrelationships.

31. SKOLNICK, Arlene. "The Family Revisited: Themes in Recent Social Science Research." _Journal of Interdisciplinary History_, 5 (1975), 703-19.
Shows that research in the social sciences has recently challenged prevailing ideas and assumptions about family systems, parenthood, family-society relationships, socialization, family conflict, and family interaction. A good introduction to current trends in family studies research.

ANTHOLOGIES

32. DE MAUSE, Lloyd, ed. _The History of Childhood_. New York: Psychohistory Press, 1974.
The best anthology to date on childhood studies and psychohistory. Contains articles which examine various historical and theoretical aspects of childhood in the United States and Europe.

33. FORSTER, Robert, and Orest RANUM, eds. _Biology of Man in History: Selections from the Annales_. Baltimore: Johns Hopkins Univ. Press, 1975.
Contains essays dealing with marriage, birth control, diet and famine, disease, and purchasing power in medieval and 18th-century Europe.

34. FORSTER, Robert, and Orest RANUM, eds. _Family and Society: Selections from the Annales_. Baltimore: Johns Hopkins Univ. Press, 1976.
Contains articles dealing with many aspects of family life in Europe from the Roman Empire to the 18th century.

35. GLASS, David Victor, and D.E.C. EVERSLEY, eds. _Population in History: Essays in Historical Demography_. Chicago: Aldine Publishing Co., 1965.
Includes articles on the history of population in the West since the 17th century.

36. GLASS, David Victor, and Roger REVELLE, eds. _Population and Social Change_. New York: Grane, Russak, 1972.
An anthology of papers presented at two international conferences on population studies in history, emphasizing Western Europe. A reprint of the Spring 1968 issue of _Daedalus_.

37. GORDON, Michael, ed. The American Family in Socio-Histor-
        ical Perspective. New York: St. Martin's Press, 1973.
     A good anthology with an excellent introductory survey of
     the development of family history and methodology, the
     meaning of modernization, and the application of modern-
     ization theory to family studies.

38. LASLETT, Peter, and Richard WALL, eds. Household and
        Family in Past Time. Cambridge: Cambridge Univ.
        Press, 1972.
     A good anthology of essays focusing primarily on house-
     hold structure and composition in historical perspective.
     The introductory essay argues that the central issue of
     family history is whether family form is influential in
     human development and related to socio-economic changes.

39. ROSENBERG, Charles E., ed. The Family in History. Phila-
        delphia: Univ. of Pennsylvania Press, 1975.
     Contains excellent essays and a suggestive introduction
     outlining an approach to past social reality based on the
     reconstruction of social options.

40. ROTBERG, Robert I., and Theodore K. RABB, eds. The Family
        in History: Interdisciplinary Essays. New York: Har-
        per & Row, 1973.
     Contains excellent articles dealing with theoretical and
     methodological issues of family history. A reprint of the
     special issue of the Journal of Interdisciplinary History
     on the history of the family, originally published in
     Autumn 1971.

41. SCIENTIFIC AMERICAN EDITORS. The Human Population: A
        Scientific American Book. San Francisco: W.H. Freeman,
        1974.
     A reprint of the September 1974 issue of Scientific Amer-
     ican which deals with the history of population, repro-
     duction and genetics, migration, mortality, population
     growth, and the status of women.

42. WRIGLEY, Edward Anthony, ed. An Introduction to English
        Historical Demography from the Sixteenth to the Nine-
        teenth Century. New York: Basic Books, 1966.
     An excellent anthology with essays on the sources and
     methods of population history, family reconstitution, and
     social structure.

43. WRIGLEY, Edward Anthony, ed. Nineteenth Century Society:
        Essays in the Use of Quantitative Methods for the Study
        of Social Data. New York: Cambridge Univ. Press, 1972.
     Contains articles which illustrate the difficulties and
     opportunities in 19th-century census analysis, and examines
     data collection methods, accuracy, and techniques in census
     analysis.

BIBLIOGRAPHIES

44. ALDOUS, Joan, and Reuben HILL. <u>International Bibliography</u>
    <u>of Research in Marriage and the Family, 1900-1964</u>.
    Minneapolis: Univ. of Minnesota Press, 1967.
    An interdisciplinary bibliography of some 12,500 scholarly
    publications on marriage and the family with a KWIC index,
    subject index, author index, and periodical index.

45. ALDOUS, Joan, and Nancy DAHL. <u>International Bibliography</u>
    <u>of Research in Marriage and the Family. Vol. II, 1965-</u>
    <u>1972</u>. Minneapolis: Univ. of Minnesota Press, 1974.
    Continues the format of the first volume to 1972, and
    contains some 12,870 entries in English and foreign languages.
    Also includes citations on the historical aspects of the
    family.

46. DAVIS, Lenwood G. <u>The History of Birth Control in the</u>
    <u>United States: A Working Bibliography</u>. Monticello,
    Ill.: Council of Planning Librarians, 1975.
    Lists basic source materials dealing with the history of
    the birth control movement in America.

47. DE MAUSE, Lloyd, et. al., eds. <u>A Bibliography of Psycho-</u>
    <u>history</u>. New York: Garland Publishing, 1975.
    Includes a wide range of entries dealing with theoretical
    models, studies of childhood, mass behavior, and leader-
    ship.

48. FREEDMAN, Ronald. <u>The Sociology of Human Fertility: An</u>
    <u>Annotated Bibliography</u>. New York: Irvington Publishers,
    1975.
    Contains 1657 selected items on human fertility published
    in the English language between 1961 and 1972, including a
    section on historical studies and demographic transition.

49. HOWARD, George Elliot. <u>The Family and Marriage: An Ana-</u>
    <u>lytical Reference Syllabus</u>. Lincoln: Univ. of Nebraska
    Press, 1914.
    Contains the syllabus of a course dealing with the insti-
    tutional development of the family from primitive society
    to the early 20th century. Also includes an excellent biblio-
    graphy of early sources on family history.

50. ISRAEL, Stanley, ed. <u>Bibliography on Divorce</u>. New York:
    Bloch Publishing, 1974.
    Includes lengthy annotations for 150 titles published since
    1940, and lists 370 other titles dealing with the legal,
    sociological, and religious aspects of divorce.

51. LUDLOW, William Linnaeus. <u>A Syllabus and a Bibliography of</u>
    <u>Marriage and the Family</u>. New Concord, Ohio: Radcliffe
    Press, 1951.
    Includes references--most dated--on the origins and evolution
    of the family, particularly the primitive, Hebrew, Roman, and

colonial American family types.

52. MCKENNEY, Mary. Divorce: A Selected Annotated Bibliography. Metuchen, N.J.: Scarecrow Press, 1975. Includes some 600 entries of scholarly and popular interest subdivided into broad subject areas. Limited to United States citations, but includes a short section on divorce outside the United States.

53. SERUYA, Flora C., et. al. Sex and Sex Education: A Bibliography. New York: Bowker Company, 1972. A comprehensive bibliography of books on sexology in all its aspects, organized topically with short annotations. Emphasizes 20th-century titles.

54. SHAW, Robert Kendall. Bibliography of Domestic Economy, in English. Albany: Univ. of the State of New York Press, 1901. Contains citations dealing with the origins and development of home economics. Useful for determining changes in domestic technology.

55. THURSTON, Flora Martha. A Bibliography on Family Relationships. New York: National Council of Parent Education, 1932. Briefly annotates books and articles published primarily between 1928 and 1932 dealing with family relationships, including family history, social changes affecting family life, parent education, family law, and family functions.

POPULATION ANALYSIS

56. BARCLAY, George W. Techniques of Population Analysis. New York: Wiley, 1958. Describes the basic techniques of population analysis, including the life table, mortality, fertility, population growth, and migration. An excellent introductory text to demography.

57. BOGUE, Donald Joseph. Principles of Demography. New York: Wiley, 1969. Discusses demographic principles and theories, and tries to promote the integration of demography with the other social sciences. Includes an excellent discussion of fertility control.

58. DRAKE, Michael. Historical Demography: Problems and Projects. Bletchley: Open Univ. Press, 1974. The second volume of the Open University's course in Historical Data and the Social Sciences. Reviews topics in population and economy, population and society, the demographic crisis, and migration. Also includes exercises and guidelines in historical demography.

8

59. POLLARD, Alfred Hurlstone, et. al. Demographic Techniques.
     Oxford: Pergamon Press, 1974.
     A good, up-to-date introduction to demographic techniques,
     including chapters on testing the accuracy of demographic
     data and estimating demographic measures from incomplete
     data.

60. PRESSAT, Roland. Demographic Analysis: Methods, Results,
     Application. Chicago: Aldine-Atherton, 1972.
     Examines the basic techniques and concepts used in demo-
     graphic analysis, notably fertility and mortality, and
     discusses ably the problems of demographic statistics.

61. SHRYOCK, Henry S., et. al. Methods and Materials of
     Demography. Washington: GPO, 1973.
     A comprehensive cookbook of demographic techniques and
     methods with emphasis on contemporary population analysis.

62. SPENGLER, Joseph John, and Otis Dudley DUNCAN, eds.
     Demographic Analysis: Selected Readings. Glencoe,
     Ill.: Free Press, 1956.
     Includes sixty articles dealing with population growth,
     vital rates, migration, utilization of human resources,
     and regional studies.

DEMOGRAPHIC HISTORY

63. ANDERSON, Michael. "The Study of Family Structure."
     Nineteenth-Century Society. Ed. Edward Anthony Wrigley.
     Cambridge: Cambridge Univ. Press, 1972, pp. 47-81.
     Discusses the principles and techniques involved in study-
     ing family structure in history, especially lower-class
     family structure, and emphasizes the importance of study-
     ing family relationships.

64. BANKS, Joseph Ambrose. "Historical Sociology and the
     Study of Population." Daedalus, 97 (1968), 397-414.
     Compares the research methods of sociologists and histor-
     ians, and contends that both disciplines must be utilized
     when examining population problems in history.

65. BEAVER, Steven E. Demographic Transition Theory Reinter-
     preted: An Application to Recent Natality Trends in
     Latin America. Lexington, Mass.: Lexington Books, 1975.
     Examines the origins and status of the theory of demographic
     transition, reviews research on demographic transition theory
     in European and non-European countries, and advocates a re-
     vised theory. Tests this theory in Latin America.

66. BERKNER, Lutz K. "The Use and Misuse of Census Data for the
     Historical Analysis of Family Structure." Journal of
     Interdisciplinary History, 5 (1975), 721-38.
     Argues that Peter Laslett's conclusions in Household and
     Family in Past Time (1972) have not proven that the

9

nuclear family has existed in most Western societies throughout history.

67. BURCH, Thomas K. "Comparative Family Structure: A Demographic Approach." Estadistica, 26 (1968), 285-93. Calls for a systematic, comparative analysis of existing census data on household and family composition. Argues that such analysis will clarify current assumptions made about the pre-modern family.

68. BURCH, Thomas K. "The Size and Structure of Families: A Comparative Analysis of Census Data." American Sociological Review, 32 (1967), 347-63. Notes that no contemporary society has large residential families and that household size reflects fertility rather than extended family structure.

69. BURCH, Thomas K. "Some Demographic Determinants of Average Household Size: An Analytic Approach." Demography, 7 (1970), 61-9. Investigates the influence of mortality, fertility, and age at marriage on mean household size under nuclear, extended, and stem family systems.

70. DAVIS, Kingsley. "The Theory of Change and Response in Modern Demographic History." Population Index, 29 (1963), 345-66. Examines demographic changes accompanying industrialization, using Japan and Ireland as examples, and argues that families faced with a high rate of natural increase will use every demographic means available to maximize new opportunities and avoid status loss.

71. DAVIS, Kingsley, and Judith BLAKE. "Social Structure and Fertility: An Analytic Framework." Economic Development and Cultural Change, 4 (1956), 211-35. Examines how some types and elements of social organization, especially in preindustrial areas, enhance or depress societal fertility.

72. FRIEDLANDER, Don. "Demographic Responses and Population Change." Demography, 6 (1969), 359-81. Proposes two hypothetical models to show the impact of modernization on a preindustrial society.

73. HENRY, Louis. "Historical Demography." Daedalus, 97 (1968), 385-96. Discusses the state of French historical demography, the accuracy of French vital statistics, the changes in demographic techniques, and the pioneers of historical demography.

74. HENRY, Louis. "The Verification of Data in Historical Demography." Population Studies, 22 (1968), 61-81. Discusses the importance of quality data in demographic

history, and cites methods of checking for systematic non-registration of births and deaths.

75. HERSHBERG, Theodore. "A Method for the Computerized Study of Family and Household Structure Using the Manuscript Schedules of the U.S. Census of Population, 1850-1880." Family in Historical Perspective Newsletter, No. 3 (Spring 1973), pp. 6-20.
Discusses the federal population manuscripts, their use in family history, and a computerized method for examining household structure and inferring relationships between household members and household head.

76. HOLLINGSWORTH, Thomas Henry. Historical Demography. Ithaca: Cornell Univ. Press, 1969.
Describes the place of demography in historical study, and surveys historical sources used for demographic analysis, namely censuses, vital statistics, surveys and tax reports, and genealogies.

77. HOLLINGSWORTH, Thomas Henry. "The Importance of the Quality of the Data in Historical Demography." Daedalus, 97 (1968), 415-32.
Stresses that accuracy of population statistics varies widely between regions and over time, and argues that demographic historians must pay attention to problems of accuracy.

78. JOHANSEN, Hans C., et. al. "Current Research in Economic History in Scandinavia: Historical Demography." Scandinavian Economic History Review, 20 (1972), 71-7.
Discusses current trends in Scandinavian demographic history, materials available, areas and periods studied, and methodological problems.

79. KNIGHTS, Peter R. "Accuracy of Age Reporting in the Manuscript Federal Censuses of 1850 and 1860." Historical Methods Newsletter, 4 (1971), 79-83.
Examines age reporting and its accuracy in American censuses, with emphasis on the methods of enumeration, the degree of accuracy, and ways of correcting errors.

80. KRAUSE, John T. "Some Implications of Recent Work in Historical Demography." Comparative Studies in Society and History, 1 (1959), 164-88.
Argues that, contrary to demographic transition theory, the birth rate and not the death rate was the major determinant of preindustrial population growth in Western Europe.

81. LAW, C. M. "Local Censuses of the Eighteenth Century." Population Studies, 23 (1969), 87-100.
Notes that local censuses in 18th-century Britain are a good source of demographic data, although they have problems of accuracy, content, and availability.

82. LEE, Roland. "Estimating Series of Vital Rates and Age
    Structures from Baptisms and Burials: A New Technique,
    With Applications to Pre-Industrial England." Pop-
    ulation Studies, 28 (1974), 495-512.
    Presents a technique for obtaining estimates of fertility,
    mortality, and age structure from long aggregate time series
    of baptisms and burials.

83. LOSCHKY, David J. "The Usefulness of England's Parish
    Registers." Review of Economics and Statistics, 49
    (1967), 471-79.
    Discusses techniques for ascertaining the worth of parish
    registers and how to overcome the problems of under-regis-
    tration.

84. MENDELS, Franklin. "Recent Research in European Historical
    Demography." American Historical Review, 75 (1970),
    1065-73.
    Discusses how recent studies have altered traditional views
    of preindustrial Europe, the process of modernization, and
    regional and national similarities and differences.

85. MILLER, Buffington Clay. "A Computerized Method of Deter-
    mining Family Structure from Mid-Nineteenth Century
    Census Data." Master's Thesis, Univ. of Pennsylvania,
    1973.
    Discusses a computerized model for inferring relationships
    between household head and household members using the
    census schedules.

86. NOONAN, John T. "Intellectual and Demographic History."
    Daedalus, 97 (1968), 463-85.
    Maintains that demographic historians need to consider ideas
    and noneconomic factors when examining population patterns
    so as to explain these patterns correctly.

87. POTTER, James. "Demography: The Missing Link in American
    History." Paper delivered at the Organization of Amer-
    ican Historians, Denver, April 1974.
    Discusses the importance of population and demographic
    patterns to historical inquiry and explanation.

88. POTTER, Robert G. "Birth Intervals: Structure and Change."
    Population Studies, 17 (1963), 155-66.
    Estimates average birth intervals in the absence of birth
    control, and discusses the effects of aging on birth inter-
    vals.

89. SCHOFIELD, Roger S. "Historical Demography: Some Possibili-
    ities and Some Limitations." Transactions of the Royal
    Historical Society, 21 (1971), 119-32.
    Reviews the current trends in demographic history and the
    limitations imposed by sources and methods of calculation.

90. SCHOFIELD, Roger S. "Representativeness and Family

Reconstitution." Annales de Demographie Historique, 1972. Ed. J. Dupaquier. Paris: Mouton, 1972, pp. 121-5.
Discusses the problems of representativeness of family reconstitution with regard to national and community population, to the adequacy of parish registers as recordings of vital statistics, and to the difficulty of generalizing from small numbers of reconstituted families.

91. THESTRUP, Poul. "Methodological Problems of a Family Reconstruction Study in a Danish Rural Parish Before 1800." Scandinavian Economic History Review, 20 (1972), 1-26.
Discusses the problems of under-registration, inadequate sampling, and identification posed by family reconstitution and presents demographic data on reconstituted families in a Danish parish from 1676 to 1801.

92. THIRSK, Joan. "Sources of Information on Population." Amateur Historian, 4 (1959), 129-33, 182-4.
Stresses the importance of local population studies, and discusses various classes of documents useful in local studies such as tax assessment and ecclesiastical censuses.

93. TILLOT, P. M. "The Analysis of Census Returns." Local Historian, 8 (1968), 2-10.
Discusses the status, trends, and problems of census analysis in demographic history.

94. VAN DE WALLE, Etienne, and Louise KÁNTROW. "Historical Demography: A Bibliographical Essay." Population Index, 40 (1974), 611-22.
Reviews definitions of historical demography, its scope, source materials used, methods of analysis, and includes a lengthy bibliography of secondary sources.

95. VANN, Richard T. "History and Demography." History and Theory, 9 (1969), 64-78.
Believes that historians need to consider more closely the relationship between demographic and historical change. Also discusses preindustrial attempts at family limitation to illustrate his point.

96. WELLS, Robert Vale. "Family History and Demographic Transition." Journal of Social History, 9 (1975), 1-20.
Examines the theory of demographic transition, how the theory might be reformulated given the historical evidence, and suggests new areas of research in family history, especially comparative studies and studies of changes in values and behavior.

97. WRIGHT, Monte D. "Demography for Historians." Rocky Mountain Social Science Journal, 7 (1970), 1-10.
Discusses techniques, trends, information sources, problems,

goals and oppotunities in demographic history.

98. WRIGLEY, Edward Anthony. "Parish Registers and Population
        History." Amateur Historian, 6 (1964), 146-51.
     Discusses the importance of population history, the inter-
     connection between economics and demography, and the prob-
     lems of parish registers and family reconstitution analysis.

99. WRIGLEY, Edward Anthony. Population and History. New York:
        McGraw-Hill, 1969.
     Demonstrates that vital statistics and marriage records can
     tell us much about social and economic history. A good in-
     troduction to basic demographic analysis and the relation-
     ship between demographic and social change.

100. WRIGLEY, Edward Anthony. "Population, Family and House-
        hold." New Movements in the Study and Teaching of His-
        tory. Ed. Charles Martin Ballard. Bloomington: In-
        diana Univ. Press, 1970, pp. 93-104.
     Discusses the importance of the family as an historical
     topic, and reviews advances in research techniques in
     family history, notably family reconstitution.

101. WRIGLEY, Edward Anthony. "Some Problems of Family Recon-
        stitution Using English Parish Register Material: An
        Example of Colyton." Third International Conference
        of Economic History. Paris: Mouton, 1972, pp. 199-221.
     Discusses the problems of English parish register records,
     especially the idea that a parish is not a closed community,
     the nature of the records themselves, and uses the family
     reconstitution of Colyton to illustrate problems.

102. WRIGLEY, Edward Anthony, and Roger S. SCHOFIELD. "Nominal
        Record Linkage By Computer and the Logic of Family Re-
        constitution." Identifying People in the Past. Ed.
        Edward Anthony Wrigley. London: Edward Arnold, 1973,
        pp. 64-101.
     Discusses nominal record linkage problems in family re-
     constitution and offers suggestions for writing algorithms
     to computerize family reconstitution.

PSYCHOLOGY OF THE FAMILY

103. ACKERMAN, Nathan Ward. The Psychodynamics of Family Life.
        New York: Basic Books, 1958.
     Argues that individual problems are often role-specific
     and stem from family relationships. Also stresses that
     therapy should consider the context of the individual's
     family.

104. BERG, Jan Hendrick van den. The Changing Nature of Man:
        Introduction to a Historical Psychology. New York:
        Norton, 1961.
     Discusses changes in the nature of man from the miracle to
     the development and rearing of children to the world of the

14

woman and the child.

105. ERIKSON, Erik Homburger. Identity and the Life Cycle:
      Selected Papers. New York: International Univ. Press,
      1959.
      Examines the unity of the human life cycle and the specific
      dynamics of each of its stages, including ego development
      and historical change, ego-identity, and the growth and
      crises of the healthy personality.

106. ERIKSON, Erik Homburger. Life History and the Historical
      Moment. New York: Norton, 1975.
      Attempts to consolidate the psychohistorical approach and
      puts forth a method for integrating psychology and history.

107. KARDINER, Abram, et. al. The Psychological Frontiers of
      Society. New York: Columbia Univ. Press, 1945.
      Discusses a technique for examining the reciprocal relations
      between personality and culture, and attempts to explain the
      origin of value systems of social goals from a psychological
      perspective.

108. KENISTON, Kenneth. "Psychological Development and Histor-
      ical Change." Journal of Interdisciplinary History, 2
      (1971), 329-45.
      Maintains that understanding the interaction between his-
      tory and psychology is difficult and presents serious con-
      ceptual problems, although current theories of developmental
      psychology offer exciting and useful possibilities to the
      historian.

109. LAING, Ronald D. The Politics of the Family and Other
      Essays. New York: Vintage, 1969.
      Shows that as an internalized space-time system, the con-
      cept of the family is a shared structure or an introjected
      set of relations between members. It gives its members
      self-identity.

110. SIMPSON, George. People in Families: Sociology, Psycho-
      analysis and the American Family. New York: Thomas Y.
      Crowell, 1960.
      Discusses the interrelationships between the sociology of
      the family and psychoanalytic interpretations of family
      life.

111. SINGER, Milton. "A Survey of Culture and Personality Theory
      and Research." Studying Personality Cross-Culturally.
      Ed. Bert Kaplan. Evanston: Northwestern Univ. Press,
      1961, pp. 9-90.
      Outlines the primary issues of cross-cultural personality
      study, and places them in an historical perspective. Also
      deals with the field of national character.

112. SKOLNICK, Arlene. "A Psychological Approach." Paper de-
      livered at the American Studies Association, San

Francisco, October 1973.
Notes that the recent research in anthropology and psychiatry, by envisioning the family as process, has questioned seriously the traditional models and concepts of the family upon which most social scientists rely, including concepts of the household, normal family behavior patterns, and the ways in which individuals view the family.

113. WEINSTEIN, Fred, and Gerald M. PLATT. The Wish to be Free: Society, Psyche, and Value Change. Berkeley: Univ. of California Press, 1969.
Develops a broad social theory to explain the modern commitment to the principles of autonomy based on the hypothesis that historically there has been a withdrawal from traditional authority on all institutional levels (especially the family) and a consequent movement toward self-determination.

SOCIOLOGY OF THE FAMILY

114. ANSHEN, Ruth Nanda, ed. The Family: Its Function and Destiny. New York: Harper & Row, 1949.
A good, but dated collection of essays focusing on the history of the family, family patterns in various cultures, and family structure.

115. BELL, Colin. Middle Class Families: Social and Geographical Mobility. London: Routlege and Kegan Paul, 1969.
Examines social and spatial mobility as independent variables, and discovers that both have distinct effects on community and family structure.

116. BELL, Norman W., and Ezra F. VOGEL, eds. A Modern Introduction to the Family. New York: Free Press, 1968.
An adequate anthology of recent sociological writings on the family with an introductory essay presenting a framework within which materials on the family may be organized.

117. BELL, Wendell. "Economic, Family, and Ethnic Status: An Empirical Test." American Sociological Review, 20 (1955), 45-52.
Tests the Shevky-Williams thesis of urban differentiation based on economic status, family status, and ethnic status. Concludes that the thesis is valid.

118. BENDER, Donald R. "A Refinement of the Concept of Household: Families, Co-Residence, and Domestic Functions." American Anthropologist, 69 (1967), 493-504.
Notes that while "household" refers to a residence group that carries out domestic functions, "family" refers to a kinship group. Argues that family, co-residence, and domestic functions are distinct kinds of social phenomena which can vary independently.

119. BLOOD, Robert O. "The Impact of Urbanization on American

Family Structure and Functioning." Sociology and
Social Research, 49 (1964), 5-16.
Argues that modern urban families possess structural
characteristics that enable them to be functionally
efficient, and that the waning of traditional functions
has been matched by new functions designed to meet social
and emotional needs of family members.

120. BURR, Wesley R. Theory Construction and the Sociology of
the Family. New York: John Wiley, 1973.
Attempts to develop theories for various aspects of the
family, notably kinship, fertility, and marital satisfaction.

121. CAPLOW, Theodore. Two Against One: Coalitions in Triads.
Englewood Cliffs: Prentice-Hall, 1968.
Contends that social interaction is triadic because one's
behavior is always subject to external influences. But
these influences can become participants in the interaction
and form dominant coalitions against one opponent. This
theory has important implications in family power relationships.

122. CONGER, John Janeway. "World They Never Knew: The Family
and Social Change." Daedalus, 100 (1971), 1105-38.
Examines the changes in the modern family and in its
relations to society, and discusses their effects upon
adolescents and their parents.

123. GOODE, William Josiah. "The Processing of Role Bargaining
in the Impact of Urbanization and Industrialization on
Family Systems." Current Sociology, 12 (1963-4), 1-13.
Argues that sociologists rely on myths of family history
and need to reexamine their assumptions about social
change, especially the diverse impact of technology on
the family of differing social classes.

124. GREENFIELD, Sidney M. "Industrialization and the Family
in Sociological Theory." American Journal of Sociology, 67 (1961), 312-22.
Argues that there is no causal relationship between small
nuclear families and urbanization or industrialization.

125. HOWARD, Ronald Lee. "A Social History of American Family
Sociology, 1865-1970." Diss. Univ. of Missouri, 1975.
Discusses sociologists' interest in the family from the
Progressives' view of the family as a flexible institution
incapable of promoting reform to the inability of contemporary sociologists to develop a comprehensive theory
which integrates family studies research.

126. LESLIE, Gerald R. The Family in Social Context. New York:
Oxford Univ. Press, 1967.
Examines the family in cross-cultural perspective, in an

historical perspective, and discusses theories of family
structure and change as well as the sociology of the family and family life cycle.

127. LEVI-STRAUSS, Claude. "The Family." Man, Culture, and
      Society. Ed. Harry L. Shapiro. New York: Oxford Univ.
      Press, 1956, pp. 261-85.
      Examines past and present anthropological assumptions
      about the family, forms of family structure and family
      bonds, and attempts to examine why the family is found
      practically everywhere.

128. LEVY, Marion J. "Aspects of the Analysis of Family
      Structure." Aspects of the Analysis of Family Structure.
      Ed. Ansley J. Coale, et. al. Princeton: Princeton Univ.
      Press, 1965, pp. 1-64.
      Examines the ideal-actual distinction as applied to kin-
      ship analysis and the role of family structure analysis
      in the general analysis of societies.

129. LITWAK, Eugene. "Geographic Mobility and Extended Family
      Cohesion." American Sociological Review, 25 (1960),
      385-94.
      Argues that extended family relations can be maintained
      in an industrial society despite geographical mobility.
      Modernization and the extended family are not incompatible.

130. LITWAK, Eugene. "Occupational Mobility and Extended Family
      Cohesion." American Sociological Review, 25 (1960),
      9-21.
      Questions Parsons' belief that there is disharmony between
      industrial society and extended family relations, and argues
      that a modified extended family is not antithetical to
      occupational mobility.

131. MCGREGOR, O. R. "Some Research Possibilities and Historical
      Materials for Family and Kinship Study in Britain."
      British Journal of Sociology, 12 (1961), 310-7.
      Reviews current trends in social history, and calls for
      studies of British family history since industrialization,
      especially functional surrogate and property law studies.

132. MIRANDE, Alfred M. "The Isolated Nuclear Family Hypothesis:
      A Reanalysis." The Family and Change. Ed. John N. Ed-
      wards. New York: Alfred A. Knopf, 1969, pp. 153-63.
      Examines the hypothesis that the contemporary family is
      relatively isolated and concludes that, with certain qual-
      ifications, socially-mobile families are less involved
      with kin.

133. PARSONS, Talcott, and Robert F. BALES. Family, Social-
      ization and Interaction Process. Glencoe, Ill.: Free
      Press, 1955.
      Discusses the problems of socialization in the family,
      the interrelations of social system, personality, and

culture, and the links between personality and structural differentiation. A major statement of the relation between the family and industrialization.

134. RAO, L. Jaganmohan. "Industrialization and the Family: A World View." International Journal of Sociology of the Family, 3 (1973), 179-89.
Reevaluates current hypotheses regarding the impact of industrialization on the family, and concludes that all are inadequate for explaining the interaction between family structure and industrialization.

135. RODMAN, Hyman, ed. Marriage, Family, and Society: A Reader. New York: Random House, 1965.
Includes clear, non-technical articles that cover topics ranging from mate selection to husband-wife relations to extended kin relations.

136. SLATER, Philip E. "Parental Role Differentiation." American Journal of Sociology, 67 (1961), 296-311.
Questions Parsons' theory of the universality of parental role differentiation along an "instrumental-expressive axis", and argues that such differentiation is optional and may be dysfunctional.

137. SUSSMAN, Marvin B., ed. Sourcebook in Marriage and the Family. Boston: Houghton-Mifflin, 1974.
A good collection of readings on the different aspects of family life from mate selection to parental problems to old age and bereavement.

138. TOMAN, Walter. Family Constellation: Its Effects on Personality and Social Behavior. 2nd ed. New York: Springer Publishing Co., 1969.
Contends that sibling position has a strong influence on an individual, his parents, his children, and his grandparents.

139. WILENSKY, Harold L. "Impact of Industrialization on Family Life." The Social Welfare Forum. New York: Columbia Univ. Press, 1956, pp. 202-19.
Explores the connections between the family and industrialism, and emphasizes that industrialization creates mobility, problems of the aged, emancipation of women, high divorce rates, and the problems of suburban, white collar living.

FAMILY LIFE-CYCLE

140. DUVALL, Evelyn Millis. Family Development. 4th ed. Philadelphia: Lippincott, 1971.
Argues that families pass through predictable stages of development--both individual and family life-cycles--which differ in length, in activity, and in intensity of family interaction.

141. EDWARDS, John N., ed. The Family and Change. New York: Knopf, 1969.
A good anthology of articles approaching the family in terms of developmental cycle or change.

142. GLICK, Paul C. "The Life Cycle of the Family." Marriage and Family Living, 17 (1955), 3-9.
Notes that demographic and economic changes mean constant readjustment of the values and habits of family members while age at marriage, family size, and individual life cycle affect patterns of family formulation and development.

143. GLICK, Paul C., and Robert PARKS. "New Approaches in Studying the Life Cycle of the Family." Demography, 2 (1965), 187-202.
Revises and updates estimates of family life cycle trends in the 20th century, and estimates typical patterns of change in family composition and economic characteristics during the cycle.

144. GOODY, John Rankin, ed. The Developmental Cycle in Domestic Groups. Cambridge: University Press, 1958.
Contains essays which examine the developmental cycle in domestic groups with regard to residence patterns, inheritance customs, and kinship relations.

145. GOVE, Walter R., et. al. "Family Life Cycle: Internal Dynamics and Social Consequences." Sociology and Social Research, 57 (1973), 182-95.
Discusses the family as a dynamic economic system which has the problem of allocating resources against potentially competing demands.

146. HAREVEN, Tamara K. "The Family as Process: The Historical Study of the Family Cycle." Journal of Social History, 7 (1974), 322-9.
Advocates a developmental or life-cycle approach to historical family studies. Argues that family structure, organization, and relationships are altered by time, socio-economic variables, and ethnicity.

147. LANSING, John B., and Leslie KISH. "Family Life Cycle as an Independent Variable." American Sociological Review, 22 (1957), 512-9.
Examines the stages of the family cycle as an independent variable for investigating variations in economic characteristics, and shows that family cycle has advantages over age as a variable.

148. OPPENHEIMER, Valerie K. "Life-Cycle Squeeze: The Interaction of Men's Occupational and Family Life Cycles." Demography, 11 (1974), 227-45.
Analyzes how the function of married women's paid employment varies at different economic levels, and relates this

variation to family life-cycle.

149. ROWE, George P. "The Developmental Conceptual Framework
to the Study of the Family." Emerging Conceptual
Frameworks in Family Analysis. Ed. Francis Ivan Nye
and Felix N. Berardo. New York: Macmillan, 1966,
pp. 198-222.
Discusses the history of the developmental approach to
family research, and evaluates the concepts and assumptions of this approach. Also includes an annotated
bibliography.

150. UHLENBERG, Peter R. "Cohort Variations in Family Life
Cycle Experiences of United States Females." Journal
of Marriage and the Family, 36 (1974), 284-92.
Develops a cohort approach for analyzing family change
and diversity, and examines the family life-cycle experiences of female cohorts as they move from age 15 to age
50.

151. YOUNG, Christabel M. "Factors Associated with the Timing
and Duration of the Leaving Home Stage of the Family
Life Cycle." Population Studies, 29 (1975), 61-73.
Studies the ages and reasons for leaving home of Austra-
lian young people, with emphasis on the effect of sex and
birth intervals.

KINSHIP

152. ADAMS, Bert N. Kinship in an Urban Setting. Chicago:
Markham Publishing Co., 1968.
Investigates kin networks and relations in the city, with
stress on the effects of sex and economic variables upon
kin relations and the roles of adult siblings, cousins,
and other kin in the life of the urbanite.

153. BOTT, Elizabeth. Family and Social Network: Roles, Norms,
and External Relationships in Ordinary Urban Families.
2nd ed. London: Tawistook Publications, 1971.
Maintains that conjugal roles are related to the family's
social network of friends, neighbors, and kin, not to
factors such as class or income.

154. FOX, Robin. Kinship and Marriage: An Anthropological
Perspective. Harmondsworth: Penguin, 1967.
Introduces kinship and marriage in terms of social anthropological theory, and contends that kinship patterns stem
from a wedding of man's physical and social attributes.

155. LITWAK, Eugene, and Ivan SZELENYI. "Primary Group Structures and Their Functions: Kin, Neighbors, and Friends."
American Sociological Review, 34 (1969), 464-81.
Argues that despite technological developments, contacts
between kin, the existence of neighborhoods, and the main-
tanance of friendships can exist, with each primary group

21

performing specific tasks.

156. PARSONS, Talcott. "The Kinship System of the Contemporary United States." American Anthropology, 45 (1943), 22-38. Attempts to describe and analyze the kinship system in structural terms and to understand the stress and psychological patterning to which it is subject.

157. WHEATON, Robert. "Family and Kinship in Western Europe: The Problem of the Joint Family Household." Journal of Interdisciplinary History, 5 (1975), 601-28. Shows that the artifical separation of household structure from kinship system presents serious analytical problems for historical family studies as does the non-consideration of the developmental cycle.

CHILDREN

158. BRAUN, Samuel J., and Esther P. EDWARDS. History and Theory of Early Childhood Education. Worthington, Ohio: Charles A. Jones Publishing Co., 1972. Attempts to examine the evolution of concepts about early childhood education and its social and intellectual context, using excerpts from the writings of early and contemporary educational theorists.

159. DE MAUSE, Lloyd. "The Evolution of Childhood." History of Childhood Quarterly, 1 (1974), 503-75. Advocates an evolutionary theory of historical change in parent-child relations--the psychogenic theory of history-- which envisages such relations as an independent source of historical change. Hypothesizes that as parents and children through time have diminished their psychic distance, new anxieties occur which are reflected in an age's childrearing modes. Simultaneously, child care has improved over time as parents increasingly met the needs of their children.

160. DE MAUSE, Lloyd. "Our Forebears Made Childhood a Nightmare." Psychology Today, April 1975, pp. 85-8. Reviews the brutal history of childhood and describes six evolutionary stages of parent-child relations in history.

161. DEMOS, John. "Developmental Perspectives on the History of Childhood." Journal of Interdisciplinary History, 2 (1971), 315-27. Maintains that an important approach to the study of childhood is to determine common experiences of childhood and childrearing in a culture or period in order to explain later adult personality. Yet to do this effectively, childhood must be viewed in a developmental perspective, seeing the child as the creator of culture.

162. ERIKSON, Erik Homburger. Childhood and Society. 2nd ed. New York: Norton, 1963. The basic introduction to ego psychology, the relationship

between psychology and history, and the life-cycle approach
to historical analysis.

163. INKELES, Alex. "Social Change and Social Character: The
     Role of Parental Mediation." Journal of Social Issues,
     11 (1955), 12-23.
     Explains that in child training, parents may rear their
     children in techniques learned in their childhood; they
     may rely on cultural surrogates or prefabricated rules;
     or they may learn from experience. In all cases the par-
     ents face the problem of how to rear children for life in
     a changed social situation.

164. LOPEZ, Manuel D. "A Guide to the Interdisciplinary Lit-
     erature of the History of Childhood." History of Child-
     hood Quarterly, 1 (1974), 463-94.
     An excellent bibliographic aid to source materials in the
     history of childhood from an interdisciplinary perspective,
     arranged by form of reference material.

165. MECHLING, Jay Edmund. "Advice to Historians on Advice to
     Mothers." Journal of Social History, 9 (1975), 44-63.
     Discusses the discrepancy between official childrearing
     advice and actual parental behavior, the problems of us-
     ing childrearing manuals as historical evidence, and pro-
     poses new uses of these manuals in social history.

166. SOMMERVILLE, C. John. "Toward a History of Childhood and
     Youth." Journal of Interdisciplinary History, 3 (1972),
     439-47.
     Surveys the literature in English relating to the history
     of youth and childhood as well as discusses some of the
     conceptual and methodological problems encountered in ex-
     amining children in history.

167. STEWART, Abigail, et. al. "Coding Categories for the Study
     of Child-Rearing from Historical Sources." Journal of
     Interdisciplinary History, 5 (1975), 687-701.
     Discusses a coding system for a content analysis of child-
     rearing manuals based on presence or absence of various
     categories.

168. TIERNO, Mark John. "American Youth: Past and Present. A
     Curriculum Unit for Secondary School Students." Diss.
     Carnegie-Mellon Univ., 1975.
     Presents a curriculum design for an interdisciplinary ap-
     proach to a family life education course at the secondary
     level. Includes rationale, bibliographic essay, student
     text, teacher's manual, and evaluation essay.

169. WHITING, John Wesley Mayhew, and Irvin L. CHILD. Child
     Training and Personality: A Cross-Cultural Study.
     New Haven: Yale Univ. Press, 1953.
     Discusses the effect of childrearing on personality, of
     personality upon culture, and of family structure upon

child training practices. A good introduction to the
interaction between personality and culture.

CHAPTER II:

THE FAMILY IN EUROPEAN HISTORY

1. The Family in Antiquity

GENERAL

170. BARDIS, Panos D. "Early Christianity and the Family."
      Sociological Bulletin, 13 (1964), 1-23.
      Discusses the influence of theology, economics, and
      philosophy on the early Christian family and its struc-
      ture and functions.

171. GOUGH, Kathleen. "The Origin of the Family." Marriage
      and the Family: A Critical Analysis and Proposals for
      Change. Ed. Carolyn Cummings Perrucci and Dena B.
      Targ. New York: McKay, 1974, pp. 71-93.
      Argues that the family was preceded by sexual indiscrim-
      inacy, and shows that women were not equal with men in
      "matriarchal" societies. Notes that sexual inequality is
      largely a matter of survival rather than the product of
      cultural impositions or the family.

172. NASH, Arnold S. "Ancient Past and Living Present." Family,
      Marriage and Parenthood. Ed. Howard Becker and Reuben
      Hill. 2nd ed. Boston: D.C. Heath, 1955, pp. 84-103.
      Surveys the historical origins of the contemporary family,
      notably the Hebrew, Greek, and Roman families as well as the
      impact of Christianity on family life.

173. WAKE, Charles Staniland. The Development of Marriage and
      Kinship. London: G. Redway, 1889.
      Questions both Morgan's thesis of the transition from matri-
      liny to patriliny and the assumption of primitive prosmis-
      cuity.

BIRTH CONTROL

174. BARDIS, Panos D. "Contraception in Ancient Egypt." Indian
      Journal of the History of Medicine, 12 (1967), 1-3.
      Describes the various methods of birth control developed by
      the ancient Egyptians and their relative effectiveness.

175. HOPKINS, Keith. "Contraception in the Roman Empire." Com-
      parative Studies in Society and History, 8 (1965), 124-51.
      Discusses fertility control in contemporary medical liter-
      ature of the Classical period, and examines circumstantial
      evidence of birth control practices and their consequences
      for Roman society.

176. MCDANIEL, Walton Brooks. Conception, Birth and Infancy in
      Ancient Rome and Modern Italy. Coconut Grove, Fla.:
      n.p., 1948.

Uses comparative analysis to examine pregnancy, birth and
babyhood of Roman society and in contemporary Italy, and
discovers an astonishing amount of parallelism, especially
superstitious ideas and practices.

177. PATLAGEAN, Evelyne. "Birth Control in the Early Byzantine
Empire." Biology of Man in History. Ed. Robert Forster
and Orest Ranum. Baltimore: Johns Hopkins Univ. Press,
1975, pp. 1-22.
Shows how a generalized religious asceticism altered attitudes toward fertility control, particularly the abandonment of the idea that procreation is the sole justifi-
cation for marriage and the spread of monastic life styles.

DEMOGRAPHY

178. HOPKINS, Keith. "The Age of Roman Girls at Marriage."
Population Studies, 18 (1965), 309-27.
Examines literary evidence to determine the modal age at
marriage of upper-class Roman girls, and finds that teenage marriage was quite common among females, although men
married considerably later.

DIVORCE

179. COLLINS, Oral. "Divorce in the New Testament." Gordon
Review, 7 (1964), 158-69.
Examines the attitudes toward marriage, divorce, and re-
marriage in the New Testament.

180. HARRELL, Pat Edwin. Divorce and Remarriage in the Early
Church: A History of Divorce and Remarriage in the
Ante-Nicene Church. London: Sweet & Maxwell, 1967.
Investigates the early Church's position on Christians and
catechumens who were divorced and remarried, and discusses
changing attitudes toward marriage from the Hellenistic
world to the Ante-Nicene Church.

DOMESTIC ARCHITECTURE

181. MCKAY, Alexander Gordon. Houses, Villas and Palaces in the
Roman World. London: Thames and Hudson, 1975.
Examines the variety of domestic architecture and interior
furnishing and decoration in the Roman Empire.

DOMESTIC LIFE AND CUSTOMS

182. BABER, Ray Erwin. "Marriage and Family Life in Ancient
Egypt." Social Forces, 13 (1935), 409-14.
Argues that the family organization of the early Egyptians
differed notably from other ancient peoples with regard to
matrilineal descent and inheritance, marriage prohibitions,
and women's status.

183. BARDIS, Panos D. "The Ancient Greek Family." Social

Science, 39 (1964), 156-75.
Examines sex roles, childrearing, housing, inheritance
laws, divorce, and sexual customs in ancient Greece.

184. BARDIS, Panos D. "Main Features of the Ancient Hebrew
      Family." *Social Science*, 38 (1963), 168-83.
Investigates the varying composition of the Hebrew Family
and types of Hebrew marriage practices as well as divorce
and sexual customs.

185. BARDIS, Panos D. "Main Features of the Ancient Roman
      Family." *Social Science*, 38 (1963), 225-40.
Discusses family composition, engagement, wedding cere-
monies, housing, sex roles, and sexuality in ancient
Rome.

186. BARDIS, Panos D. "Marriage and Family Customs in Ancient
      Egypt: An Interdisciplinary Study." *Social Science*,
      41 (1966), 229-45.
Discusses the ancient Egyptian family in terms of marriage
practices, childrearing, divorce, sex roles, and family
composition.

187. BARDIS, Panos D. "Selected Aspects of Family Life in
      Ancient Egypt." *International Review of History and
      Political Science*, 3 (1966), 1-16.
Examines family size, the ethical principles influencing
marriages, and sex roles in ancient Egypt.

188. BLUMNER, Hugo. *The Home Life of the Ancient Greeks*. New
      York: Cooper Square, 1966.
Reviews various facets of Greek domestic relations, with
emphasis on birth and infancy, women, diet, clothing, and
leisurely activities.

189. BURGMANN, D. M. "A Study of the Family in Athens in the
      Fifth and Fourth Centuries, B.C." Undergraduate Thesis,
      Oxford Univ., 1951.
Uses literary sources to examine the Athenian family, its
customs, and role in Greek society.

190. CARCOPINO, Jerome. *Daily Life in Ancient Rome: The People
      and the City at the Height of the Empire*. New Haven:
      Yale Univ. Press, 1940.
Includes a chapter on marriage, women, and the family with
emphasis on Roman marriage law, parental authority, marriage
customs, sex roles, and family instability.

191. DAVIES, J. K. "Athenian Propertied Families, 600-300, B.C."
      Diss. Oxford Univ., 1965.
Describes the life and customs of the rich and powerful
Athenian families and their role in Greek society.

192. GREENGUS, S. "Old Babyonian Marriage Ceremonies and Rites."
      Journal of Cuneiform Studies, 2 (1966), 55-72.

Discusses a recently discovered text and its descriptions
of Old-Babylonian marriage customs and ceremonies.

193. LACEY, Walter Kirkpatrick. The Family in Classical Greece.
      Ithaca: Cornell Univ. Press, 1968.
      Compares family life in various Greek city-states, and
      examines marriage customs, property relationships, and
      attitudes toward women in ancient Greece.

194. LIPIN, L. A. "The Assyrian Family in the Second Half of
      the Second Millennium B.C." Journal of World History,
      6 (1960), 628-43.
      Argues that the power of the pater familias in the Middle
      Assyrian period increased and that the law did not protect
      Assyrian women from abuse.

195. MENDELSOHN, I. "The Family in the Ancient Near East."
      Biblical Archaelogist, 11 (1948), 24-40.
      Discusses the Near Eastern family in terms of monogamy and
      polygamy, marriage and divorce, women and children.

196. NIEDZIELSKI, Zygmunt. "The Athenian Family from Aeschylus
      to Aristotle." Diss. Univ. of Chicago, 1955.

197. PATAI, Raphael. Sex and Family in the Bible. New York:
      Doubleday, 1959.
      Compares marriage customs and laws in the Bible to 19th-
      and 20th-century patterns of the Middle East. Argues that
      there has been much fluidity in family structure over time.

198. RAWSON, Beryl. "Family Life among the Lower Classes at
      Rome in the First Two Centuries of the Empire." Clas-
      sical Philology, 61 (1966), 71-83.
      Discusses the opportunities for marriage, types of mar-
      riages, family stability, and parent-child relationships
      among the slaves, freedmen, and poor freeborn.

199. RORDORF, Willy. "Marriage in the New Testament and in the
      Early Church." Journal of Ecclesiastical History, 20
      (1969), 193-210.
      Investigates the relation between marriage and eschatology,
      and examines attitudes toward adultery, divorce, second
      marriages, and women in the early Church. Also discusses
      the belief in the sacramentality of marriage.

200. SAVAGE, Charles Albert. The Athenian Family: A Socio-
      logical and Legal Study. Baltimore: Lord Baltimore
      Press, 1907.
      Discusses the attitudes of the Greek state toward the fam-
      ily, the position of women, the ideals of marriage, re-
      lations between parent and child, and the Athenian inher-
      itance system. Concludes that Athenian family life was
      full of peril.

201. SCOTT, Nora Elizabeth. Home Life of the Ancient Egyptians.

New York: Metropolitan Museum, 1947.

202. SLATER, Philip Elliot. The Glora of Hera: Greek Mythology
and the Greek Family. Boston: Beacon Press, 1968.
Examines the domination of Greek women over the child's
early years, the mother-son relationship, and makes psycho-
analytical interpretations of classical Greek mythology and
social organization.

203. SLATER, Philip Elliot. "The Greek Family in History and
Myth." Arethusa, 7 (1974), 9-44.
Shows how the low status of females and the male's fear of
women were mutually reinforcing in Hellenic society. Argues
that women were powerful in the Greek household.

204. THEOPHANE, Sister M. "Family Customs in the Old Testament."
American Catholic Sociological Review, 16 (1955), 198-
210.
Examines the structure of the ancient Jewish family and
finds that the family was extended and patriarchal with
strong kin ties.

205. WILLIAMS, Gordon. "Some Aspects of Roman Marriage Ceremonies and Ideals." Journal of Roman Studies, 48 (1958),
16-29.
Traces early Roman marriage ceremonies and customs as well
as ideals of marriage, notably wifely obedience to a husband, faithfulness to one man, and the marriage bond con-
ceived of as eternal.

FAMILY LAW AND INHERITANCE

206. HARRISON, Alick Robin Walsham. The Law of Athens: The
Family and Property. Oxford: Clarendon Press, 1968.
Analyzes the law of Athens concerning the family and property, including husband-wife relations, dowries, adoption,
succession, and guardianship.

207. NEUFELD, Ephram. Ancient Hebrew Marriage Law. London:
Longmans, Green, and Co., 1944.
Surveys the laws and customs relating to marriage among
Hebrews as revealed in the Old Testament, including the
forms of marriage, mate selection, impediments to mar-
riage, and the status of parents and children.

208. PESTMAN, Pieter Willem. Marriage and Matrimonial Property in Ancient Egypt: A Contribution to Establishing
the Legal Position of the Woman. Leiden: E.J. Brill,
1961.
Examines matrimonial law and the law regarding matrimonial property in Egypt to the Roman period, including the
celebration and dissolution of marriage and the legal effects of marriage and divorce with regard to property law.

209. RABINOWITZ, Jacob J. "Marriage Contracts in Ancient

Egypt in the Light of Jewish Sources." <u>Harvard Theo-</u>
<u>logical Review</u>, 46 (1953), 91-8.
Finds many similarities between Egyptian, Demotic, Greek,
and Jewish marriage contracts from the late 4th century
B.C. onward. This indicates that legal rules and form-
ulae were derived from a common source: the Jews.

210.   SCHAPS, David. "Women in Greek Inheritance Law." <u>Clas-</u>
<u>sical Quarterly</u>, 25 (1975), 53-7.
Discusses the basic principles of Greek inheritance law
in which women inherit in the absence of males.

211.   SKAIST, Aaron Jacob. "Studies in Ancient Mesopotamian
Family Law Pertaining to Marriage and Divorce." Diss.
Univ. of Pennsylvania, 1963.
Examines the forms and characteristics of marriage as
reflected in Mesopotamian marriage contracts and their
changes through time and between region.

212.   WESTRUP, Carl Wium. <u>Family Property and Patria Potestas</u>.
New York: Oxford Univ. Press, 1934.
Discusses domestic relations and parent-child relation-
ships in Roman law.

213.   WOLFF, Hana Julius. "Marriage Law and Family Organization
in Ancient Athens." <u>Traditio</u>, 2 (1944), 43-95.
Deals with the problem of the changing relation between
solemn marriage and unions concluded informally with respect to the law of Athens.

KINSHIP

214.   ELLIS, Alfred Burdon. "Marriage and Kinship Among the
Ancient Israelites." <u>Popular Science Monthly</u>, 42
(1893), 325-37.
Examines the extent to which the Israelites conformed to
the "normal" phases of the evolution of marriage and ar-
rived at a system of kinship through males.

215.   SMITH, William Robertson. <u>Kinship and Marriage in Early</u>
<u>Arabia</u>. Cambridge: Macmillan, 1885.
Discusses the origins of the system of male kinship and
the laws of marriage in Arabia during the time of Mohammed.

SEXUALITY

216.   AMUNDSEN, Darrel W., and Carol J. DIERS. "The Age of Menarche in Classical Greece and Rome." <u>Human Biology</u>, 41
(1969), 125-32.
Examines contemporary and modern accounts to determine the
age of menarche in the Classical period.

217.   AMUNDSEN, Darrel W., and Carol J. DIERS. "The Age of Menopause in Classical Greece and Rome." <u>Human Biology</u>, 42
(1970), 79-86.

Examines statements by eight Greek and Roman authors to
determine the age of menopause in the Classical period.

218. BARDIS, Panos D. "Incest in Ancient Egypt." Indian
Journal of the History of Medicine, 12 (1967), 14-20.
Argues that to 330 B.C. brother-sister unions, while
common among the Pharaohs, were rare among the common
people in Egypt, but during the Roman period incestuous
marriages gained in popularity among the masses.

219. BARDIS, Panos D. "Sex in Ancient Rome." Sexology, 32
(1966), 637-41.
Describes sexual relations and customs in Roman society.

220. BRANDT, Paul. Sexual Life in Ancient Greece. 1931; rpt.
New York: Barnes & Noble, 1952.
Surveys rather incompetently and unhistorically the sex
customs of the Greeks.

221. CERNY, Jaroslav. "Consanguineous Marriages in Pharaonic
Egypt." Journal of Egyptian Archaeology, 40 (1954),
23-9.
Discusses the current belief in the commonality of marriages between brothers and sisters in ancient Egypt, and
concludes that such marriages were uncommon if non-existent
among workmen.

222. DOVER, K. J. "Classical Greek Attitudes to Sexual Behavior." Arethusa, 6 (1973), 59-74.
Discusses changing Greek attitudes toward sexual enjoyment
with emphasis on inhibition, sex segregation and adultery,
commercial sex, self-control, and homosexuality.

223. EGLINTON, J. Z. Greek Love. New York: Oliver Layton
Press, 1964.
Discusses the theory, practice, history, and literature of
Greek love as well as boy-love in European and American
history.

224. FLACELIERE, Robert. Love in Ancient Greece. 1960; rpt.
New York: Crown, 1962.
Examines various aspects of sexuality in ancient Greece
as well as marriage age, sex roles, marriage customs, and
family life.

225. GRIMAL, Pierre. Love in Ancient Rome. New York: Crown,
1967.
Examines Roman marriage, love and religion, free love,
imperial amours, and concludes that Rome did not fall
because of immorality.

226. KIEFER, Otto. Sexual Life in Ancient Rome. London: Routledge & Kegan Paul, 1950.
Describes the development of Roman sexual life, religion
and philosophy in relation to sexual life, and women and

marriage practices.

227. LIGHTMAN, Marjorie. "The Social Legitmacy of Various Sexual Relationships during the Late Roman Republic." Paper delivered at the American Historical Association, San Francisco, December 1973.

228. MIDDLETON, Russell. "Brother-Sister and Father-Daughter Marriage in Ancient Egypt." American Sociological Review, 27 (1962), 603-11.
Presents evidence concerning the marriage of near kin among royalty and commoners in the Pharaonic, Ptolemaic, and Roman periods of Egyptian history, and questions the universality of the incest taboo.

229. PIKE, Edgar Royston. Love in Ancient Rome. London: Frederick Muller, 1965.
Discusses wedding customs, sexual habits and practices of the Romans. Argues that under the Romans the patriarchal forms of the family began to disintegrate and respect for women began to appear.

230. WICK, Terry E. "The Importance of the Family as a Determiner of Sexual Mores in Classical Athens." Societas, 5 (1975), 133-45.
Considers the nature and function of the family in classical Athens, and argues that there existed a closs correlation between acceptable sexual behavior and the interests of the individual family and state.

231. WOLFF, Hans Julius. "The Background of the Post-Classical Legislation on Illegitimacy." Seminar, 3 (1945), 21-45.

232. ZEISEL, William. "Family Structure and Christian Morality: A Transformation of Greco-Roman Values." Paper delivered at the American Historical Association, San Francisco, December 1973.

WOMEN

233. POMEROY, Sarah B. "Selected Bibliography on Women in Antiquity." Arethusa, 6 (1973), 135-43.
Includes citations on women, the family, and sexual mores.

234. REED, Evelyn. Woman's Evolution: From Matriarchal Clan to Patriarchal Family. New York: Pathfinder Press, 1975.
Discusses matriarchal society and the transition to patriarchy, and contends that woman's inferiority did not stem from primitive society.

2. The Medieval Family

235. BURR, David. "Olivi on Marriage: The Conservative as
     Prophet." _Journal of Medieval and Renaissance Studies_,
     2 (1972), 183-204.
     Discusses the doubts of Petrus Olivi on sacramentality of
     marriage, his staunch advocacy of the superiority of vir-
     ginity/celibacy, and his position in pre-Reformation in-
     tellectual history.

236. DELHAYE, Philippe. "The Development of the Medieval
     Church's Teaching on Marriage." _Concilium_, May 1970,
     pp. 83-8.
     Argues that the Church acquired control over marriage by
     the 11th century when canon law teaching on marriage and
     the idea of marriage as a sacrament crystalized.

237. HEANEY, Seamus P. _The Development of the Sacramentality
     of Marriage from Anselm of Laon to Thomas Aquinas_.
     Washington: Catholic Univ. Press, 1963.
     Traces the development of the doctrine of the sacrament-
     ality of marriage from the early scholastic period to the
     writings of St. Thomas Acquinas. Also reviews Augustinian
     definitions of marriage, and concludes that sacramentality
     of marriage resulted from the application of the definition
     of _sacramentum_ to marriage.

238. HERLIHY, David. "What We Know About Medieval Marriages."
     Paper delivered at Historians and the Family: A Sym-
     psium, Mount Holyoke College, April 1975.

239. SCHERMERHORN, Richard A. "Family Carry-overs of Western
     Christendom." _Family, Marriage, and Parenthood_. Ed.
     Howard Becker and Reuben Hill. Boston: D.C. Heath,
     1955, pp. 104-30.
     Discusses the evolution of European family life from the
     sacred to the secular, from early barbaric to bourgeois
     family life of the 16th century.

240. SHEEHAN, Michael M. _Family and Marriage in Medieval Europe_:
     A Working Bibliography. Vancouver: Medieval Studies
     Committee, 1976.
     Provides an excellent introduction to the bibliographical
     materials in medieval demography and kinship, family and
     marriage, women and children.

241. WESTMAN, Barbara Hanawalt. "The Peasant Family and Crime
     in Fourteenth-Century England." _Journal of British
     Studies_, 13 (1974), 1-18.
     Examines the frequency of familial and non-familial crimes,
     the specific types of crimes involving family and kin mem-
     bers, and the tensions in rural society and within the med-
     ieval peasant family which contributed to family crime.

33

BIRTH CONTROL

242. FLANDRIN, Jean-Louis. "Contraception, Marriage, and Sexual Relations in the Christian West." Biology of Man in History. Ed. Robert Forster and Orest Ranum. Baltimore: Johns Hopkins Univ. Press, 1975, pp. 23-47.
Argues that illicit relations were not limited to specific social groups during the middle ages, but were widespread and involved contraceptive measures. Thus, before birth control was practiced in marriage, it was characteristic of illicit relationships.

243. NOONAN, John Thomas. Contraception: A History of its Treatment by the Catholic Theologians and Canonists. Cambridge: Harvard Univ. Press, 1965.
Discusses the development of the Catholic Church's teaching on birth control, and suggests that a more liberal view of contraception is possible without a rejection of tradition.

CHILDREN

244. GOODRICH, Michael. "Childhood and Adolescence Among the Thirteenth-Century Saints." History of Childhood Quarterly, 1 (1973), 285-309.
Analyzes the childhood and adolescence of saints to understand why the youthful rebellions in the middle ages take an ascetic religious form.

245. GRANSDEN, Antonia. "Childhood and Youth in Medieval England." Nottingham Medieval Studies, 16 (1972), 3-19.
Notes that in some respects the behavior of young people and attitudes toward them resembled modern trends and that in the 12th and 13th centuries generational tensions existed, especially over religious issues.

246. HOLMES, Urban T. "Childhood in the Twelfth and Thirteenth Centuries." Paper delivered at the American Historical Association, New York, December 1966.

247. KELLUM, Barbara A. "Infanticide in England in the Later Middle Ages." History of Childhood Quarterly, 1 (1974), 367-88.
Maintains that infanticide in late medieval England was not only the consequence of economic pressures but was possibly an ingrained part of the medieval personality.

248. LYMAN, Richard B. "Barbarism and Religion: Late Roman and Early Medieval Childhood." The History of Childhood. Ed. Lloyd de Mause. New York: Psychohistory Press, 1974, pp. 75-100.
Shows that against the folk-customs of infanticide, abortion, sale of children, and abandonment, the gains in medieval children were minimal. There is evidence, however, that mother-child affection was increasing, albeit slowly.

249. MCLAUGHLIN, Mary Martin. "Survivors and Surrogates:
      Children and Parents from the Ninth to the Thirteenth
      Centuries." The History of Childhood. Ed. Lloyd
      de Mause. New York: Psychohistory Press, 1974, pp.
      101-82.
      Illustrates how children were abused and neglected during
      the late middle ages, although churchmen increasingly op-
      posed such practices and tried to insill more humane at-
      titudes.

DEMOGRAPHY

250. RUSSELL, Josiah Cox. British Medieval Population. Albu-
      querque: Univ. of New Mexico Press, 1948.
      Examines demographic problems and sources in medieval
      England, and estimates the sex ratio, age at marriage,
      fertility rates, time of birth, and infant and child
      mortality rates.

DOMESTIC ARCHITECTURE

251. EAMES, P. "The Character and Use of Domestic Furnishings
      in England as Discernable from Documentary and Archae-
      logical Evidence from the 11th-15th Centuries." Master's
      Thesis: Univ. of Liverpool, 1969.
      Discusses the use of medieval household furnishings as an
      indicator of English social and family life.

252. FAULKNER, P. A. "Domestic Planning from the Twelfth to
      the Fourteenth Centuries." Archaeological Journal,
      115 (1958), 150-83.
      Examines some of the remaining structural evidence for a
      domestic planning typology in medieval England, and dis-
      cusses in detail the end hall house and its purposes and
      functions in medieval society.

253. WOOD, Margaret. The English Mediaeval House. London:
      Phoenix House, 1965.
      Surveys the evolution of the medieval house, and examines
      how its growth was influenced by changing social conditions.

DOMESTIC LIFE AND CUSTOMS

254. BEECH, George T. "Personal Names and the Study of Family
      and Social History in Western France, 800-1200." Paper
      delivered at the American Historical Association, New
      York, December 1968.
      Examines personal names as a guide for determining the fam-
      ily origins and membership of unidentifiable people at a
      time when only one name was given.

255. BROOKE, C. N. L. "Gregorian Reform in Action: Clerical
      Marriage in England, 1050-1200." Cambridge Historical
      Journal, 12 (1956), 1-21.
      Examines the attempts to limit clerical marriage and the

parallel rise of the Romantic ideal in the 12th century.

256. FRANK, Roberta. "Marriage in Twelfth- and Thirteenth-Century Iceland." Viator, 4 (1973), 473-84.
Finds in Icelandic prose sagas that women were constantly present and were vitally important to the family's continuity and well-being, and notes that canon law had little impact on Icelandic marriage behavior.

257. GELLINEK, Christian. "Marriage by Consent in Literary Sources of Germany." Studia Gratiana: Collectanea Stephan Kuttner, 12 (1967), 557-79.
Shows that marriages by deliberate consent of the participants were practiced in Southern Germany during the 11th and 12th centuries.

258. GIRARD, Rene. "Marriage in Avignon in the Second Half of the Fifteenth Century." Speculum, 28 (1953), 485-98.
Examines marriage laws and customs in Southern France, especially marriage age, the status of women, the wedding ceremony, remarriage, and marriage stability.

259. HASKELL, Ann S. "The Paston Women on Marriage in Fifteenth Century England." Viator, 4 (1973), 459-71.
Examines the Paston family correspondence, and finds tensions between parents and children over mate selection, but notes that parental-controlled marriages were common in medieval England.

260. HOMANS, George Caspar. English Villagers of the Thirteenth Century. Cambridge: Harvard Univ. Press, 1941.
Discusses inheritance customs, marriage ceremonies, wardship, and family life of English villagers of the Middle Ages.

261. HUGHES, Diane Owen. "Domestic Ideals and Social Behavior: Evidence from Medieval Genoa." The Family in History. Ed. Charles E. Rosenberg. Philadelphia: Univ. of Pennsylvania Press, 1975, pp. 115-43.
Examines notarial records to discern the role of the household in medieval Genoa and the relations between ideals and behavior.

262. HUGHES, Diane Owen. "Toward Historical Ethnography: Notarial Records and Family History in the Middle Ages." Historical Methods Newsletter, 7 (1974), 61-71.
Discusses the validity of notarial chartularies as data sources for family history and social structure of southern Europe.

263. NOONAN, John Thomas. "Power to Choose." Viator, 4 (1973), 419-34.
Argues that although arranged marriages were common in Western Europe, some freedom of choice did exist and was discussed and recognized by religious and legal authorities.

264. SCAMMELL, Jean. "Freedom and Marriage in Medieval England."
     Economic History Review, 27 (1974), 523-37.
     Examines the increasing tendency toward liberty among medi-
     eval English peasants with regard to marriage control,
     morality, and inheritance patterns.

265. THRUPP, John. _The Anglo-Saxon Home: A History of the Do-_
     mestic Institutions and Customs of England. From the
     Fifth to the Eleventh Century. London: Longman, Green,
     1862.
     Discusses the wife and child in medieval England, includ-
     ing restrictions on marriage, matrimonial rights, infan-
     ticide, parental authority, and divorce.

266. THURSTON, Herbert. "Mediaeval Matrimony." _Dublin Review,_
     171 (1922), 44-57.
     Discusses medieval marriage customs, parental control of
     marriages, child marriages, and tensions in marriage.

FAMILY COMPOSITION AND STRUCTURE

267. BRITTON, Edward. "The Peasant Family in Fourteenth-Cen-
     tury England." _Peasant Studies_, April 1976, pp. 2-7.
     Reviews current theories of the peasant family in medieval
     England--notably the stem and joint family systems--and
     emphasizes the importance of non-inheriting sons, family
     structure, and the dwelling unit in the understanding pea-
     sant families.

268. COLEMAN, Emily R. "Medieval Marriage Characteristics: A
     Neglected Factor in the History of Medieval Serfdom."
     Journal of Interdisciplinary History, 2 (1971), 205-20.
     Observes that medieval French families were small, nuclear
     families. The existence of a high sex ratio did not, how-
     ever, give women an advantage in the marriage market since
     the woman herself passed social status to her children.

269. HALLAM, H. E. "Some Thirteenth Century Censuses." _Economic_
     History Review, 10 (1958), 340-61.
     Analyzes censuses at Spalding, Lincolnshire and finds the
     prominence of relatively large nuclear families, but notes
     the close relationship between family size and inheritance
     customs.

270. HERLIHY, David. "Family Solidarity in Medieval Italian
     History." _Economy, Society and Government in Medieval_
     Italy. Ed. David Herlihy, et. al. Kent, Ohio: Kent
     State Univ. Press, 1969, pp. 173-84.
     Examines data on family structure and solidarity in various
     Italian cities, and calls into question current theories of
     progressive nuclearization.

271. HERLIHY, David. "Mapping Households in Medieval Italy."
     Catholic Historical Review, 58 (1972), 1-24.
     Discusses the composition and size of households in Florence

37

in the 15th century through the use of mapping the extension of the household collaterally, generationally, and in terms of the service dimension.

272. HUGHES, Diane Owen. "Urban Growth and Family Structure in Medieval Genoa." Past & Present, February 1975, pp. 3-28.
Argues that the impact of urbanization on family structure in Genoa depended on the family's economic and social role, but generally urbanization strengthened family bonds.

273. KRAUSE, John. "The Medieval Household: Large or Small?" Economic History Review, 9 (1957), 420-32.
Analyzes the methods, assumptions, and conclusions of recent studies of medieval population history, with emphasis on household size.

274. TRANSANO, Vincent Antone. "The Rural Noble Family of Southern Tuscany (800-1350)." Diss. Univ. of California at Davis, 1974.
Analyzes the organization, composition, function, and evolution of the noble family and its interaction with feudalism and economics.

275. WEINBERGER, Stephen. "Peasant Households in Provence: ca. 800-1100." Speculum, 47 (1973), 247-57.
Examines a 813-814 polyptych to determine size and structure of peasant families, their marriage and land patterns, and class distinctions among the peasantry, and notes that the extended family was prevalent.

FAMILY LAW AND INHERITANCE

276. BRUNDAGE, James A. "Concubinage and Marriage in Medieval Canon Law." Journal of Medieval History, 1 (1975), 1-17.
Discusses the ambiguity of medieval law toward concubinage as canonists who morally disapproved of concubinage sought to assimilate the status of the concubine with that of married women. But Tridentine reforms abolished earlier recognition of non-marital unions.

277. ENGDAHL, David E. "Medieval Metaphysics and English Marriage Laws." Journal of Family Law, 8 (1968), 381-97.
Examines the shift from the empirical to the metaphysical conception of marriage and the displacement of English law by Roman canon law with regard to validity in marriage.

278. FAITH, Rosamond Jane. "Peasant Families and Inheritance Customs in Medieval England." Agricultural History Review, 14 (1966), 77-95.
Discusses the variety of peasant inheritance customs and their waning emphasis on family landholding in the 14th and 15th centuries as more land became available.

279. FALK, Ze'ev Wilhelm. Jewish Matrimonial Law in the Middle

<u>Ages</u>. London: Oxford Univ. Press, 1966.
Examines changing Jewish family law in terms of monogamy,
matrimony, the matrimonial match, divorce, and the status
of women.

280. GOTTLIEB, Beatrice. "Getting Married in Pre-Reformation
Europe: The Doctrine of Clandestine Marriage and Court
Cases in Fifteenth-Century Champagne." Diss. Columbia
Univ., 1974.
Contends that problems surrounding non-church marriages,
as revealed in medieval court cases, usually involved be-
trothal and that the normal way to get married--at least
for artisans and peasants--involved several distinct steps.

281. GOTTLIEB, Beatrice. "The Problem of Clandestine Marriage."
Paper delivered at the American Historical Association,
New Orleans, December 1972.
Discusses non-church marriages and their problems, notably
betrothal.

282. HELMHOLZ, Richard H. <u>Marriage Litigation in Medieval Eng-
land</u>. Cambridge: Cambridge Univ. Press, 1974.
Examines English ecclesiastical court records to determine
the evolution of the Church's law of marriage, the frequency of private marriages, and the litigation involving
these marriages.

283. HERLIHY, David. "Land, Family and Women in Continental
Europe, 701-1200." <u>Traditio</u>, 18 (1962), 89-120.
Explores how lay propertied families managed their estates,
and how family structure was affected by socio-economic
changes. Also illustrates the important role medieval
women played in the management of family property.

284. KELLY, Henry Ansgar. "Clandestine Marriage and Chaucer's
<u>Troilus</u>." <u>Viator</u>, 4 (1973), 435-58.
Discusses the nature and prevalence of clandestine marriage in 14th-century England, and argues that the exchange of marriage vows away from a priest still meant
that the marriage contract was binding and valid.

285. KITTEL, Margaret Ruth. "Common Law Limitations on the
Canon Law of Marriage." Paper delivered at the American
Historical Association, San Francisco, December 1973.
Discusses the difficulties faced by medieval English
women in marrying the man of their choice.

286. KITTEL, Margaret Ruth. "Married Women in Thirteenth-Century England: A Study in Common Law." Diss. Univ. of
California at Berkeley, 1973.
Argues that parents and lords exercised much control over
the marriages of medieval women, nor did married women
have complete control over their land. But the position
of married women in criminal law improved with time.

287. NOONAN, John T. "Marital Affection in the Canonists."
      Studia Gratiana: Collectanea Stephan Kuttner, 12
      (1967), 479-509.
      Discusses the changing interpretations of the term "mar-
      italis affectio" by the canonists from Justinian to In-
      nocent III.

288. PAINTER, Sidney. "The Family and the Feudal System in
      Twelfth Century England." Speculum, 35 (1960), 1-16.
      Explores the effects of family relationships on property
      distribution and their influence on political and mili-
      tary activities.

289. RITZER, Korbinian. "Secular Law and the Western Church's
      Concept of Marriage." Concilium, May 1970, pp. 67-75.
      Discusses marriage ideals as well as the extension of im-
      pediments to marriage by Church reformers in the early
      Middle Ages.

290. SHEEHAN, Michael M. "The Formation and Stability of Mar-
      riage in Fourteenth-Century England: Evidence of an
      Ely Register." Mediaeval Studies, 33 (1971), 228-63.
      Argues that most court cases concerning marriages involved
      clandestine marriage, that the court was not an instrument
      of easy annulment but a body for the defence of marriage,
      and that an individualistic attitude toward marriage ex-
      isted in the 14th century.

291. SHEEHAN, Michael M. "The Influence of Canon Law on the
      Property Rights of Married Women in England." Mediaeval
      Studies, 25 (1963), 109-24.
      Argues that the canonists opposed the traditional prin-
      ciples of chattel ownership by defending the property
      rights of women, but their position was not accepted.

292. SHEEHAN, Michael M. "Marriage and Family in English Con-
      ciliar and Synodal Legislation." Essays in Honor of
      Anton Charles Pegis. Ed. J. Reginald O'Donnell.
      Toronto: Pontifical Institute of Medieval Studies,
      1974, pp. 205-14.
      Deals with the Church's conception of religious life as
      an alternative to marriage, the ideal of marriage, and
      Church statues governing marriage in medieval England.

293. SMITH, Charles Edward. Papal Enforcement of Some Medieval
      Marriage Laws. University, La.: Louisana State Univ.
      Press, 1940.
      Discusses impediments to medieval marriages--particularly
      consanguity and affinity--and enforcement and relaxation
      by the Church of laws forbidding marriages between relatives.

KINSHIP

294. LOYN, H. R. "Kinship in Anglo-Saxon England." Anglo-Saxon
      England, 3 (1973), 197-209.

Examines the problems of kinship and the role of kin in Anglo-Saxon England.

295. ROSENTHAL, Joel T. "Marriage and the Blood Feud in 'Heroic' Europe." British Journal of Sociology, 17 (1966), 133-44.
Discusses the institution of the blood feud in medieval Europe and the use of woman, through her marriage, to heal such a feud.

SEXUALITY

296. AMUNDSEN, Darrel W., and Carol J. DIERS. "The Age of Menarche in Medieval Europe." Human Biology, 45 (1973), 363-9.
Examines medieval sources from the 6th through the 15th century to estimate the age of menarche, and finds that the ages ranged from the 12th to the 15th years.

297. DONALDSON, E. Talbot. "The Myth of Courtly Love." Ventures, 5 (1965), 16-23.
Reviews the history of the concept of courtly love, and concludes that it did not exist in the Middle Ages.

298. MATHEW, Gervase. "Marriage and Amour Courtois in Late Fourteenth-Century England." Essays Presented to Charles Williams. Ed. C. S. Lewis. London: Oxford Univ. Press, 1947, pp. 128-35.
Analyzes the relationship between the ideal of marriage and that of courtly love in terms of changing social structure.

299. MOLLER, Herbert. "The Meaning of Courtly Love." Journal of American Folklore, 73 (1960), 39-52.
Examines the influence of courtly love on upper class behavior and argues that its underlying idea was that biological energies should be channeled into culturally desirable ends.

300. MOLLER, Herbert. "The Social Causation of the Courtly Love Complex." Comparative Studies in Society and History, 1 (1958), 137-63.
Argues that courtly love as a configuration of specific anxieties and wishful fantasies appealed to secular upper class men because differential opportunities and a high sex ratio created strains in the knightly class. These strains found outlets in courtly love.

301. MOORE, John C. "Love in Twelfth-Century France: A Failure in Synthesis." Traditio, 24 (1968), 429-43.
Discusses 12th-century French students of love--the clergy, scholars, and courtly writers--and their failure to integrate traditional and contemporary perceptions of love into a coherent world-view.

302. NEWMAN, F. X., ed. The Meaning of Courtly Love. Albany:

State Univ. of New York Press, 1968.
A collection of essays which examine the concept of courtly
love and its usefulness/uselessnes in medieval social history. Also includes bibliography of recent writings on the
subject.

303. PARMISANO, Fabian. "Love and Marriage in the Middle Ages."
New Blackfriars, 50 (1969), 599-608, 649-60.
Argues that beginning in the 14th century some theologians,
principally Nicole Oresme, began to question the Augustin-
ian notion that procreation was the only motive for conjugal intercourse and to emphasize the bond of love in marriage. These views were also adopted by Thomas Aquinas.

304. POST, J. B. "Ages at Menarche and Menopause: Some Medieval
Authorities." Population Studies, 25 (1971), 83-7.
Examines medical works of the Middle Ages to determine mean
age at menarche and menopause, and finds similarities between these ages and those of the 20th century.

WOMEN

305. BULLOUGH, Vern L. "Medieval Medical and Scientific Views of
Women." Viator, 4 (1973), 485-501.
Discusses antifeminine attitudes among medieval medical writers who contended that women were inferior to men because of
their sinfulness and anatomy.

306. ERICKSON, Carolly, and Kathleen CASEY. "Women in the Middle Ages: A Working Bibliography." Mediaeval Studies,
37 (1975), 340-59.
Includes some 300 entries covering all aspects of women's
role in medieval society.

307. HERLIHY, David. "Life Expectancies for Women in Medieval
Society." The Role of Woman in the Middle Ages. Ed.
Rosmarie Thee Morewedge. Albany: State Univ. of New
New York Press, 1975, pp. 1-22.
Discusses the influence on women of life expectancies,
and examines sex ratios and the survival and treatment
of medieval women.

308. KAUFMAN, Michael W. "Spare Ribs: The Conception of Woman
in the Middle Ages and Renaissance." Soundings, 56
(1973), 139-63.
Argues that women had a higher social role in medieval society
than previously imagined and that women's subjection did not
solidify until the 16th century.

309. MCNAMARA, Jo Ann, and Suzanne WEMPLE. "The Power of Women
Through the Family in Medieval Europe, 500-1100." Clio's
Consciousness Raised: New Perspectives on the History of
Women. Ed. Mary Hartman and Lois W. Banner. New York:
Harper & Row, 1974, pp. 103-18.
Maintains that the social and economic status of women

during the Middle Ages increased as public power was assumed by the great families of the age. But as this power
was recaptured by royalties, women's roles and status
shrank.

3. The Early Modern Family

GENERAL

310. AVELING, Dom Hugh. "The Marriages of Catholic Recusants,
        1559-1642." Journal of Ecclesiastical History, 14 (1963),
        68-83.
      Analyzes the clandestine marriages of Catholic recusants
      as revealed in the York ecclesiastical court cases.

311. BARRATT, Harold S. "'The Rose Distilled': Virginity,
        Fertility, and Marriage in Shakespeare." Diss. Univ.
        of Western Ontario, 1975.
      Shows that Shakespeare emphasized the need for prenuptial
      virginity as a pre-requisite for marriage and did not per-
      ceive a polarity between virginity and marriage. Instead,
      he rejected permanent virginity and believed in the sacred-
      ness and redeeming qualities of marriage.

312. COCKE, Emmett W. "Luther's View of Marriage and Family."
        Religion in Life, 42 (1973), 103-15.
      Notes that Luther envisioned marriage as a part of divine
      creation and believed in the idea of freedom to marry,
      yet he regarded marriage as an antidote to sin.

313. CROFTS, Richard A. "Radical Views of Marriage: The Left
        Wing of the Reformation." Paper delivered at the Amer-
        ican Historical Association, New Orleans, December 1972.

314. FINN, Dorothy Mercedes. "Love and Marriage in Renaissance
        Literature." Diss. Columbia Univ., 1955.
      Argues that Renaissance writers had two attitudes toward
      the relation between love and marriage. Some writers,
      turning to the classical tradition, discussed marriage in
      a rational, detached manner and gave romantic love little
      importance. Others, in the medieval tradition, regarded
      love more important than marriage.

315. GORNALL, J. F. G. "Marriage and Property in Jane Austen's
        Novels." History Today, 17 (1967), 805-11.
      Notes that one of Austen's concerns was the marriage cus-
      toms of the 18th-century English landed gentry, the role
      of mutual affections, and legal provisions in marriage
      contracts.

316. GORNALL, J. F. G. "Marriage, Property, and Romance in
        Jane Austen's Novels." Hibbert Journal, 65 (1967),
        151-6; 66 (1967), 24-9.
      Examines Jane Austen's depiction of the social life of

the English landed gentry in which marriage was not only
a matter of mutual affection, but an institution through
which the gentry maintained and increased their economic
status.

317. HALLER, William. "'Hail Wedded Love'." ELH: A Magazine
      of English Literary History, 13 (1946), 79-97.
      Examines the ideas of love, marriage, and divorce in 17th
      century England and their impact on John Milton.

318. HAYDEN, Mark A. Vander. "Erasmus on Marriage." Paper
      delivered at the American Historical Association, New
      Orleans, December 1972.

319. JOHNSON, James Turner. "The Covenant Idea and the Puritan
      View of Marriage." Journal of the History of Ideas, 32
      (1971), 107-18.
      Examines the covenant idea in relation to the Puritan view
      of marriage, and shows how husband-wife relations were
      based on models derived from covenantal theology.

320. JOHNSON, James Turner. "English Puritan Thought on the
      Ends of Marriage." Church History, 38 (1969), 429-36.
      Discusses Puritan writings on the ends of marriage, and
      concludes that a major strand in the Puritan tradition
      counters the Book of Common Prayer marriage doctrine,
      especially in terms of the ends of marriage and the
      heightened conception of woman.

321. JOHNSON, James Turner. A Society Ordained by God: English
      Puritan Marriage Doctrine in the first half of the Seven-
      teenth Century. Nashville: Abingdon, 1970.
      Argues that the Puritans' covenantal conception of marriage
      contrasted with traditional procreation-based marriage doc-
      trines, and the premium placed on mutual compatibility led
      to the acceptance of divorce on the grounds of incompat-
      ibility.

322. ROOT, Robert Lathrop. "The Problematics of Marriage: Eng-
      lish Comedy, 1688-1710." Diss. Univ. of Iowa, 1975.
      Contends that English comedy of the late-17th century was
      preoccupied with marriage, although pre-Revolutionary com-
      edy was endowed with a libertine outlook while the post-
      Revolutionary comedy was based on an optimistic or exem-
      plary outlook.

323. SJOBERG, Gideon. "Familial Organization in the Preindus-
      trial City." Marriage and Family Living, 18 (1956),
      30-6.
      Examines the high premium placed upon family life in the
      preindustrial city and the efforts to sustain the familial
      system.

324. STONE, Lawrence. "The Rise of the Nuclear Family in Early
      Modern England." The Family in History. Ed. Charles E.

Rosenberg. Philadelphia: Univ. of Pennsylvania Press,
1975, pp. 13-57.
Argues that during the 16th and 17th centuries the English
family shifted from a kin-oriented to a nuclear structure,
that the economic functions of the family declined, and
that patriarchal authoritarianism temporarily increased.

325. VANN, Richard T. "Nurture and Conversion in the Early
Quaker Family." Journal of Marriage and the Family,
31 (1969), 639-43.
Demonstrates that English Quakers in the 17th and 18th
centuries were drawn from younger children of mobile families who would not benefit from primogeniture. Also
shows that conversion to Quakerism depended upon adher-
ence to customs transmitted through the family, leading
to a decline in numbers.

BIRTH CONTROL

326. BLACKER, J. G. C. "Social Ambitions of the Bourgeoisie
in 18th-Century France, and Their Relation to Family
Limitation." Population Studies, 11 (1957), 46-63.
Examines the reluctance of those who were socially mobile
to divide their property between a large number of family
members.

327. SCHNUCKER, Robert V. "Elizabethan Birth Control and Puritan Attitudes." Journal of Interdisciplinary History,
5 (1975), 655-67.
Demonstrates that the Puritans, although aware of contraceptive methods, rejected birth control as antithetical
to God's will, and their preachers at least took their
beliefs seriously as evidenced by their large families.

328. WRIGLEY, Edward Anthony. "Family Limitation in Pre-Industrial England." Economic History Review, 19 (1966),
82-109.
Shows how fertility in pre-modern Colyton, Devon went
through three phases. From 1550 to 1640 there was a surplus of baptisms over burials; from 1640 to 1780 burials
usually exceeded baptisms; and from 1780 to 1830 there
was a large surplus of baptisms. Family limitation was
practiced even among the lower classes.

CHILDREN

329. BAYNE-POWELL, Rosamond. The English Child in the Eighteenth
Century. New York: E. P. Dutton, 1939.
Examines various aspects of English childhood from education
to children's literature to the child and the law. Argues
that 18th-century parents began to consider children in a
kinder spirit and in a less harsh manner.

330. BEDFORD, Jessie. English Children in the Olden Time. 2nd
ed. London: Methuen & Co., 1907.

Discusses infancy, nursery lore, games, pastimes, and
educational theories in 17th and 18th century England.

331.   BERRY, Boyd Midi. "The First English Pediatricians and
           Tudor Attitudes Toward Childhood." Journal of the
           History of Ideas, 35 (1974), 561-77.
        Argues that beginning in the 16th century there arose in
        England a literature which expressed a new concern for
        children as unique and different from adults, a concern
        triggered largely by socio-economic dislocations.

332.   GIBSON, Lois Rauch. "Attitudes Toward Childhood in
           Eighteenth-Century British Fiction." Diss. Univ. of
           Pittsburgh, 1975.
        Illustrates that 18th-century adults increasingly valued
        children as more emphasis was placed on the child as a
        creature of passion and imagination. But as the passions
        gained preeminence, the child moved from being a creature
        to be saved to the source of salvation.

333.   HARADA, Mary Ault. "Family Values and Child Care during
           the Reformation Era: A Comparative Study of Hutterites
           and Some Other German Protestants." Diss. Boston Univ.,
           1968.
        Discusses family and educational concepts and the progress
        of elementary-vernacular education within Protestantism
        and the evangelical Anabaptism of the Hutterites.

334.   HARADA, Mary Ault. "The Training of Children Among German
           Speaking Protestants and Hutterites." Paper delivered
           at the American Historical Association, New Orleans,
           December 1972.

335.   HELMHOLZ, Richard H. "Infanticide in the Province of Can-
           terbury During the Fifteenth Century." History of
           Childhood Quarterly, 2 (1975), 379-90.
        Argues that infanticide was practiced in 15th-century Eng-
        land despite prosecution by Church courts. The punish-
        ment, however, was less severe than homicide.

336.   HOLMAN, J. R. "Orphans in Pre-Industrial Towns--The Case
           of Bristol in the Late Seventeenth Century." Local
           Population Studies, Autumn 1975, pp. 40-4.
        Compares the proportion of children in married couple and
        widow/widower-headed households, and notes that 23.7% of
        Bristol's children were orphans in 1696.

337.   HUNT, David. Parents and Children in History: The Psycho-
           logy of Family Life in Early Modern France. New York:
           Basic Books, 1970.
        Examines the psychodynamics of childhood and family life
        in 17th-century France, with emphasis on Cardinal Richelieu
        and Louis XIII.

338.   LASLETT, Peter. "Parental Deprivation in the Past: A Note

46

on the History of Orphans in England." Local Population
Studies, Autumn 1974, pp. 11-8.
Addressed the question, are there more parentally deprived
children today than there were in preindustrial England,
and concludes that orphanage was more widespread in the
18th century than today.

339. LORENCE, Bogna W. "Parents and Children in Eighteenth-Century Europe." History of Childhood Quarterly, 2 (1974),
1-30.
Observes that attitudes of 18th-century parents toward
their children varied from indifference with minimal parent-child interaction to intrusiveness with rigid attempts
at character molding to the egalitarian emphasis on parent-child mutuality.

340. MCGRAW, Patricia Marie. "Ideas About Children in Eighteenth-Century British Fiction." Diss. Univ. of Connecticut, 1976.
Examines the impact of Locke and Rousseau on British writers
and discusses the nature-nurture debate in fiction. Notes
that children in the 18th century were not yet sentiment-
alized.

341. MARVICK, Elizabeth Wirth. "Nature Versus Nurture: Patterns
and Trends in Seventeenth-Century French Child-Rearing."
The History of Childhood. Ed. Lloyd de Mause. New York:
Psychohistory Press, 1974, pp. 259-302.
Illustrates that childrearing practices in 17th-century
France were remarkably stable as were demographic patterns
of high mortality and remarriage. But the gradual diminution
of parental power over children, fostered by Catholic reformers, resulted in a new morality emphasizing self-direction
and individuality.

342. PINCHBECK, Ivy. "The State and the Child in Sixteenth
Century England." British Journal of Sociology, 7 (1956),
273-85; 8 (1957), 59-74.
Argues that the state in Tudor England, similar to the contemporary Welfare State, was concerned with the problems of
maintaining and training children of the poor, although middle and upper class children were little affected.

343. PINCHBECK, Ivy, and Margaret HEWITT. Children in English
Society: From Tudor Times to the Eighteenth Century.
London: Routledge & Kegan Paul, 1969.
Deals with changing social attitudes toward children and
the consequential influences on social policy and legislation, especially the alternating patterns of benevolence
and indifference.

344. PLUMB, J. H. "The New World of Children in Eighteenth-Century England." Past & Present, May 1975, pp. 64-95.
Examines changing attitudes toward children by childrearing

theorists, educators, educational institutions, writers
of children's literature, and changing developments of
children's amusements.

345. ROE, Frederic Gordon. The Georgian Child. London:
      Phoenix House, 1961.
      Discusses 18th-century English children in terms of toys,
      manners and punishments, clothing, books, school, and past-
      times.

346. ROSS, James Bruce. "The Middle-Class Child in Urban
      Italy, Fourteenth to Early Sixteenth Century." The His-
      tory of Childhood. Ed. Lloyd de Mause. New York:
      Psychohistory Press, 1974, pp. 183-228.
      Describes how growing up in Renaissance Italy was marked by
      severe shocks caused by wet-nursing, educational practices,
      apprenticeship, and familial mobility--all of which demand-
      ed great physical and emotional adjustments on the part of
      children.

347. SAFFADY, William. "The Effect of Childhood Bereavement and
      Parental Remarriage in Sixteenth-Century England: The
      Case of Thomas More." History of Childhood Quarterly,
      1 (1973), 310-36.
      Discusses the effect of parental death and remarriage on
      Thomas More and speculates on their effects on his adult
      personality.

348. SCHNUCKER, Robert V. "The English Puritans and Pregnancy:
      Delivery and Breast Feeding." History of Childhood
      Quarterly, 1 (1974), 637-58.
      Shows how the Puritans were sensitive to the needs of
      pregnant women and were aware of the dangers accompany-
      ing delivery. Although breast feeding was the ideal,
      there were physical and psychological problems that pre-
      vented its realization.

349. TREXLER, Richard C. "The Foundings of Florence, 1395-1455."
      History of Childhood Quarterly, 1 (1973), 259-85.
      Argues that although Florentine society tried to control
      infanticide through the establishment of institutions, these
      institutions failed to reintegrate the unwanted into society
      and perhaps stimulated the desertion of children.

350. TREXLER, Richard C. "Infanticide in Florence: New Sources
      and First Results." History of Childhood Quarterly, 1
      (1973), 98-116.
      Illustrates that infanticide and child abandonment were not
      uncommon in Renaissance Florence and reveal vividly the
      tragic history of childhood.

351. TREXLER, Richard C. "Ritual in Florence: Adolescence and
      Salvation in the Renaissance." The Pursuit of Holiness
      in Late Medieval and Renaissance Religion. Ed. Charles
      Trinkaus and Heiko A. Oberman. Leiden: E. J. Brill,

1974, pp. 200-64.
Discusses the creation in urban Florence of confraternities of boys whose purpose was adolescent acculturation. As the monasteries declined, new means for the social control of youth were developed.

352. TUCKER, M. J. "The Child as Beginning and End: Fifteenth and Sixteenth Century English Childhood." The History of Childhood. Ed. Lloyd de Mause. New York: Psycho-history Press, 1974, pp. 229-58.
Argues that children during the 15th and 16th centuries were thought of little importance and that childhood was a state to be endured rather enjoyed. But attitudes toward children, especially physical care, became more humane.

353. WRIGHTSON, Keith. "Infanticide in Earlier Seventeenth-Century England." Local Population Studies, Autumn 1975, pp. 10-22.
Argues that infanticide can best be understood as a combination of a crime by temporarily unbalanced mothers and a socially sanctioned form of population control. The practice was known and practiced infrequently in 17th century rural England.

DEMOGRAPHY

354. BERRY, Boyd Midi, and Roger S. SCHOFIELD. "Age at Baptism in Pre-Industrial England." Population Studies, 25 (1971), 453-63.
Examines the changing length of the interval between birth and baptism in forty-three English parish registers to determine the accuracy of baptism registers as a record of births.

355. BRADLEY, Leslie. "An Enquiry into Seasonality in Baptisms, Marriages, and Burials." Local Population Studies, Spring 1970, pp. 21-40; Autumn 1970, pp. 18-35; Spring 1971, pp. 15-31.
Examines seasonality in 12 English parishes to discern the effect of unemployment on marriage, the influence of church prohibitions of marriages during specific periods, the impact of winter on conceptions, the rates of pre-marital pregnacy, and the relationship of seasonality and cause of death.

356. CARTER, Ian. "Marriage Patterns and Social Sectors in Scotland Before the Eighteenth Century." Scottish Studies, 17 (1973), 51-60.
Shows that marriages between clans in the Highland and Lowland sectors during the years 1500-1700 were few; thus the Highland was an autonomous social and political area.

357. CHAMBERS, Jonathan David. Population, Economy, and Society in Preindustrial England. New York: Oxford Univ. Press, 1972.

Discusses the uniqueness of European marriage patterns,
fluctuating fertility patterns, and their relationship
to preindustrial economic development.

358. COHEN, Joel E. "Childhood Mortality, Family Size, and
     Birth Order in Pre-Industrial Europe." Demography,
     12 (1975), 35-55.
     Examines the relations among completed family size, birth
     order, childhood mortality, and parental cohort mortality
     in France and Switzerland between 1550 and 1900.

359. COWGILL, Ursula M. "The People of York: 1538-1812."
     Scientific American, 222 (1970), 104-12.
     Examines the cycles in marriage and childbearing, their
     relationship to the religious calendar and the seasons,
     and also analyzes childhood survivorship, age at marriage,
     and age of childbearing in an English community.

360. DEPREZ, Paul. "The Demographic Development of Flanders in
     the Eighteenth Century." Population in History: Essays
     in Historical Demography. Ed. David Victor Glass and
     D. E. C. Eversley. Chicago: Aldine, 1965, pp. 608-30.
     Reviews the general development of the population, age at
     marriage, birth intervals, the relationship between fertil-
     ity and marriage, and infant mortality in Flanders.

361. DRAKE, Michael. "An Elementary Exercise in Parish Register
     Demography." Economic History Review, 14 (1962), 427-55.
     Examines 16th and 17th century parish registers from West
     Riding to discern patterns and interaction of vital rates.

362. DYRVIK, Stale. "Historical Demography in Norway, 1660-1801:
     A Short Survey." Scandinavian Economic History Review,
     20 (1972), 27-44.
     Reviews current trends in Norwegian demographic history as
     well as summarizes recent findings on marriage, growth rates,
     and population trends.

363. EVERSLEY, D. E. C. "A Survey of Population in an Area of
     Worcestershire from 1660-1850 on the Basis of Parish
     Records." Population Studies, 17 (1963), 253-79.
     Examines the practicality of using parish registers to dis-
     cern 18th-century population trends, notably population
     growth, vital rates, and infant mortality.

364. GILLE, H. "The Demographic History of the Northern Eur-
     opean Countries in the Eighteenth Century." Population
     Studies, 3 (1949), 3-65.
     Shows that most Scandinavian adults in the 18th century
     married and that there was high legitimate and low ille-
     gitimate fertility as well as high infant mortality. Mar-
     riage rates, birth rates, and death rates began to decline
     in the late 18th century.

365. GOUBERT, Pierre. "Legitimate Fecundity and Infant Mortality

50

in France During the Eighteenth Century: A Comparison." <u>Daedalus</u>, 97 (1968), 593-603.
Shows that family reconstitution methods applied to 18th century Brittany reveal that most births were legitimate, that child-bearing began late and ended early, and that levels of infant mortality and marital fertility were high in Brittany but markedly lower in Southwest France.

366. HAMMEL, Eugene A. "The Zadruga as Process." <u>Household and Family in Past Time</u>. Ed. Peter Laslett and Richard Wall. Cambridge: Cambridge Univ. Press, 1972, pp. 335-73.
Analyzes kinship and kinship process in relation to household structure in the Balkans and asks how Balkan households are similar to other complex households.

367. HOSKINS, W. G. "The Population of an English Village, 1086-1801: A Study of Wigston Magna." <u>Transactions of the Leicestershire Archaeological and Historical Society</u>, 33 (1957), 15-35.

368. JACKSON, Donald. <u>Intermarriage in Ireland, 1550-1650</u>. Montreal: Cultural and Educational Productions, 1970.
Traces genealogies of Irish families to determine the rate of intermarriage between colonists and indigenous families, intermarriage being a proxy for cultural exchange and assimilation.

369. JONES, R. E. "Parish Registers and Population History: North Shropshire, 1538-1837." Diss. London School of Economics, 1972.
Uses parish registers to determine the vital rates and demographic changes and responses of an English village.

370. KERMACK, W. R. "Did the Marriage Age of Scottish Brides Decrease in the Eighteenth Century?" <u>Scottish Genealogist</u>, 18 (1971), 21-2.
Examines the marriages of 100 Scottish brides and finds that age of marriage decreases from a mean of 25.25 in the first quarter to 23.28 in the last eighth of the 18th century.

371. KRIER, Donald F. "Population Movements in England, 1650-1812: A Family Reconstitution Study of Three Eighteenth Century Lancashire Parishes." Diss. Boston Univ., 1969.
Analyzes whether demographic characteristics were responsive to factors such as employment, new occupational structures or changes in income. Concludes that completed family size was a function of occupational status.

372. KUCHEMAN, C. F., et. al. "A Demographic and Genetic Study of a Group of Oxfordshire Villages." <u>Human Biology</u>, 39 (1967), 251-76.
Uses parish registers and census schedules to analyze the birth rate, age at marriage, birth intervals, family size, and infant mortality from 1578 to the present.

373. LASLETT, Peter. The World We Have Lost: England Before
      the Industrial Age. London: Methuen, 1971.
      Examines preindustrial English social structure, notably
      class divisions, demographic changes, family structure,
      economic organization, and literacy.

374. LITCHFIELD, R. Burr. "Demographic Characteristics of
      Florentine Patrician Families, Sixteenth to Nineteenth
      Centuries." Journal of Economic History, 29 (1969),
      191-205.
      Examines the diminishing number of prominent Florentine
      families and the demographic reasons for their decrease
      in numbers, notably limitation of marriages.

375. LOSCHKY, David J., and Donald F. KRIER. "Income and Fam-
      ily Size in Three Eighteenth-Century Lancashire Parishes:
      A Reconstitution Study." Journal of Economic History,
      29 (1969), 429-48.
      Compares seven income groups in terms of age at marriage,
      average number of births per family, and age intervals
      between spouses.

376. MALTBY, Bessie. "Easingwold Marriage Horizons." Local
      Population Studies, Spring 1969, pp. 36-9.
      Discusses marriage distances in Easingwold parish from
      1644 to 1812, and finds that most marriages took place
      between parish residents. Marriage partners from outside
      the parish came from a relatively short distance away.

377. MENDELS, Franklin Frits. "Industry and Marriages in Flanders
      Before the Industrial Revolution." Population and Eco-
      nomics. Proceedings of Section V of the Fourth Congress
      of the International Economic History Association, 1968.
      Ed. Paul Deprez. Winnipeg: Univ. of Manitoba Press,
      1970, pp. 81-93.
      Examines the effects of industrial export demand on mar-
      riages in 18th-century Flanders, and illustrates that the
      oscillations in marriage rates were correlated with changes
      in the grain market as well as the international linen
      market.

378. OHLIN, G. "Mortality, Marriage and Growth in Pre-Industrial
      Populations." Population Studies, 14 (1961), 190-7.
      Discovers that the institutional pattern connecting marriage
      with inheritance in preindustrial populations also linked
      the control of fertility to mortality.

379. SOGNER, Solvi. "Aspects of the Demographic Situation in 17
      Parishes in Shropshire, 1711-60." Population Studies,
      17 (1963), 126-46.
      Analyzes parish registers to determine illegitimacy, place
      of residence of marriage partners, and births per marriage.

380. SPEAKE, R. "The Historical Demography of the Ancient Parish
      of Audley, 1538-1801." North Staffordshire Journal of

Field Studies, 11 (1971), 65-80.
Discerns population trends from Audley parish registers as
well as population estimates and migration patterns.

381. SPEAKE, R. "The Historical Demography of Warton Parish
Before 1801." Historic Society of Lancashire and Che-
shire Transactions, 122 (1970), 43-65.
Uses parish registers from Warton to discern 17th and 18th
century occupational structure, population movement, vital
rates, and population estimates.

382. STONE, Lawrence. "Marriage Among the English Nobility in
the 16th and 17th Centuries." Comparative Studies in
Society and History, 3 (1961), 182-206.
Discusses the changes in mate selection, age at marriage,
duration of marriage, and socio-economic motives for marriage among English elites.

383. TURNER, Derek. "The Effective Family." Local Population
Studies, Spring 1969, pp. 47-52.
Discusses a refinement of the fertility rate--the 'effective family'--which is the number of children per family
who themselves married. Presents data that show the effective family in England remaining small and stable until
the mid-18th century.

384. UTTERSTROM, Gustaf. "Some Population Problems in Pre-Industrial Sweden." Scandinavian Economic History Review,
2 (1954), 103-65.
Argues that population fluctuations in 18th and 19th century Sweden were not a product of changes in the means of
subsistence but the result of factors such as climate and
living conditions.

385. VAN BATH, Bernard H. Slicher. "Historical Demography and
the Social and Economic Development of the Netherlands."
Daedalus, 97 (1968), 604-21.
Discusses the changing population characteristics of the
Netherlands between 1500 and 1800, including fertility,
mortality, family structure, age distribution, and age at
marriage.

386. WRIGLEY, Edward Anthony. "Marriage and Fertility in Pre-
Industrial England." Listener, 75 (1966), 199-201.
Discusses advances in the techniques of historical demography, notably family reconstitution, and analyzes the
results of a pilot reconstitution study at Colyton, including changing age at marriage, family size, birth
control practices, and pre-marital pregnancy.

DIVORCE

387. GUTHRIE, Charles John. "The History of Divorce in Scotland." Scottish Historical Review, 8 (1910), 39-52.
Compares English and Scottish divorce laws and the origins

53

of divorce reform with emphasis on the Reformation period.

388. MUELLER, Gerhard O. W. "Inquiry Into the State of a Divorce-
      less Society: Domestic Relations, Law and Morals in Eng-
      land From 1660-1857." University of Pittsburgh Law
      Review, 18 (1957), 545-78.
      Discusses the divorceless period of English history and
      how judges shaped the law to remedy hardships, how people
      sought non-divorce solutions to marital problems, and how
      popular pressure led to the Matrimonial Causes Act of 1857.

DOMESTIC ARCHITECTURE

389. GOLDTHWAITE, Richard A. "The Florentine Palace as Domestic
      Architecture." American Historical Review, 77 (1972),
      977-1012.
      Argues that the Florentine palace reflected a new esthetic
      consciousness of the patrician and the changed conditions
      of 14th-century family life. It symbolized the ideals of
      privacy and intimacy.

DOMESTIC LIFE AND CUSTOMS

390. ALBERTI, Leone Battista. The Family in Renaissance Flor-
      ence. Columbia, S.C.: Univ. of South Carolina Press,
      1969.
      Examines the problems of paternal responsibility, conjugal
      love, household management, and the proper external re-
      lations of the household head in the Italian family. Ori-
      ginally published in the early 15th century.

391. ASHLEY, Maurice. "Love and Marriage in Seventeenth-Century
      England." History Today, 8 (1958), 667-75.
      Examines 17th-century sex roles, marriage customs and court-
      ship practices, and attitudes toward love among the varying
      social classes of England.

392. BEDFORD, Jessie. Home Life Under the Stuarts, 1603-1649.
      New York: E. P. Dutton, 1903.
      Examines various aspects of 17th-century upper class Eng-
      lish family life, including the nursery, children's games,
      schools, courtship practices, the housewife, clothing, and
      domestic architecture.

393. BURTON, Elizabeth. The Elizabethans at Home. London:
      Secker & Warburg, 1958.
      Describes the homes, furniture, food, medical care, cloth-
      ing, and pastimes of 16th-century Englishmen.

394. BURTON, Elizabeth. The Georgians at Home, 1714-1830. London:
      Longmans, 1967.
      Discusses domestic architecture, furniture and interior
      decoration, dietary habits, folk-medicine, amusements, and
      clothing of mid-18th-century Englishmen.

395. BURTON Elizabeth. The Jacobeans at Home. London: Secker
     & Warburg, 1962.
     Examines the homes, furniture, dietary patterns, recreations,
     clothing, and medical care of 17th-century Englishmen.

396. CLARK, Cumberland. Shakespeare and Home Life. London:
     Williams & Norgate, 1935.
     Describes Elizabethan home life with emphasis on houses,
     furniture, diet, home duties, leisure activities, and
     dress.

397. HECHT, J. Jean. The Domestic Servant Class in Eighteenth
     Century England. London: Routledge & Paul, 1956.
     Explores the composition, size, and structure of the ser-
     vant class and its relation to 18th-century society, as
     well as the means of recruitment, working and living con-
     ditions, and servants' hopes and ambitions.

398. HOLE, Christina. English Home-Life, 1450 to 1800. London:
     B. T. Batsford, 1947.
     Examines the daily habits and home-life of country-dwellers
     in England, including furnishings, childrearing, domestic
     dwellings, diet, and servants.

399. KATZ, Jacob. "Family, Kinship, and Marriage Among Ashken-
     azim in the Sixteenth to Eighteenth Centuries." Jewish
     Journal of Sociology, 1 (1959), 4-22.
     Discusses the functions and structure of the Jewish fam-
     ily, including the interplay between economics and the
     family as well as age at marriage and arranged marriages.

400. LOCHHEAD, Marion. The Scots Household in the 18th Century:
     A Century of Scottish Domestic and Social Life. Edinburgh:
     Moray Press, 1948.
     Discusses all aspects of Scottish housekeeping, including
     manners, diet, social life, childrearing, leisurely activ-
     ities, and domestic manufacturing.

401. PEARSON, Lu Emily. Elizabethans at Home. Stanford: Stan-
     ford Univ. Press, 1957.
     Discusses Elizabethan domestic life from all aspects--domestic
     architecture, childrearing, clothing, courtship, parent-child
     relationships, sex roles, and family life.

402. PLANT, Marjorie. The Domestic Life of Scotland in the
     Eighteenth Century. Edinburgh: Edinburgh Univ. Press,
     1952.
     Uses account-books, diaries, and reminiscences to describe
     the upper class Scottish home, family life, diet, furnish-
     ings, servants, childrearing, and family celebrations.

403. POWELL, Chilton Latham. English Domestic Relations, 1487-
     1653. New York: Columbia Univ. Press, 1917.
     Discusses the laws, practices, and customs of marriage
     as well as varying religious positions on marriage and

divorce. Also examines domestic conduct books and attitudes toward women.

404. SCHUCKING, Levin Ludwig. The Puritan Family: A Social Study from the Literary Sources. 1929; rpt. New York: Schocken Books, 1970.
Discusses the family as depicted in Puritan literature, especially conduct books, and concludes that the achievement of the bourgeoisie was their transformation of the family into a real community.

405. SLATER, Miriam. "Marriage in an Upper Gentry Family in 17th Century England." Paper delivered at Historians and the Family: A Symposium, Mount Holyoke College, April 1975.

406. SLATER, Miriam. "The Weightiest Business: Marriage in an Upper Gentry Family." Paper delivered at the American Historical Association, Chicago, December 1974.

407. THOMPSON, Charles John Samuel. Love, Marriage and Romance in Old London. London: Heath Cranton, 1936.

408. TRUMBACH, Randolph Earl. "The Aristocratic Family in England, 1690-1780: Studies in Childhood and Kinship." Diss. Johns Hopkins Univ., 1972.
Examines three generations of the 160 families whose heads sat in the House of Lords in terms of sex roles, birth control, childrearing, attitudes toward children, kinship, and inheritance.

409. WHEATON, Robert. "Bordeaux before the Fronde: A Study of Family, Class, and Social Structure." Diss. Harvard Univ., 1973.
Finds that small, nuclear families were prevalent in Bordeaux in the 1640s, although multiple family households did exist at all social levels. Notes that the kin group was also small, and that social position was largely determined by one's family. Also discusses family tensions.

FAMILY COMPOSITION AND STRUCTURE

410. BERKNER, Lutz Karl. "Family, Social Structure, and Rural Industry: A Comparative Study of the 'Waldviertel' and the 'Pays de Caux' in the Eighteenth Century." Diss. Harvard Univ., 1973.
Compares the social structure and rural household organization of two regions in Germany and France where the rural cotton textile industry developed in the 18th century to determine the impact of industry on social structure and the role of social structure in the development of rural industry.

411. BERKNER, Lutz Karl. "The Stem Family and the Developmental Cycle of the Peasant Household: An 18th-Century Austrian

Example." <u>American Historical Review</u>, 77 (1972),
398-418.
Illustrates that when family cycle is taken into consid-
eration, the proportion of stem families in preindustrial
societies significantly increases. Argues that the stem
family is related to demographic and economic variables,
especially land and labor.

412. BIRABEN, Jean-Noel. "A Southern French Village: The Inhabitants of Montplaisant in 1644." <u>Household and Family in Past Time</u>. Ed. Peter Laslett <u>and Richard Wall</u>.
Cambridge: Cambridge Univ. Press, 1972, pp. 237-54.
Examines household structure and composition in a 17th
century French village.

413. DUPAQUIER, Jacque, and Louis JADIN. "Structure of Household and Family in Corsica, 1769-71." <u>Household and
Family in Past Time</u>. Ed. Peter Laslett <u>and Richard
Wall</u>. Cambridge: Cambridge Univ. Press, 1972, pp.
283-97.
Examines household structure by age of household, and finds
wide variations, although most of the households consist
of conjugal families.

414. KLAPISCH, Christiane. "Household and Family in Tuscany in
1427." <u>Household and Family in Past Time</u>. Ed. Peter
Laslett <u>and Richard Wall</u>. Cambridge: Cambridge Univ.
Press, 1972, pp. 267-81.
Uses the catasto of 1427 to reveal information about the
number and composition of households, age and sex composition, rural-urban differentials, and distribution of
households by sex and marital status in 15th-century Tuscany.

415. LASLETT, Peter. "The Comparative History of the Household
and Family." <u>Journal of Social History</u>, 4 (1970),
75-87.
Suggests that the extended household was uncommon in pre-
industrial societies and that household size is not a good
indicator of family structure. Industrialization, thus,
did not create the nuclear family.

416. LASLETT, Peter, and John HARRISON. "Clayworth and Cogenhoe." <u>Historical Essays, 1600-1750, Presented to David
Ogg</u>. Ed. Henry E. Bell and R. L. Ollard. London: A.
and C. Black, 1963, pp. 157-84.
Discusses the register of Clayworth and Cogenhoe censuses
of 1676 and 1688. Examines household size and composition,
and finds the existence of small households. Also analyzes
the vital rates and mobility of Cogenhoe.

417. LASLETT, Peter, and Marilyn CLARK. "Houseful and Household
in an Eighteenth-Century Balkan City. A Tabular Analysis
of the Listing of the Serbian Sector of Belgrade in 1733-4."
<u>Household and Family in Past Time</u>. Ed. Peter Laslett and

Richard Wall. Cambridge: Cambridge Univ. Press, 1972, pp. 375-400.
Reveals the pattern of domestic groups in 18th-century Belgrade and compares the results with preindustrial households in Western Europe.

418. MCARDLE, Frank. "Another Look at 'Peasant Families East and West'." Peasant Studies Newsletter, 3 (1974), 11-4.
Notes that central Italian peasant families of the 18th century were similar to those in the Baltic Province of Kurland. Stresses that comparative studies of peasant families need to consider settlement patterns and local domestic architecture.

419. PLAKANS, Andrejs. "Peasant Families East and West: A Comment on Lutz K. Berkner's 'Rural Family Organization in Europe: A Problem in Comparative History'." Peasant Studies Newsletter, 2 (1973), 11-6.
Discusses the preliminary results of a study of the 1797 census in the Baltic Province of Kurland, with emphasis on mean unit size of peasant groups and frequency of family structures.

420. PLAKANS, Andrejs. "Peasant Farmsteads and Households in the Baltic Littoral, 1797." Comparative Studies in Society and History, 17 (1975), 2-35.
Emphasizes that family life in Eastern Europe differed markedly from Western Europe with respect to organizational and structural patterns, family and individual life cycle, and the interaction between family life and the preindustrial economic system.

421. PLAKANS, Andrejs. "Seigneurial Authority and Peasant Family Life: The Baltic Area in the Eighteenth Century." Journal of Interdisciplinary History, 5 (1975), 629-54.
Observes that Baltic family life revolved around large cores consisting of a conjugal family, married and unmarried relatives, and others. This pattern of co-residency may have been the result of cultural proclivities or landowner interference.

422. SABEAN, David Warren. "Rural Family Structure in Traditional Southwest German Society in the Seventeenth and Eighteenth Centuries." Paper delivered at the American Historical Association, New York, December 1971.

423. TRANTER, N. L. "Population and Social Structure in a Bedfordshire Parish: The Cardingon Listing of Inhabitants, 1782." Population Studies, 21 (1967), 261-82.
Notes that almost all 18th-century English cottage dwellers married and lived in one-family households. But also shows that rural English society was fraught with broken marriages or remarriages, high infant mortality, and excessive turnover rates.

424. VAN DER WOUDE, A. M. "Variations in the Size and Structure
      of the Household in the United Provinces of the Nether-
      lands in the Seventeenth   and Eighteenth Centuries."
      Household and Family in Past Time. Ed. Peter Laslett
      and Richard Wall. Cambridge: Cambridge Univ. Press,
      1972, pp. 299-318.
      Finds regional variations in household size and a possible
      correlation between the farming system and the presence of
      extended families.

425. WALL, Richard. "Mean Household Size in England from Print-
      ed Sources." Household and Family in Past Time. Ed.
      Peter Laslett and Richard Wall. Cambridge: Cambridge
      Univ. Press, 1972, pp. 159-203.
      Presents the opinions and assumptions of English social
      and political leaders concerning household size to il-
      lustrate that 18th-century writers did not suppose that
      multiple or extended family households existed to a large
      extent.

FAMILY LAW AND INHERITANCE

426. BERKNER, Lutz Karl. "Rural Family Organization in Europe:
      A Problem in Comparative History." Peasant Studies
      Newsletter, 1 (1972), 145-56.
      Examines the impact of inheritance patterns and marriage
      laws on family organization, especially that of peasants,
      and cautions against comparative family studies without
      controlling variables.

427. CLAY, Christopher. "Marriage, Inheritance, and the Rise of
      Large Estates in England, 1660-1815." Economic History
      Review, 21 (1968), 503-18.
      Shows that from the 17th to the 18th century, marriage and
      inheritance did not favor English magnates more than gentry
      because of female inheritance patterns. But as less land
      came on the market large estates slowly came into being.

428. HABAKKUK, H. J. "Marriage Settlements in the Eighteenth
      Century." Transactions of the Royal Historical Society,
      32 (1950), 15-30.
      Illustrates that 18th-century marriage settlements of the
      English elite were based on primogeniture in which the
      eldest son inherited the family estate, with jointures and
      portions provided for daughters and younger sons.

429. HARVEY, Judith Walters. "The Influence of the Reformation
      on Nuernberg Marriage Laws, 1520-1535." Diss. Ohio State
      Univ., 1972.
      Examines the extent to which the Reformation influenced the
      interpretation of existing marriage laws or promoted the
      passage and application of new legislation which conformed
      to Protestant marriage doctrine.

430. HOWELL, Cicely. "Stability and Change, 1300-1700: The

Socio-Economic Context of the Self-Perpetuating Family
Farm in England." <u>Journal of Peasant Studies</u>, 2 (1975),
468-82.
Notes that the change in inheritance patterns aided in
bringing about the transformation of the medieval peasantry into small-holders of respected status.

431. HURSTFIELD, Joel. <u>The Queen's Wards: Wardship and Marriage</u>
       <u>Under Elizabeth I</u>. London: Longmans, Green & Co., 1958.
       Examines the origins and the personal and social consequences
       of the revival of feudal wardship and marriage as well as its
       effects upon government in 16th and 17th century England.

432. HURSTFIELD, Joel. "Wardship and Marriage Under Elizabeth
       I." <u>History Today</u>, 4 (1954), 605-12.
       Discusses the royal right of wardship and marriage, the
       decline of the feudal significance of these rights, and
       their growing economic importance.

433. KENT, F. W. <u>Under the Shadow of One Will: Lineage and</u>
       <u>Family in the Renaissance</u>. Melbourne: Australian Broad-
       casting Commission, 1972.
       Discusses the importance of lineage and inheritance of
       property in prominent families of the Renaissance.

434. MCLAREN, Dorothy. "The Marriage Act of 1653: Its Influ-
       ence on the Parish Registers." <u>Population Studies</u>, 28
       (1974), 319-27.
       Maintains that the Act of 1653, generally thought to be
       ineffectual, resulted in stricter control over wedlock
       with regard to solemnization and registration of English
       marriages.

435. SABEAN, David Warren. "Family and Land Tenure: A Case
       Study of Conflict in the German Peasants' War (1525)."
       <u>Peasant Studies Newsletter</u>, 3 (1974), 1-15.
       Discusses the effect of rising population and its effects
       on land tenure and usage, and examines the status of per-
       sonal bondage--<u>Leibeigenschaft</u>--and its implications for
       rights in land.

436. WRIGLEY, Edward Anthony. "Clandestine Marriage in Tetbury
       in the Late 17th Century." <u>Local Population Studies</u>,
       Spring 1973, pp. 15-21.
       Analyzes the changes in non-church celebrated marriages in
       an English parish and their relations to social and politi-
       cal changes between 1660 and 1719.

KINSHIP

437. CHOJNACKI, Stanley. "Dowries and Kinsmen in Early Renais-
       sance Venice." <u>Journal of Interdisciplinary History</u>,
       5 (1975), 571-600.
       Maintains that during the dowry inflation of the 14th and
       15th centuries, male commitment to lineage persisted while

females increasingly left property to female relatives because of personal affection (kin ties) and an indifference to lineage.

438. MACFARLANE, Alan. The Family Life of Ralph Josselin:
      A Seventeenth-Century Clergyman: An Essay in Historical Anthropology. Cambridge: Cambridge Univ.
      Press, 1970.
      Examines the diary of a 17th-century English clergyman,
      using the methods of social anthropology, to determine
      Ralph Josselin's social and economic activities and kinship relations.

439. SABEAN, David Warren. "Family and Kinship Among Swabian
      Peasants." Paper delivered at the Conference on the
      Family, Social Structure and Social Change, Worcester,
      April 1972.

SEXUALITY

440. ASHLEY, Maurice Perry. The Stuarts in Love, With Some Reflection on Love and Marriage in the Sixteenth and Seventeenth Centuries. London: Hodder & Stoughton, 1963.
      Explores the love affairs of English kings and queens in
      the context of the general attitudes toward love and marriage, and finds many similarities to modern ideas.

441. HAIR, P. E. H. "Bridal Pregnancy in Earlier Rural England
      Further Examined." Population Studies, 24 (1970), 59-70.
      Argues that bridal pregnancy decreased from the 17th to the
      18th centuries and was the product of courting conventions,
      not sexual license. Nor was it common among teenagers or
      widows.

442. HAIR, P. E. H. "Bridal Pregnancy in Rural England in Earlier Centuries." Population Studies, 20 (1966), 233-43.
      Notes that marriage and baptism records in rural England
      from 1540 to 1835 reveal that about one-third of all brides
      were pregnant, but the frequency of bridal pregnancy varied
      greatly between regions.

443. HALLER, William, and Malleville HALLER. "The Puritan Art
      of Love." Huntington Library Quarterly, 5 (1942), 235-72.
      Discusses the teachings of the Puritan pulpit concerning
      love and marriage, especially the sentimental and idealistic
      aspects.

444. RODIS, Themistocles C. "Morals: Marriage, Divorce, and Illegitimacy during the French Revolution, 1789-1795."
      Diss. Case Western Reserve, 1968.
      Analyzes the transition from an ecclesiastical to a secular
      control of marriage, divorce, and illegitimacy, and finds
      few changes in French morality from 1789 to 1795.

445. ESHLEMAN, Michael K. "Diet During Pregnancy in the Sixteenth and Seventeenth Centuries." _Journal of the History of Medicine_, 30 (1975), 23-39.
Examines the importance of diet during pregnancy, the goals of prenatal diet, and how these goals were accomplished.

446. FORBES, Thomas Roger. _The Midwife and the Witch_. New Haven: Yale Univ. Press, 1966.
Discusses supersitions surrounding birth and the role of the midwife in history, especially her resort to superstitious practices and her regulation.

447. FORBES, Thomas Roger. "The Regulation of English Midwives in the Sixteenth and Seventeenth Centuries." _Medical History_, 8 (1964), 235-44.
Discusses the attempt by the Church to regulate and license English midwives.

448. GEORGE, Margaret. "From 'Good-Wife' to 'Mistress': The Transformation of the Female in Bourgeois Culture." _Science and Society_, 37 (1973), 152-77.
Argues that in the 17th-century bourgeois English society, the status of women deteriorated from the woman as a socially integrated and important individual to the woman-as-dutiful wife and social inferior.

449. HOLE, Christina. _The English Housewife in the Seventeenth Century_. London: Chatoo & Windus, 1953.
Describes the domestic activities of the English housewife, her household chores and pastimes, and her legal rights. Also discusses childrearing, diet, and clothing.

450. HUFTON, Olwen. "Women and the Family Economy in Eighteenth Century France." _French Historical Studies_, 9 (1975), 1-22.
Discusses the role of the daughter in working-class families, her employment and marriage prospects, and the extent and significance of women's contribution to the family economy.

451. THOMPSON, Roger. _Women in Stuart England and America: A Comparative Study_. London: Routledge, 1974.
Compares women in the 17th-century colonies with those in England in terms of responses to the "woman question", treatment and economic opportunity, and specific institutions such as the family and law.

452. WOODS, Margaret Louisa. "The English Housewife in the Seventeenth Century." _Fortnightly Review_, 88 (1910), 823-33.
Examines a 17th-century English domestic manual to reveal social customs, diet, and functions of the English housewife.

4. The Modern Family   (1800-1945)

GENERAL

453. AGREN, Kurt. et. al., eds. Aristocrats, Farmers, Prole-
     tarians: Essays in Swedish Demographic History. Up-
     psala: Esselte Studium, 1973.
     Contains essays covering fertility, family formation, and
     migration in Sweden since 1600 and their relation to socio-
     economic variables.

454. BARDIS, Panos D. "Family Forms and Variations Historically
     Considered." Handbook of Marriage and the Family. Ed.
     Harold T. Christensen. Chicago: Rand McNally & Co.,
     1964, pp. 403-61.
     Discusses the origin and evolution of family sociology,
     and surveys the development of family forms from the He-
     brew family to the present.

455. BERKNER, Lutz Karl. "Recent Research on the History of
     the Family in Western Europe." Journal of Marriage
     and the Family, 35 (1973), 395-405.
     Illustrates how recent European historiography has ap-
     proached the family in terms of social class, demographic
     history and household analysis, and regional and local
     studies. Argues that variation in household size and
     composition can be explained in large measure by socio-
     economic or political variables.

456. BOSANQUET, Helen Dendy. The Family. New York: Macmillan
     Company, 1906.
     Examines the history of the family as an institution, fol-
     lowing closely the arguments of Howard, and traces the
     waning of the patriarchal family and the relation of the
     family to industry, property, and the state.

457. BRIFFAULT, Robert. The Mothers: The Matriarchal Theory
     of Social Origins. 3 vol. 1927; rpt. New York: Mac-
     millan, 1960.
     Examines the matriarchal theory of social evolution, es-
     pecially the impact of woman on primitive and ancient
     societies and the development of civilization.

458. CONNELL, Kenneth Hugh. Irish Peasant Society: Four
     Historical Essays. Oxford: Clarendon Press, 1968.
     Includes essays on pre-famine illegitimacy and post-famine
     Catholic attitudes toward marriage.

459. GLOAG, John Edwards, and C. T. WALKER. Home Life in His-
     tory: Social Life and Manners in Britain, 200 B.C.
     to A.D. 1926. New York: Coward-McCann, 1928.
     Surveys very broadly representative samples of home life
     in Britain, with emphasis on domestic architecture, meals,
     manners, and conversation.

63

460. GOODSELL, Willystine. A History of the Family as a Social
      and Educational Institution. New York: Macmillan, 1915.
      Calls for a gentic study of the family, and traces the evolu-
      tion of the family from the primitive family to the patri-
      archal family to the modern family.

461. GOUBERT, Pierre. "Historical Demography and the Reinter-
      pretation of Early Modern French History: A Research
      Review." Journal of Interdisciplinary History, 1 (1971),
      37-48.
      Notes that French demographic historiography is the product
      of two distinct groups: social and economic historians and
      demographers. Both have noted a transformation in 18th
      century French society as mobility, birth control, ille-
      gitimacy, premarital pregnancy increased and the infant
      death rate declined.

462. GRONSETH, Erik. "Notes on the Historical Development of
      the Relation Between Nuclear Family, Kinship System and
      the Wider Social Structure in Norway." Families in
      East and West. Ed. Reuben Hill and Rene Konig. Paris:
      Mouton, 1970, pp. 225-47.
      Traces the structural and functional patterns of the kin-
      ship and family system in Norway from 3000 B.C. to the
      mid-19th century, with emphasis on the relation between
      the nuclear family and the wider kinship structure.

463. HOWARD, George Elliot. A History of Matrimonial Insti-
      tutions. 3 vol. Chicago: Univ. of Chicago Press, 1904.
      Examines the literature and theories of primitive matri-
      monial institutions, the early history of divorce and
      marriage in England, and the development of matrimon-
      ial institutions in the United States.

464. HOWINGTON, Nolan P. "The Historic Attitude of the Chris-
      tian Churches Concerning Marriage, Divorce, and Remar-
      riage." Diss. Southern Baptist Theological Seminary,
      1948.

465. HOWSE, Marguerite. A Short History of Christian Marriage.
      London: A. R. Mowbray, 1933.

466. JAMES, Edwin Oliver. Marriage Customs Through the Ages.
      New York: Collier Books, 1965.
      Discusses the institutional development of marriage, with
      emphasis on the transition from primitive to religious to
      civil marriages.

467. KOVALEVSKII, Maksim Maksimovich. "Matrimonial Customs
      and Usages of the Russian People and the Light They
      Throw on the Evolution of Marriage." Modern Customs
      and Ancient Laws of Russia. London: David Nutt,
      1891, pp. 1-31.
      Examines the evolution of marriage in Russia from early
      promisuous origins to the imposition of rigid ecclesiastical

codes, from the matriarchal to the patriarchal family.

468. LETOURNEAU, Charles Jean Marie. The Evolution of Mar-
      riage and of the Family. New York: C. Scribner's
      Sons, 1891.

469. LOCKOCK, Herbert Mortimer. History of Marriage, Jewish
      and Christian in Relation to Divorce & Certain For-
      bidden Degrees. New York: Longmans, Green & Co.,
      1894.

470. SHORTER, Edward. The Making of the Modern Family. New
      York: Basic Books, 1975.
      Examines the shift from the traditional to the modern
      family in terms of a revolution in courtship sentiment,
      in the mother-child relationship, and in the line between
      family and community.

471. THWING, Charles Franklin, and Carrie F. BUTLER. The
      Family: An Historical and Social Study. Boston:
      Lothrop, Lee & Shephard, 1913.
      Uses an institutional approach to trace the history of
      the family from pre-historic to Christian to modern
      times. Is concerned with the breakdown of the modern
      family and why such a breakdown has occurred.

472. TURNER, Ernest Sackville. The History of Courting.
      New York: E. P. Dutton, 1955.
      Traces the history of courtship practices in Western Civ-
      ilization, and shows how courtship adjusted itself to
      changing conceptions of love and new codes of manners.

473. UNWIN, J. D. "Marriage in Cultural History." Hibbert
      Journal, 26 (1928), 687-706.
      Surveys the shift from parental-controlled marriages to
      marriages based on mutual consent.

474. URLIN, Ethel Lucy Hargreave. A Short History of Marriage:
      Marriage Rites, Customs, and Folklore in Many Countries
      and All Ages. London: W. Rider & Son, 1913.
      Summarizes the marriage customs of nations worldwide and
      in historical perspective. Includes an examination of prim-
      itive marriage, Greek and Roman marriage, Western and Eastern
      marriage customs, old English marriage customs and super-
      stitions, and the wedding-ring.

475. WERNICK, Robert, et. al. The Family. New York: Time-Life
      Books, 1975.
      Surveys the changing role and function of the family, and
      presents a popular account of the family in past and present
      societies worldwide.

476. WESTERMARCK, Edvard Alexander. History of Human Marriage.
      1891; rpt. London: Macmillan and Co., 1921.
      Surveys the origins of marriage, its frequency and marriage

age, endogamy and exogamy, marriage rites, group marriage
and polygyny, and divorce.

BIRTH CONTROL

477. BANKS, Joseph Ambrose. Prosperity and Parenthood: A
      Study of Family Planning among the Victorian Middle
      Classes. London: Routledge Paul, 1954.
      Argues that the rising standard of living, beginning with
      Malthusian controversies and continuing through the em-
      phasis on conspicuous consumption, was largely respons-
      ible for the declining birth rate among Victorian middle
      classes.

478. BANKS, Joseph Ambrose, and Olive BANKS. Feminism and
      Family Planning in Victorian England. New York:
      Schocken Books, 1964.
      Believes that the emancipation of women was not a causal
      factor in the decline in fertility rates. Argues that
      birth control was an individual revolt by women against
      a passive role in family decision making.

479. CAMPBELL, Flann. "Birth Control and the Christian Churches."
      Population Studies, 14 (1960), 131-47.
      Notes that although Christian Churches have traditionally
      opposed contraceptive measures as sinful, in the 20th cen-
      tury Churches became aware of demographic problems and have
      begun to modify their views.

480. CARLSSON, G. "Nineteenth Century Fertility Oscillations."
      Population Studies, 24 (1970), 413-22.
      Shows that Swedish population data from 1830 to 1879 re-
      veal that birth control was extensively practiced before
      the decline in marital fertility.

481. DOWSE, Robert E., and John PEEL. "The Politics of Birth
      Control." Political Studies, 13 (1965), 179-97.
      Argues that the middle class in Britain championed birth
      control and not political parties. Also traces the de-
      velopment of the advocacy of birth control on general
      humanitarian and democratic grounds.

482. FINCH, Bernard Ephraim, and Hugh GREEN. Contraception
      Through the Ages. London: Peter Owen, 1963.
      Discusses the idea of contraception, and traces the de-
      velopment and use of various contraceptive methods. Views
      the advancement of contraception as a science.

483. FRYER, Peter. The Birth Controllers. New York: Stein
      and Day, 1966.
      Describes the pioneers of birth control, their public
      activities, and the opposition to family limitation from
      the 17th century to the present.

484. GAUNT, David. "Family Planning and the Preindustrial

Society: Some Swedish Evidence." <u>Aristocrats, Farmers,
Proletarians: Essays in Swedish Demographic History</u>.
Ed. Kurt Agren, et. al. Uppsala: Esselte Studium,
1973, pp. 28-59.
Applies the methods of family reconstitution to preindustrial Swedish parish records, and discusses vital rates,
age at first marriage, family limitation, and family size.

485. GITTINS, Diana G. "Married Life and Birth Control Between
the Wars." <u>Oral History</u>, Autumn 1975, pp. 53-64.
Uses oral history to conclude that a perceived standard of
living influenced attempts at family limitation and that
birth control knowledge was not diffused from the middle
to the lower classes. Rather, it was withheld from the
the working classes.

486. GREEN, Shirley. <u>The Curious History of Contraception</u>.
New York: St. Martin's Press, 1971.
Discusses the history of birth control practices and the
origins of the birth control movement, but draws heavily
from Himes and adds little new material.

487. HIMES, Norman E. <u>Medical History of Contraception</u>. Baltimore: Williams & Wilkins, 1936.
Contends that the history of birth control is the ageless
story of man struggling to achieve "adequate parenthood"
and of the democratization of contraceptive practices.
Notes that attempts at birth limitation are the result of
perceived or unconscious needs, not rhetoric or advocacy.
The major work to date on the history of birth control.

488. JEGER, L. M. "The Politics of Family Planning." <u>Political
Quarterly</u>, 33 (1962), 48-58.
Discusses the history of the birth control movement in Britain from the trial of Bradlaugh and Besant in 1877 to the
establishment of the National Birth Control Council in 1930.

489. LANGER, William L. "The Origins of the Birth Control Movement in England in the Early Nineteenth Century." <u>Jour-
nal of Interdisciplinary History</u>, 5 (1975), 669-86.
Shows that the birth control movement grew out of a con-
certed attempt by political economists to counteract the
problems of increasing poverty, a poverty attributed to a
superabundance of workers.

490. LIVI-BACCI, Massimo. "Fertility and Population Growth in
Spain in the Eighteenth and Nineteenth Centuries."
<u>Daedalus</u>, 97 (1968), 523-35.
Argues that the declining birth rate in Spain was the pro-
duct of voluntary birth control.

491. PEEL, John. "Contraception and the Medical Profession."
<u>Population Studies</u>, 18 (1964), 133-45.
Discusses the changing attitudes of the British medical
profession toward birth control in the 19th and 20th

67

centuries.

492. RANUM, Orest, and Patricia RANUM, ed. Popular Attitudes
     toward Birth Control in Pre-Industrial France and
     England. New York: Harper & Row, 1972.
     An anthology of essays examining when Western Europe
     began to practice or become familiar with family limit-
     ation.

493. SHORTER, Edward. "Female Emancipation, Birth Control, and
     Fertility in European History." American Historical
     Review, 78 (1973), 605-40.
     Explains how changing attitudes toward birth control and
     the new sexual freedom led to a rising illegitimacy among
     young European women from 1750 to 1880. But notes that
     from 1880 to 1940, fertility declined among all women due
     to a sense of female emancipation and independence and to
     increased access to contraceptives.

494. SJOVALL, Hjalmar. "Abortion and Contraception in Sweden,
     1870-1970." Zeitschrift fur Rechtsmedizin, 70 (1972),
     197-209.
     Shows that birth control has been practiced in Sweden since
     at least 1870, and that modern Sweds have adopted an ef-
     fective system of family limitation.

495. TIETZE, Christopher. "History of Contraceptive Methods."
     Journal of Sex Research, 1 (1965), 69-85.
     Surveys the development of birth control methods and pre-
     scriptions from Biblical times to the present.

496. VAN DE WALLE, Etienne. "Marriage and Marital Fertility."
     Daedalus, 97 (1968), 486-501.
     Examines the transition in Western Europe from uncontrolled
     to controlled marital fertility, and finds that marital
     fertility declined despite trends toward earlier marriage,
     indicating a change in the attitude toward fertility control.

497. VAN DE WALLE, Etienne, et. al. "The Decline of Non-Marital
     Fertility in Europe, 1880-1940." Population Studies, 25
     (1971), 375-93.
     Notes that illegitimate fertility rates in Europe dropped
     drastically after 1880 and paralleled declines in marital
     fertility. The drop indicates a greater acceptance of con-
     traception or abortion.

498. WOOD, Clive, and Beryl SUITTERS. The Fight for Acceptance:
     A History of Contraception. Aylesbury: Medical and
     Technical Publishing Co., 1970.
     Examines the medical history of contraception, the develop-
     ment of the birth control movement, and man's desire to
     control fertility.

499. ARIES, Philippe. Centuries of Childhood: A Social History
     of Family Life. New York: Vintage, 1962.
     Maintains that childhood as a distinct state of life is a
     modern discovery. Before modern times, the child was re-
     garded as a miniature adult and the family was integrated
     into community life. Now there is age segmentation and
     the family has become a child-centered, private institution,
     segregated from outside society.

500. DUNN, Patrick P. "Fathers and Sons Revisited: The Child-
     hood of Vissarion Belinskii." History of Childhood
     Quarterly, 1 (1974), 389-408.
     Speculates that the warm, nurturant attitude of some Rus-
     sian fathers towards their sons may have helped create the
     social climate necessary for revolution.

501. DUNN, Patrick P. "'That Enemy is the Baby': Childhood in
     Imperial Russia." The History of Childhood. Ed. Lloyd
     de Mause. New York: Psychohistory Press, 1974, pp.
     383-406.
     Contends that Russian childhood was a difficult stage of
     life because of parental indifference, high infant mortal-
     ity, and poor physical care. The increasing acceptance of
     childhood autonomy fostered, in part, the revolutionary
     inclinations of the intelligentsia.

502. GILLIS, John P. Youth and History: Tradition and Change
     in European Age Relations, 1770 to the Present. New
     York: Academic Press, 1974.
     Examines European youth from preindustrial society where
     youth was in a semi-independent state to the "discovery"
     of adolescence and the current emergence of "post-modern"
     youth.

503. KNODEL, John, and Etienne VAN DE WALLE. "Breast Feeding,
     Fertility and Infant Mortality: An Analysis of Some
     Early German Data." Population Studies, 21 (1967),
     109-31.
     Demonstrates that large regional variations existed in the
     proportion of children breast-fed and in the duration of
     breast-feeding. High infant mortality is associated with
     the absence of breast feeding.

504. LANGER, William L. "Infanticide: A Historical Survey."
     History of Childhood Quarterly, 1 (1974), 353-66.
     Shows that infanticide has had a long and disreputable
     tradition in Western Civilization despite ceaseless ad-
     monishments by the Church and civil authorities.

505. MEAD, Margaret, and Elena CALAS. "Child-training Ideals
     in a Postrevolutionary Context: Soviet Russia."
     Childhood in Contemporary Cultures. Ed. Margaret Mead
     and Martha Wolfenstein. Chicago: Univ. of Chicago

Press, 1955, pp. 179-203.
Shows that the rigid and structured modes of childrearing
in the Soviet Union are designed to produce a personality
which accepts unquestioningly a Marxist world-view, the
goals of the state, and is unreceptive to external influences

506. METRAUX, Rhoda. "Parents and Children: An Analysis of Contemporary German Child-Care and Youth-Guidance Literature." Childhood in Contemporary Cultures. Ed. Margaret Mead and Martha Wolfenstein. Chicago: Univ. of
Chicago Press, 1955, pp. 204-28.
Illustrates how childrearing practices in modern Germany
prepare the child to become an obedient, independent individual who accepts social mores.

507. MUSGROVE, Frank. "Population Changes and the Status of the
Young in England Since the Eighteenth Century." Sociological Review, 11 (1963), 69-93.
Explores the changing influence of demographic factors and
compulsory education on age at marriage and independent income of the 10-20 age cohort.

508. PINCHBECK, Ivy, and Margaret HEWITT. Children in English
Society: From the Eighteenth Century to the Children
Act, 1948. London: Routlege and Kegan Paul, 1973.
Discusses institutional attitudes and care of children,
notably child labor, juvenile reform, pauperism, and
child abuse.

509. ROBERTS, Elizabeth. "Learning & Living--Socialisation Outside School." Oral History, Autumn 1975, pp. 14-28.
Focuses on the period 1890-1914 and is concerned with informal education that urban English children received outside the elementary schools. Concludes that children left
school well able to survive in adult world and accepted
unquestioningly the social order.

510. ROBERTSON, Priscilla. "Home as a Nest: Middle Class Childhood in Nineteenth-Century Europe." The History of Childhood. Ed. Lloyd de Mause. New York: Psychohistory Press,
1974, pp. 407-31.
Notes that under the impact of Rousseau, 19th-century Eur-
opeans began reexamining their notions about children.
What resulted was a new approach to children which took
into account their needs and demands. This transition also
was brought about by the cult of domesticity which stressed
the woman's childrearing role.

511. ROE, Fredrick Gordon. The Victorian Child. London:
Phoenix House, 1959.
Examines Victorian childhood in terms of the nursery, toys,
punishments, clothing, children's literature, and education.

512. SUSSMAN, George D. "The Wet-Nursing Business in Nineteenth
Century France." French Historical Studies, 9 (1975),

70

304-28.
Examines the practice of wet-nursing in 19th-century
France, its extent and development, and its regulation
by French authorities.

513. THOMPSON, Paul. "The War With Adults." Oral History,
Autumn 1975, pp. 29-38.
Uses oral history to determine the extent of English
children's resistance to adults and the handicaps that
children suffered from the 1880s onward.

514. VIGNE, Thea. "Parents and Children, 1890-1918: Distance
and Dependence." Oral History, Autumn 1975, pp. 6-13.
Discusses patterns of dependence and separation in British working-class families, and offers suggestions as to
why some families differed from the norm.

515. VIGO, Giovanni. "Infant Mortality in a Pre-Industrial
District (Cantone di Bassano, 1798-1802)." Journal
of European Economic History, 3 (1974), 121-5.
Examines data on births, deaths, and survivals for children
of several Italian parishes in Bassano.

DEMOGRAPHY

516. ANDERSON, Olive. "The Incidence of Civil Marriages in
Victorian England and Wales." Past & Present, November
1975, pp. 50-87.
Examines the ways in which Victorians chose to get married so as to determine the geographical distribution
of denominational strength, the progress of de-Christian-
ization in England, and the nature of the heterogeneity
produced by industrialization.

517. ANGENOT, L. H. J. "The Fertility of the Female Population
of Rotterdam between 1870 and 1940." International
Population Conference: London 1969. Liège: n.p.,
1971, IV, pp. 2387-91.
Concludes that the decline in Rotterdam's fertility did not
begin with the decline in the crude birth rate, and notes
that older women first contributed to the decline in fertility, followed by younger women.

518. ASPBURY, George Frederick. "Marriage and Migration:
Spatial Mobility and Modernization in Cordoba, Spain,
1920-1968." Diss. Univ. of Michigan, 1975.
Argues that spatial mobility and interaction increase
with modernization as the constraining effects of distance are decreased, and shows that spatial mobility is
a function of socio-economic class.

519. BELL, Rudolph M. "The Transformation of a Rural Village:
Istria, 1870-1972." Journal of Social History, 7 (1974),
243-70.
Argues that traditional peasant society was not static as

evidenced by cycles of vital events, occupational structure, political development, and emigration patterns.

520. BEVERIDGE, William H. "Marriage and Birth Seasons."
    Economica, 3 (1936), 133-61.
    Compares seasonal fluctuations in the marriage and birth
    rates in early 20th-century England and Wales with those
    rates of the mid-19th century.

521. BUISSINK, J. D. "Regional Differences in Marital Fertility in the Netherlands in the Second Half of the
    Nineteenth Century." _Population Studies_, 25 (1971),
    353-74.
    Concludes that birth control was practiced in some provinces of the Netherlands by the mid-19th century, and
    notes that religious convictions determined largely the
    extent of birth control practices.

522. CAMP, Wesley D. _Marriage and the Family in France Since
    the Revolution: An Essay in the History of Population._
    New York: Bookman Associates, 1961.
    Attempts to discern changing patterns in age structure
    through marriage formation and dissolution, and argues
    that demographic trends do not indicate a weakening of
    the French social fabric.

523. COALE, Ansley J. "The Decline in Fertility in Europe
    from the French Revolution to World War II." _Fertility
    and Family Planning: A World View._ Ed. Samuel J.
    Behrman, et. al. Ann Arbor: Univ. of Michigan
    Press, 1969, pp. 3-24.
    Notes that prior to widespread resort to birth control
    in Europe there occurred a nuptiality pattern that reduced fertility, namely a decrease in the proportion married and the voluntary desire to reduce marital fertility.
    Also presents the overall trends in fertility decline.

524. CONNELL, Kenneth Hugh. "Peasant Marriage in Ireland After
    the Great Famine." _Past & Present_, 12 (1957), 176-91.
    Argues that the increased age at marriage after 1846 is a
    product of emigration, the consolidation of land holdings,
    and a rising standard of living.

525. CONNELL, Kenneth Hugh. "Peasant Marriage in Ireland: Its
    Structure and Development Since the Famine." _Economic
    History Review_, 14 (1962), 502-23.
    Examines the delaying of or aversion to marriage by Irish
    peasants, the importance of land and inheritance patterns
    in peasant marriages, and the impact of emigration on marriage.

526. DEMENY, Paul. "Early Fertility Decline in Austria-Hungary:
    A Lesson in Demographic Transition." _Daedalus_, 97 (1968),
    502-22.
    Examines the stages of demographic transition in Austria-

Hungary from 1880 to 1960, and discusses critically various
explanations of fertility decline and demographic transition
theory.

527. DRAKE, Michael. "Age at Marriage in the Pre-Industrial
West." Population Growth and the Brain Drain. Ed. Frank
Bechhofer. Edinburgh: Edinburgh Univ. Press, 1969,
pp. 196-208.
Discusses the importance of age at marriage in understanding population growth and the industrial revolution. Discovers wide variations in age at marriage in Western pre-
dustrial societies, although these ages were generally
higher than those in many contemporary under-developed
countries.

528. DRAKE, Michael. "The Growth of Population in Norway,
1735-1855." Scandinavian Economic History Review,
13 (1965), 97-142.
Discusses changing birth, death, and marriage rates, and
compares the Norwegian experience with Western Europe.

529. DRAKE, Michael. "Marital Age Patterns in Peasant Societies:
Ireland and Norway, 1800-1900." Third International
Conference of Economic History. Paris: Mouton, 1972,
pp. 55-66.
Examines and criticizes K. H. Connell's study of Irish
population change. Also reviews age at marriage patterns
in 19th-century Norway, and concludes that differences in
economic opportunities do not affect the age at marriage
of women in the same way as that of men.

530. DRAKE, Michael. "Marriage and Population Growth in Ireland, 1750-1845." Economic History Review, 16 (1963),
301-13.
Argues that pre-Famine age at marriage was late, that the
age at which men marry is not directly linked to the age
of their brides, and that a trend toward later marriages
in the 1830s probably did not occur.

531. DRAKE, Michael. Population and Society in Norway, 1735-
1865. Cambridge: Cambridge Univ. Press, 1969.
Explores the changes in vital rates in preindustrial Norway, the interplay of marriage, economics, and social
customs, regional variations in demographic trends, and
family and household structure.

532. HAJNAL, J. "European Marriage Patterns in Perspective."
Population in History. Ed. David Victor Glass and D. E.
C. Eversley. Chicago: Aldine, 1965, pp. 101-46.
Shows that there is a distinctive West European marriage
pattern of higher age at marriage and higher proportion
of persons who never marry. These traits distinguish West
from East European marriage configurations.

533. HALPERN, Joel M., and David ANDERSON. "The Zadruga: A

Century of Change." Antropologia, 12 (1970), 83-97.
Examines the historical demography of a Serbian village
from 1863 to 1961 and the relationships between increasing longevity, declining fertility, and household size.

534. HARRISON, G. A., et. al. "Social Class and Marriage
Patterns in Some Oxfordshire Populations." Journal
of Biosocial Science, 3 (1971), 1-12.
Finds that more individuals married out of their class
in 1901-1967 than in 1837-1900, thus social status is
becoming a minor factor in mate selection.

535. HEER, D. M. "The Demographic Transition in the Russian
Empire and the Soviet Union." Journal of Social His-
tory, 1 (1968), 193-240.
Considers the impact of birth control, modernization,
education, child welfare policies, the role of women in
Russian demographic history from 1861 to 1965.

536. HOLLINGSWORTH, Thomas H. "The Demography of the British
Peerage." Population Studies, 18 (1964), supplement.
Shows that the British peerage from 1600 to 1938 tends
to lead demographic trends, with the general population
about a generation behind.

537. KNODEL, John E. The Decline of Fertility in Germany,
1871-1939. Princeton: Princeton Univ. Press, 1974.
Discusses the geographical patterns of fertility and
fertility decline by variables in Germany. Fertility
decline occurred in every part of Germany even with an
increase in the proportion married.

538. KNODEL, John E. "Infant Mortality and Fertility in Three
Bavarian Villages: An Analysis of Family Histories
From the Nineteenth Century." Population Studies,
22 (1968), 297-318.
Notes that Bavarian practices of breast feeding prolonged
birth intervals, yet the impact of infant mortality on
birth intervals is inconclusive. Marital fertility between
families with low child mortality and those with high rates
was surprisingly similar.

539. KNODEL, John E. "Law, Marriage and Illegitimacy in Nineteenth-Century Germany." Population Studies, 20 (1967),
279-94.
Shows that some German states, concerned about overpop-
ulation and poverty, restricted marriage to the morally
and financially able. But such legislation prevented marriage rather than limited fertility as evidenced by declining illegitimacy rates.

540. KNODEL, John E. "Malthus Amiss: Marriage Restrictions in
19th-Century Germany." Social Science, 27 (1972), 40-5.
Notes that although Malthus believed in population control
by marriage postponement and some German states passed laws

to delay and restrict marriages, such laws were ineffective
in limiting fertility.

541. KNODEL, John E. "Two and a Half Centuries of Demographic
     History in a Bavarian Village." Population Studies,
     24 (1970), 353-76.
     Illustrates that age at marriage and illegitimacy decreased
     during the 19th century, but marital fertility and infant
     mortality remained high until 1900, suggesting the absence
     of birth control.

542. KRAUSE, John T. "Changes in English Fertility and Mor-
     tality, 1781-1850." English History Review, 11 (1958),
     52-70.
     Argues that population growth was a product of rising fer-
     tility, resulting in part from higher marriage and ille-
     gitimacy rates.

543. LANGER, William L. "Checks to Population Growth, 1750-
     1850." Scientific American, February 1972, pp. 92-9.
     Notes that there is evidence of widespread celibacy and
     infanticide, practices which checked the rapid population
     growth of Europe between 1750 and 1850.

544. LEE, Joseph. "Marriage and Population in Pre-famine
     Ireland." Economic History Review, 21 (1968), 283-95.
     Argues that Drake (1963) is correct is positing a high
     median male age at marriage in early 19th-century Ire-
     land, but his conclusion that contradictions exist be-
     tween literary and statistical sources needs modification.

545. LIVI-BACCI, Massimo. "Fertility and Nuptiality Changes in
     Spain from the Late Eighteenth Century to the Early
     Twentieth Century." Population Studies, 22 (1968),
     83-102, 211-35.
     Shows that marital fertility dropped steadily, with re-
     gional variations, in Spain from the 1760s onward, pos-
     sibly due to birth control practices. Moreover, the pro-
     portion of unmarried has generally decreased since 1787
     except in those areas of high out-migration.

546. LIVI-BACCI, Massimo. "The Fertility of Marriages in
     Tuscany During the XIXth Century: Results and Method-
     ology." Saggi di Demografia Storica. Ed. Carlo A.
     Corsini, et. al. Firenze: Universita, Dipartimento
     Statistico-Matematico, 1969, pp. 51-64.
     Agues that the decline in family size after 1820 can be
     explained neither by changes in mortality nor modifications
     in the age at marriage, but rather a change in attitude.
     Uses the average number of children per marriage to ex-
     amine fertility decline.

547. MCKENNA, Edward Emmanuel. "Marriage and Fertility in
     Postfamine Ireland: A Multivariate Analysis." Amer-
     ican Journal of Sociology, 80 (1974), 688-705.

Examines Irish censuses from 1851 to 1911 to test K. H.
Connell's theory of postfamine demographic trends, and
argues that variations in marital fertility, nonagricul-
tural occupations, and inheritance patterns were more
influential in structuring fertility than falling marriage rates.

548. MCKENNA, Edward Emmanuel. "Social Change, Marriage, and
Fertility in Ireland, 1851-1961." Diss. Purdue Univ.,
1972.
Examines factors related to fertility decline in postfamine Ireland, notably agrarian economic and social
institutions such as inheritance, farm size, and type of
agricultural emphasis.

549. MALKIN, H. J. "Observations on Social Conditions, Fertility and Family Survival in the Past." Proceedings
of the Royal Society of Medicine, 53 (1960), 117-32.
Examines the royal families of England to determine changes
in life expectancy, fertility, and family size.

550. MATRAS, Judah. "Social Strategies of Family Formation:
Data for British Female Cohorts Born 1831-1906."
Population Studies, 19 (1965), 167-82.
Proposes a procedure for comparing age at marriage and
fertility control patterns of female birth cohorts using
number of children ever born.

551. NORBERG, Anders, and Sune AKERMAN. "Migration and the
Building of Families: Studies on the Rise of the
Lumber Industry in Sweden." Aristocrats, Farmers,
Proletarians: Essays in Swedish Demographic History.
Ed. Kurt Agren, et. al. Uppsala: Esselte Studium,
1973, pp. 88-119.
Analyzes the complex relationship between migratory movements and the formation of families, particularly the way
migration affected the formation of families in northern
provinces of Sweden, and argues that the family played a
central role in the migrants' process of adjustment.

552. OGDEN, Philip. "Patterns of Marriage Seasonality in Rural
France." Local Population Studies, Spring 1973, pp.
53-64.
Discusses the fundamental changes undergone by the seasonal
pattern of marriages in France in the period 1860-1970 and
how such a study is useful in guaging the nature of social
activity in local areas.

553. OUTHWAITE, R. B. "Age at Marriage in England from the Late
Seventeenth to the Nineteenth Century." Transactions of
the Royal Historical Society, 23 (1973), 55-70.
Criticizes existing estimates on age at marriage based on
family reconstitution, and presents new evidence derived
from selected English marriage licenses.

554. PEARCE, Carol G. "Expanding Families: Some Aspects of
        Fertility in a Mid-Victorian Community." Local Pop-
        ulation Studies, Spring 1973, pp. 22-35.
     Compares fertility, birth spacing, and premarital preg-
     nancy between unskilled laborers and retail trade work-
     ers in Ashford, Kent, England in the mid-19th century.

555. PEEL, R. F. "Local Intermarriage and the Stability of
        Rural Populations in the English Midlands." Geography,
        27 (1942), 22-30.
     Uses parish registers to study the range of intermarriage
     reflected in place of residence from 1600 to 1940, and
     finds localism in marriages to 1900.

556. PERRY, P. J. "Working-Class Isolation and Mobility in
        Rural Dorset, 1837-1936: A Study of Marriage Dis-
        tances." Institute of British Geographers, Trans-
        actions, March 1969, pp. 121-41.
     Analyzes the everyday mobility of working-class inhabitants
     of Dorset through the use of marriage registers to dis-
     cern rural isolation and mobility.

557. SHORTER, Edward, et. al. "The Decline of Non-Marital
        Fertility in Europe, 1880-1940." Population Studies,
        25 (1971), 375-93.
     Notes that the decline in non-marital fertility para-
     lleled drops in overall fertility, reflecting an in-
     creasing resort to contraception and abortion. Urban-
     ization or industrialization were non-explanatory var-
     iables.

558. SILVER, Morris. "Births, Marriages, and Income Fluct-
        uations in the United Kingdom and Japan." Economic
        Development and Cultural Change, 14 (1966), 302-33.
     Shows that from the late 19th century to the present,
     births and marriages in Britain and Japan have been
     positively correlated to business cycles.

559. SKLAR, June L. "Marriage Behavior and Nonmarital Fer-
        tility: A Comparative Analysis of Ireland and Sweden
        in the 1880s and Early 1890s." Paper delivered at the
        American Sociological Association, San Francisco,
        August 1975.

560. SKLAR, June L. "The Role of Marriage Behavior in the
        Demographic Transition: The Case of Eastern Europe
        Around 1900." Population Studies, 28 (1974), 231-47.
     Examines patterns of marriage behavior--age at marriage
     and celibacy--in Eastern Europe and their relation to
     population growth.

561. SMITH, Daniel Scott. "A Homeostatic Demographic Regime:
        Patterns in West-European Family Reconstitution Stud-
        ies." Paper delivered at the Conference on Behavioral
        Models in Historical Demography, Philadelphia, October

1974.
Examines 38 West-European family reconstitution studies, and finds that a low level of marital fertility was associated with early female age at marriage and a low level of mortality; the ecological pattern was not present at the level of individual couples.

562. THOMAS, D. N. "Marriage Patterns in the British Peerage in the Eighteenth and Nineteenth Centuries." Master's Thesis: London School of Economics, 1969.
Describes the limited marriage patterns of British peers and their sons.

563. THOMAS, D. N. "The Social Origins of Marriage Partners of the British Peerage in the 18th and 19th Centuries." Population Studies, 26 (1972), 99-112.
Argues that the majority of marriages by peers and their sons were outside the peerage but within a narrow social elite.

564. TURNER, Christopher. "Developmental Cycles and Transformations in Social Structure: Family Life and Social Relationships in XVII and XIXth England." Paper delivered at the International Seminar of the Committee on Family Research of the International Sociological Association, Paris, September 1973.

565. WALSH, Brendan M. "Marriage Rates and Population Pressure: Ireland, 1871 and 1911." Economic History Review, 23 (1970), 148-62.
Argues that high marriage fertility, emigration, and aspirations to higher living standards lowered marriage rates in the western counties of Ireland after 1880.

566. WOJTUN, Bronislaw. "Trends in Fertility in West Poland in the Nineteenth Century." Susquehanna University Studies, 8 (1967), 69-78.
Discusses the turning points and trend lines in fertility of West Poland as a whole and of five regencies.

DIVORCE

567. GLASS, David Victor. "Divorce in England and Wales." Sociological Review, 26 (1934), 288-308.
Discusses historical trends of divorce in Britain since 1858, and concludes that rising divorce rates reflect the maladjustment of families in an urbanized setting.

568. KITCHIN, Shepherd Brainthwaite. A History of Divorce. London: Chapman & Hall, 1912.
Explains the origin of the diversity of laws and opinions about divorce, including Roman and early Christian divorce, and divorce in modern American and European history.

569. LATEY, William. The Tide of Divorce. London: Longman,

1970.
Traces the history of divorce laws in England from early
Roman law until the present, with emphasis on divorce law
reform and the breakdown of marriage.

570. MCGREGOR, Oliver Ross. _Divorce in England: A Centenary_
      Study. London: Heinemann, 1957.
      Examines the changing religious, moral, and legal opinion
      about divorce in England, including the Victorian family
      and the Morton Commission.

571. ROWNTREE, Griselda, and Norman H. CARRIER. "The Resort
      to Divorce in England and Wales, 1858-1957." _Pop-_
      ulation Studies, 11 (1958), 188-233.
      Argues that the increase of divorce in England and Wales
      is not indicative of marital breakdown, but reflects the
      greater ability and willingness of couples to take ad-
      vantage of the legal means to terminate their marriages.

572. WOODHOUSE, Margaret K. "The Marriage and Divorce Bill of
      1857." _American Journal of Legal History_, 3 (1959),
      260-75.
      Reviews English divorce laws before 1857, and discusses
      the background and controversy of the 1857 Marriage and
      Divorce Bill.

DOMESTIC ARCHITECTURE

573. DUTTON, Ralph. _The Victorian Home: Some Aspects of_
      Nineteenth-Century Taste and Manners. London: B.T.
      Batsford, 1954.
      Examines the Victorian home, its social symbolism, the
      standards of furnishings, and changing taste among Eng-
      lish middle classes of the 19th century.

574. PARR, Albert Eide. "Heating, Lighting, Plumbing and
      Human Relations." _Landscape_, Winter 1970, pp. 28-9.
      Speculates on the impact of technical innovations in
      heating, lighting, and plumbing on floor patterns, the
      arrangement of room interiors, and social interaction
      of family members.

DOMESTIC LIFE AND CUSTOMS

575. ARENSBERG, Conrad M., and Solom T. KIMBALL. _Family and_
      Community in Ireland. 2nd ed. Cambridge: _Harvard_
      Univ. Press, 1968.
      Examines the social organization of Irish small farmers,
      with emphasis on intra-family relationships and relation-
      ships between community and individual.

576. BEALES, H. L. "The Victorian Family." _Ideas and Beliefs_
      of the Victorians: An Historic Revaluation of the Vic-
      torian Age. London: Sylvan Press, 1949, pp. 343-50.
      Shows that among the middle classes, the Victorian family

was a self-sufficient sanctuary from society but was
threatened by the re-definition of women's social role
and by individualism. Although the state increasingly
usurped family functions, this process affected the
lower classes most directly and most adversely.

577. BURTON, Elizabeth. The Early Victorians at Home, 1837-
       1861. London: Longmans, 1972.
       Deals with the middle and upper class English, and de-
       scribes the homes, decor, recreations, gardens, medicine,
       and food of the early Victorians.

578. DAWES, Frank Edward. Not in Front of the Servants:
       Domestic Service in England, 1850-1939. London:
       Wayland, 1973.
       Describes the attitudes of servants and employers, ranks
       amd divisions of the servant class, work load and living
       conditions, recruitment, and pastimes of servants.

579. ELNETT, Elaine Pasvolsky. Historic Origin and Social De-
       velopment of Family Life in Russia. New York: Colum-
       bia Univ. Press, 1927.
       Discusses the changes in the organization of Russian fam-
       ily life and their relation to other social institutions.

580. FRANKLE, Barbara Stein. "The Genteel Family: High-Vic-
       torian Conceptions of Domesticity and Good Behavior."
       Diss. Univ. of Wisconsin, 1969.
       Argues that the English middle classes, faced with ten-
       sions and problems of adjustment resulting from urban-
       ization, mobility, and improved social status, attempted
       to adopt a life-style which emphasized civility, stabil-
       ity, privacy, and secure personal contacts.

581. GATHORNE-HARDY, Jonathan. The Rise and Fall of the British
       Nanny. London: Hodder & Stoughton, 1972.
       Traces the nanny's emergence from wet-nurses, her rise in
       the Victorian age, her function in the British household,
       and the psychological effect of nannies on children.

582. HOLMSEN, Andreas, et. al. "The Old Norwegian Peasant Com-
       munity." Scandinavian Economic History Review, 4
       (1956), 17-81.
       Discusses the family, inheritance patterns, social status,
       and marriage in Norwegian peasant communities.

583. HORN, Pamela. The Rise and Fall of the Victorian Servant.
       Dublin: Gilland Macmillan, 1975.
       Examines the largest source of 19th-century female employ-
       ment, and notes that domestics had contented relationships
       with their employers, making the rise of feminism difficult.

584. HURVITZ, Nathan. "Courtship and Arranged Marriages Among
       Eastern European Jews Prior to World War I as Depicted
       in a Briefenshteller." Journal of Marriage and the

Family, 37 (1975), 422-30.
Analyzes a book of sample letters to discern courtship
patterns and evidence of arranged marriages among Eastern
European Jews in the early 20th century.

585. KARPIS, Melvin Roland. "The Victorian Family." New England
        Social Science Bulletin, 19 (1961), 20-4.
     Discusses the moral and social concepts that characterized
     the Victorian family.

586. KOOMEN, Willem. "A Note on the Authoritarian German Fam-
        ily." Journal of Marriage and the Family, 36 (1974),
        634-6.
     Analyzes the assumption that the pre-WWII German family
     was more authoritarian than its American counterpart,
     and finds no major differences in German and American
     parental control except that German parents exercised
     more rigid control over their daughters.

587. LOCHHEAD, Marion. The Victorian Household. London:
        John Murray, 1964.
     Portrays the Victorians at home and the relation between
     house and owner. Also examines the changing pattern of
     living within the house.

588. MCBRIDE, Theresa Marie. "Rural Tradition and the Process
        of Modernization: Domestic Servants in Nineteenth-Cen-
        tury France." Diss. Rutgers Univ., 1973.
     Examines the servant class, its relationship to middle
     class life styles, the role of domestic service as a chan-
     nel for urban mobility, and its role in the modernization
     process.

589. MCBRIDE, Theresa Marie. "Social Mobility for the Lower
        Class: Domestic Servants in France." Journal of Social
        History, 8 (1974), 63-78.
     Discusses how domestic service was an important channel
     for social and geographical mobility during the period of
     urbanization and a transitional stage in the lives of many
     individuals.

590. MUSGROVE, Frank. "The Family as an Educational Institution,
        1760-1860." Diss. Univ. of Nottingham, 1958.
     Discusses the role of the family as educator in early
     19th-century British society.

591. MUSGROVE, Frank. "Middle Class Families and Schools,
        1780-1880: Interaction and Exchange of Function Be-
        tween Institutions." Sociological Review, 7 (1959),
        169-78.
     Investigates the transition from the family as educator
     to the development of school systems to meet new social
     needs.

592. ODDY, D. J. "The Working Class Diet, 1886-1914." Diss.

London School of Economics, 1970.
Describes the working-class diet in England and speculates on its possible socio-economic consequences.

593. ODDY, D. J. "Working-Class Diets in Late Nineteenth-Century Britain." Economic History Review, 23 (1970), 314-23.
Shows that the diet of working-class families as revealed in their budgets illustrates that while real wages increased, health and nutrition standards remained low.

594. PETERSON, William. "The Evolution of Soviet Family Policy." Problems of Communism, 5 (1956), 29-36.
Examines the history of Soviet governmental policy towards morality, birth control, and the family since the Revolution.

595. REDDY, William M. "Family and Factory: French Linen Weavers in Belle Epoque." Journal of Social History, 8 (1975), 102-12.
Notes that 19th-century French linen workers wished to continue the domestic system of production in the factory, the family wage system, and opposed new techniques to protect the family's position in the factory.

596. REDDY, William M. "Laborers and Their Families: Community, Kinship, and Social Protest in a French Factory Town in 1903." Diss. Univ. of Chicago, 1974.
Contends that employment of women and children in factories not only stemmed from physical necessity, but also resulted from the work ethic since French linen workers defended vigorously their right to hire and work with their own kin.

597. RICHARDSON, S. J. "'The Servant Question': A Study of the Domestic Labour Market, 1851-1917." Master's Thesis: Bedford College, Univ. of London, 1966.
Discusses the changing role and status of English servants as well as their relationship to the shifting occupational structure of the late 19th century.

598. SIDGWICK, Cecily Ullman. Home Life in Germany. New York: Macmillan, 1908.
Discusses children, marriage, housewives, foods, and leisurely activities of early 20th century Germans.

599. SMELSER, Neil J. "Sociological History: The Industrial Revolution and the British Working-Class Family." Journal of Social History, 1 (1967), 17-35.
Maintains that the working-class family increasingly had its economic, educational and social functions usurped by other institutions during industrialization.

600. SMITH, Cecil O. "The Parisian Bourgeoisie Under Louis XVI and Louis Phillippe: Education and Marriage." Diss. Harvard Univ., 1959.
Examines the social impact of the French Revolution by

tracing changes in the structure of the Parisian bourgeoisie, in female education in the bourgeoisie, and in
parental authority and marrying. Concludes that marriage
loses its position as a social escalator and that parental
authority shifted from positive to negative, from the
choosing of a daughter's husband to preventing objection-
able marriages.

601. THOMPSON, Derek. "Courtship and Marriage Between the
   Wars." Oral History, Autumn 1975, pp. 39-44.
Discusses courtship and marriage customs of English lower
middle and working classes during the Depression.

602. VOLIN, Lazar. "The Peasant Household Under the Mir and
   the Kolkhoz in Modern Russian History." The Cultural
   Approach to History. Ed. Caroline Farrar Ware. New
   York: Columbia Univ. Press, 1940, pp. 125-39.
Compares the impact of the Russian land commune on the
peasant family in the 19th century with that of collectiv-
ism in the 20th century.

FAMILY COMPOSITION AND STRUCTURE

603. ANDERSON, Michael. Family Structure in Nineteenth Century
   Lancashire. London: Cambridge Univ. Press, 1971.
Examines the impact of urban-industrial life on the kinship system and changes in household structure in an English working-class community.

604. ANDERSON, Michael. "Household Structure and the Industrial
   Revolution: Mid-Nineteenth Century Preston in Comparative Perspective." Household and Family in Past Time.
   Ed. Peter Laslett and Richard Wall. Cambridge: Cambridge Univ. Press, 1972, pp. 215-35.
Finds that households in mid-19th-century England had a
larger proportion of kin in residence than those in pre-
industrial England, and that these kin served important
social and economic functions in the family, especially
caring for children of working mothers.

605. ARMSTRONG, W. A. "A Note on the Household Structure of
   Mid-Nineteenth-Century York in Comparative Perspective."
   Household and Family in Past Time. Ed. Peter Laslett and
   Richard Wall. Cambridge: Cambridge Univ. Press, 1972,
   pp. 205-14.
Compares the household structure of mid-19th-century York
with preindustrial communities and finds great similarities.

606. BLAYO, Yves. "Size and Structure of Households in a Northern French Village Between 1836 and 1861." Household
   and Family in Past Time. Ed. Peter Laslett and Richard
   Wall. Cambridge: Cambridge Univ. Press, 1972, pp.
   255-65.
Compares changing household size and composition in 19th
century France, and finds a definite movement toward

smaller family size although the mean number of children per family remained constant.

607. CHAPLIN, David. "Household, Family Structure and Domestic Service in Mid-Nineteenth-Century London." Paper delivered at the National Council on Family Relations, Portland, November 1972.

608. HALPERN, Joel M. "Town and Countryside in Serbia in the Nineteenth Century, Social and Household Structure as Reflected in the Census of 1863." Household and Family in Past Time. Ed. Peter Laslett and Richard Wall. Cambridge: Cambridge Univ. Press, 1972, pp. 401-27.
Compares household size and composition between rural and urban areas in 19th-century Serbia.

609. HELIN, Etienne. "Size of Households Before the Industrial Revolution: The Case of Liege in 1801." Household and Family in Past Time. Ed. Peter Laslett and Richard Wall. Cambridge: Cambridge Univ. Press, 1972, pp. 319-34.
Examines the problems of the 1801 census, and reveals that household size in Liege in 1801 was small.

610. ILIEVA, Nicolina. "Changes in the Family Cycle of the Bulgarian Family Since the End of the Nineteenth Century." Paper delivered at the International Seminar of the Committee on Family Research of the International Sociological Association, Paris, September 1973.

611. LASLETT, Peter. "The Decline of the Domestic Group in England." Population Studies, 24 (1970), 449-54.
Reviews methodological procedures dealing with mean size of domestic group, and shows that domestic group size did begin to fall sharply from 1891 onward in England, with fundamental changes occurring between 1921 and 1951.

612. LASLETT, Peter. "The Family Cycle, Period of Childbearing and the Differences Between Eastern and Western Societies, Industrial and Pre-Industrial Societies." Paper delivered at the International Seminar of the Committee on Family Research of the International Sociological Association, Paris, September 1973.
Rewritten as "Characteristics of the Western Family Considered Over Time" and found in Laslett's Family Life and Illicit Love in Earlier Generations, forthcoming.

613. LASLETT, Peter. "Mean Household Size in England Since the Sixteenth Century." Household and Family in Past Time. Ed. Peter Laslett and Richard Wall. Cambridge: Cambridge Univ. Press, 1972, pp. 125-58.
Discusses the importance of mean household size (MHS) in social research, and presents evidence showing the constancy of MHS in history.

614. LASLETT, Peter. "New Light on the History of the English
    Family." Listener, 75 (1966), 233-4.
    Reviews findings to date of the Cambridge Group concerning
    the history of the family, and concludes that there is lit-
    tle difference in household size between country and city,
    or between period and period. But notes that the presence
    or absence of servants largely determines household size.

615. LASLETT, Peter. "Size and Structure of the Household in
    England Over Three Centuries." Population Studies,
    23 (1969), 199-223.
    Shows that mean household size in England has remained
    constant from the 16th century to 1911, that demographic
    or industrial shifts have not affected substantially
    household size, and that the nuclear family has been the
    dominant familial form in the past.

616. LEES, Lynn H. "Migration and the Irish Family Economy."
    Paper delivered at Historians and the Family: A Sym-
    posium, Mount Holyoke College, April 1975.
    Compares family patterns in pre-famine Ireland with those
    of Irish migrants in mid-19th-century London.

617. LEES, Lynn H. "Patterns of Lower-Class Life: Irish Slum
    Communities in Nineteenth-Century London." Nineteenth
    Century Cities: Essays in the New Urban History. Ed.
    Stephan Therstrom and Richard Sennett. New Haven:
    Yale Univ. Press, 1969, pp. 359-85.
    Demonstrates that the London Irish poor, although appear-
    ing to have a disorganized, marginal existence, in actual-
    ity had structural regularities, a pattern of social dif-
    ferentiation, and a family system which readily adapted to
    poverty--all creating a cohesive way of life.

618. MOSELY, Philip E. "The Peasant Family: The Zadruga, or
    Communal Joint-Family in the Balkans, and Its Recent
    Evolution." The Cultural Approach to History. Ed.
    Caroline Farrar Ware. New York: Columbia Univ. Press,
    1940, pp. 95-108.
    Defines the various regional types of zadruga found in the
    Balkans and places these in their social environment.

619. PARISH, William L., and Moshe SCHWARTZ. "Household Com-
    plexity in Nineteenth Century France." American Socio-
    logical Review, 37 (1972), 154-72.
    Examines the effects of landholding, illiteracy, and set-
    tlement patterns on household complexity, and the effects
    of household complexity on various demographic variables.

620. SABEAN, David Warren. "Household Formation and Geographical
    Mobility: A Family Register Study for a Wuerttenberg
    Village, 1760-1900." Annales de Demographie Historique,
    1970. Paris: Mouton, 1971, pp. 275-94.
    Relates questions of geographical mobility to occupation and
    family structure, especially household formation, in a German

village. Concludes that the range of family contacts was
quite restricted.

621. SMITH, Roger. "Early Victorian Household Structure: A
      Case Study of Nottinghamshire." International Review
      of Social History, 15 (1970), 69-84.
      Compares household structure in three socially and econom-
      ically contrasting districts in Nottinghamshire in 1851.

622. TRANTER, N. L. "The Social Structure of a Bedfordshire
      Parish in the Mid-Nineteenth Century: The Cardington
      Census Enumerators' Books, 1851." International Re-
      view of Social History, 18 (1973), 90-106.
      Argues that although the demographic changes in this ag-
      ricultural community were minor, there was a trend towards
      a balanced sex ratio, a growth in household size and num-
      ber of children, and a decrease in the proportion of mar-
      ried persons.

FAMILY LAW AND INHERITANCE

623. ARNOLD, J. C. "The Marriage Law of England." Quarterly
      Review, 288 (1950), 486-99.
      Reviews the historical background of the Marriage Act of
      1949 with emphasis on the evolution of the statute law
      of marriage.

624. BEHRMAN, Cynthia Fansler. "The Annual Blister: A Side-
      light on Victorian Social and Parliamentary History."
      Victorian Studies, 11 (1968), 483-502.
      Discusses the history of the law prohibiting marriage with
      a deceased wife's sister.

625. BERKNER, Lutz Karl, and Franklin Frits MENDELS. "Inher-
      itance Systems, Family Structure, and Demographic Pat-
      terns in Western Europe (1700-1900)." Historical Studies
      of Changing Fertility. Ed. Charles Tilly. Princeton:
      Princeton Univ. Press, forthcoming.
      Reviews the effects of inheritance systems on nuptiality
      and migration. Shows that the contrasting models of par-
      tible and impartible inheritance are strongly influenced
      by economic factors. Test cases from Flanders, Normandy,
      Lower Saxony, and 19th-century France are presented as
      examples.

626. HABAKKUK, H. J. "Family Structure and Economic Change in
      Nineteenth Century Europe." Journal of Economic History,
      15 (1955), 1-12.
      Discusses the rules and customs of inheritance and their
      significance for economic development, population growth,
      and population mobility in the 19th century.

627. LANDES, David. "Bleichroders and Rothschilds: The Prob-
      lem of Continuity in the Family Firm." The Family in
      History. Ed. Charles E. Rosenberg. Philadelphia:

Univ. of Pennsylvania Press, 1975, pp. 95-114.
Examines the Bleichroder and Rothschild families in terms
of why family business enterprises, even with all the
elements of continuity present, sometimes rupture.

628. POWELL, Raphael. "The Concept of Marriage in Ancient and
      Modern Law." Current Legal Problems, 3 (1950), 46-64.
      Discusses the problem of whether procreation of children
      can be regarded as a fundamental purpose of marriage.
      Examines literary evidence and marriage law to show that
      the procreation of children is necessary for marriage.

629. RODMAN, Karl M. "A Brief History of Marriage and Divorce."
      Oregon Law Review, 23 (1944), 249-63.
      Sees the general history of marriage and divorce divided
      into three epochs: prechurch customs, church-controlled
      law, and civil procedure. Discusses the control of hus-
      band over wife and children as well as the trend toward
      divorce reform.

630. SHINN, William T. "The Law of the Russian Peasant House-
      hold." Slavic Review, 20 (1961), 601-21.
      Discusses the development of the customary law of the
      peasant household from its initial recognition in the
      late 19th-century to its present embodiment in Soviet
      collective-farm law.

631. SVERDLOV, G. M. "Milestones in the Development of Soviet
      Family Law." American Review on the Soviet Union,
      August 1948, pp. 3-27.
      Discusses how the Soviet authorities after 1917 began to
      reconstruct marriage and family relationships.

632. TRAER, James F. "Marriage and the Family in French Law
      and Social Criticism from the End of the Ancien Regime
      to the Civil Code." Diss. Univ. of Michigan, 1970.
      Explores the development of French law and social crit-
      icism concerning marriage and the family to understand
      the social impact of the French Revolution.

SEXUALITY

633. BEALES, H. L., and Edward GLOVER. "Victorian Ideas of
      Sex." Ideas and Beliefs of the Victorians: An His-
      toric Revaluation of the Victorian Age. London:
      Sylvan Press, 1949, pp. 358-64.
      Argues that despite the conspiracy of silence which shrouded
      the sexual attitudes of the Victorian Age, sexual irregular-
      ities were prevalent throughout Victorian society.

634. BLOCH, Iwan. Sexual Life in England Past and Present.
      London: F. Aldor, 1938.

635. COMINOS, Peter T. "Innocent Femina Sensualis in Unconscious
      Conflict." Suffer and Be Still: Women in the Victorian

Age. Ed. Martha Vicinus. Bloomington: Indiana Univ.
Press, 1972, pp. 155-72.
Examines the model of Femina Sensualis upon which the
social character of upper class women was formed and her
unconscious conflict and mechanism of sexual repression.

636. COMINOS, Peter T. "Late-Victorian Sexual Respectability
and the Social System." *International Review of Social
History*, 8 (1963), 18-48, 216-50.
Contends that there was an integration of the normative
sexual codes that stressed restraint and self-control
with capitalism which also emphasized self-discipline.
But this emphasis was at odds with the prevailing double
standard and thwarted equal spouse relationships. It resulted ultimately in modern psychology's revolt against
formalism.

637. CUTRIGHT, Phillips. "Historical and Contemporary Trends
in Illegitimacy." *Archives of Sexual Behavior*, 2 (1972),
97-118.
Reviews historical trends in illegitimacy rates in European populations after 1750. Argues that changes in
illegitimacy rates since WWII are related closely to patterns of marital fertility control and changes in the
age at marriage and age of legitimate childbearing.

638. DIERS, Carol J. "Historical Trends in the Age of Menarche
and Menopause." *Psychological Reports*, 34 (1974),
931-7.
Reviews recent research and contemporary medical writings
to show the peaking of the age for menarche in the early
19th century. Notes that age for menopause has remained
around age 50 throughout history, although the data are
incomplete.

639. HARRISON, Brian. "Underneath the Victorians." *Victorian
Studies*, 10 (1967), 239-62.
Reviews attitudes of sex held by the Victorians and the
treatment by historians of Victorian sexual mores.

640. JOHNSON, Wendell Stacy. *Sex and Marriage in Victorian
Poetry*. Ithaca: Cornell Univ. Press, 1975.
Deals with the Victorian poets' awareness of sexual drives,
sexual frustrations, and sexism as well as attitudes towards
marriage and sexual relations.

641. KERN, Stephen. *Anatomy and Destiny: A Cultural History of
the Human Body*. Indianapolis: Bobbs-Merrill, 1975.
Examines Victorian scientific studies of the human body
in terms of the middle class attempt to avoid their biological and sexual nature. Also discusses sexual morality,
fashions, gender roles, and public hygiene.

642. KERN, Stephen. "Explosive Intimacy: Psychodynamics of the
Victorian Family." *History of Childhood Quarterly*, 1

(1974), 437-62.
Argues that the Victorian family, far from being a stable,
protective institution, was fraught with tensions and contradictions. It was, in short, the source of anxiety and
conflict.

643. LASLETT, Peter. "Age of Menarche in Europe since the
Eighteenth Century." Journal of Interdisciplinary
History, 2 (1971), 221-36.
Reveals that teenage marriage records and census documents
can be used with reservations to ascertain the age at menarche in history. But notes that menarchal age varies
greatly with time, social class, and nutritional level.

644. LASLETT, Peter, and Karla OOSTERUEEN. "Long-Term Trends
in Bastardy in England: A Study of the Illegitimacy
Figures in the Parish Registers and in the Reports of
the Registrar General, 1561-1960." Population Studies,
27 (1973), 255-86.
Discusses the reliability of parish registers with regard
to illegitimcy, and finds cycles of illegitimacy peaking
around 1600, 1800, and in the mid-20th century. Also
hypothesizes the existence of a subsociety especially prone
to illegitimacy.

645. LEWINSOHN, Richard. History of Sexual Customs. New York:
Harper & Row, 1959.
Surveys various sexual customs and attitudes in Western
Civilization from the ancients to the present.

646. MCLAREN, Angus. "Some Secular Attitudes Toward Sexual
Behavior in France: 1760-1860." French Historical
Studies, 8 (1974), 604-25.
Examines the secular opposition to birth control in France.
Argues that this opposition denounced contraception as un-
natural and socially detrimental, although birth control
was in reality widely practiced.

647. MADISON, Bernice. "Russia's Illegitimate Children Before
and After the Revolution." Slavic Review, 22 (1963),
82-95.
Discusses the size and scope of illegitimacy in Russia from
1706 to the present and the government's attitude toward
and attempts to cope with the problem.

648. MARCUS, Steven. The Other Victorians: A Study of Sexual-
ity and Pornography in Mid-Nineteenth Century England.
New York: Basic Books, 1964.
Discusses the official views of sexuality held by the
Victorians, pornographic novels, literature of flagel-
lation, and the anonymous autobiography, My Secret Life.

649. MURSTEIN, Bernard I. Love, Sex, and Marriage Through the
Ages. New York: Springer Publishing, 1974.
Examines the symbolic meaning of sex, love, and marriage

in history using an interdisciplinary approach. Emphasizes
the Western World.

650. NEUMAN, Robert Paul. "Industrialization and Sexual Behav-
      ior: Some Aspects of Working-Class Life in Imperial
      Germany." Modern European Social History. Ed. Robert
      J. Bezucha. Lexington, Mass.: D. C. Heath, 1972,
      pp. 270-98.
      Uses workers' autobiographies to suggest the contrasts
      in sexual behavior between urban and rural dwellers, and
      emphasizes that such contrasts were not as great as pre-
      viously assumed. The changes in sexual habits were a re-
      sult of modernization, not of urban-industrial life.

651. NEUMAN, Robert Paul. "Masturbation, Madness, and the Modern
      Concepts of Childhood and Adolescence." Journal of Social
      History, 8 (1975), 1-27.
      Argues that anxiety about masturbation stems from a con-
      fused response to the early onset of puberty in Western
      Europe and from middle-class sexual concepts that reflected
      wider social and economic concerns. Attitudes toward mas-
      turbation also reflected and influenced the development
      of modern concepts of childhood and adolescence.

652. NEUMAN, Robert Paul. "The Sexual Question and Social
      Democracy in Imperial Germany." Journal of Social His-
      tory, 7 (1974), 271-86.
      Discusses how the Social Democratic Party attacked bour-
      geois sexual morality and marriage, yet reiterated tradi-
      tional sexual attitudes under the guise of science and
      self-sacrifice for the class struggle.

653. NEUMAN, Robert Paul. "Socialism, the Family and Sexual-
      ity: The Marxist Tradition and Germany Social Demo-
      cracy Before 1914." Diss. Northwestern Univ., 1972.
      Examines the tension between theory and practice on
      questions related to marriage, the family, and sexual
      attitudes in the German Social Democratic movement and
      its Marxist forerunners.

654. PEARSALL, Ronald. The Worm in the Bud: The World of
      Victorian Sexuality. New York: Macmillan, 1969.
      Analyzes Victorian sexuality from prudery to marriage,
      including birth control, prostitution, perversion, and
      pornography.

655. PHAYER, J. Michael. "Lower-Class Morality: The Case of
      Bavaria." Journal of Social History, 8 (1974), 79-95.
      Argues that after 1800 the sexual revolution had its im-
      pact on the rural lower-class in Germany. But the reasons
      for this shift in morality lay not in a decline in re-
      ligion but in changing class attitudes that emphasized
      individuality.

656. PUTNAM, George F. "Vasilii V. Rozanov: Sex, Marriage

and Christianity." <u>Canadian Slavic Studies</u>, 5 (1971), 302-26.
Argues that the Russian intellectual, Vasilii, believed that the family was the remedy to all social ills. But he stressed that more liberal attitudes toward sex were needed within the context of Christianity.

657. ROBINSON, Paul A. "Romantic Sexual Theory." Paper delivered to the American Historical Association, Boston, December 1970.
Argues that the Romantics synthesized the two major sexual traditions of the 18th century: the libertine tradition (represented by Sade) and the sentimental tradition (represented by Richardson). They advocated greater sexual freedom, but only within a significant psychological context.

658. SHORTER, Edward. "Capitalism, Culture, and Sexuality: Some Competing Models." <u>Social Science Quarterly</u>, 53 (1972), 338-56.
Examines traditional assumptions and models of the connection between capitalism and sexuality. Concludes that capitalism fostered a change in mentality, namely a rejection of family and community controls over sexual behavior, the development of a working-class subculture with emphasis on personal self-fulfillment, and the enlarging of the material basis of independence for young women.

659. SHORTER, Edward. "Illegitimacy, Sexual Revolution, and Social Change in Modern Europe." <u>Journal of Interdisciplinary History</u>, 2 (1971), 237-72.
Argues that the increase in illegitimacy beginning in the mid-18th century indicates a liberalization of sexual mores, a trend related closely to changing social and cultural variables, a change in mentalities, the growth of capitalism, and residential mobility.

660. SHORTER, Edward. "Sexual Change and Illegitimacy: The European Experience." <u>Modern European Social History</u>. Ed. Robert J. Bezucha. Lexington, Mass.: D. C. Heath, 1972, pp. 231-69.
Discusses the rapid increase in illegitmate births between 1750 and 1850 in terms of modernization theory and as a reflection of changing sexual patterns. Also proposes a model linking sexual change and modernization.

661. SHORTER, Edward. "Towards a History of <u>La Vie Intime</u>: The Evidence of Cultural Criticism in Nineteenth-Century Bavaria." <u>The Emergence of Leisure</u>. Ed. Michael Robert Marrus. New York: Harper & Row, 1974, pp. 38-68.

662. SIMONS, G. L. <u>A History of Sex</u>. London: New English Library, 1970.

663. TANNER, J. M. "Earlier Maturation in Man." Scientific American, January 1968, pp. 21-7.
Shows that there has been an uptrend in adult size and that a progressive decline in the age at menarche has occurred in Europe since at least the mid-19th century and in America since at least 1900. Thus, children today are reaching puberty progressively earlier. Notes also that the age of menarche is significantly related to the number of children in the family.

664. TAYLOR, Gordon Rattray. Sex in History: The Story of Society's Changing Attitudes to Sex Throughout the Ages. New York: Vanguard Press, 1954.
Examines changes in sexual manners and attitudes through history and relates these changes to the larger social context.

665. THOMAS, Keith. "The Double Standard." Journal of the History of Ideas, 20 (1959), 195-216.
Examines the history of the idea that unchastity is for a man a mild and pardonable offense, but for a woman a most serious matter.

666. TOMASSON, Richard F. "A Millennium of Sexual Permissiveness in the North." American Scandinavian Review, 62 (1974), 370-8.
Argues that there is a comparatively high degree of premarital sexual permissiveness in the Scandinavian countries, a trend which has deep historical roots.

667. VEITH, Ilza. "'Education for Morality': Sex Education-- Victorian Style." Bulletin of the Menninger Clinic, 34 (1970), 292-303.
Discusses the issue of teaching the realities of sex to the young, beginning with the writings of English physician, Thomas Beddoes. Also includes a discussion of American physician, Elizabeth Blackwell, and her advocacy of sex education.

668. YOUNG, Wayland Hinton. Eros Denied: Sex in Western Society. New York: Grove Press, 1964.
Considers the phenomenon of excluded words, erotic art and literature, sex customs, and inquires as to why our culture excludes certain words, people, actions, and images.

669. ZELDIN, Theodore. "The Conflict of Moralities: Confession, Sin, and Pleasure in the Nineteenth Century." Conflicts in French Society: Anticlericalism, Education, and Morals in the Nineteenth Century. London: George Allen & Unwin, 1970, pp. 13-51.
Investigates the extent to which the French Catholic Church and its enemies advocated conflicting forms of personal conduct and morality in the 19th century.

670. BRANCA, Patricia. "Health and Households; Material
     Culture of Middle-Class Women in Nineteenth-Century
     Britain." Diss. Rutgers Univ., 1973.
     Explores the role of the middle-class woman in the family,
     as mistress of the house, mistress of domestic servants,
     and as mother.

671. BRANCA, Patricia. "Image and Reality: The Myth of the
     Idle Victorian Woman." Clio's Consciousness Raised:
     New Perspectives on the History of Women. Ed. Mary
     Hartman and Lois W. Banner. New York: Harper & Row,
     1974, pp. 179-91.
     Argues that Victorian women were not frivolous, irrational,
     and helpless creatures of fashion. Rather, most middle-
     class women were deeply absorbed in household and child-
     rearing matters, had limited financial resources, and
     lacked formal schooling.

672. BRANCA, Patricia. Silent Sisterhood: Middle Class Women
     in the Victorian Home. Pittsburgh: Carnegie-Mellon
     Univ. Press, 1975.
     Examines the ordinary married middle-class woman in her
     family setting and the impact of modernization on such
     women. Argues that Victorian women played an important
     and fulfilling family role.

673. BULLOUGH, Vern I. The Subordinate Sex: A History of At-
     titudes Toward Women. Urbana: Univ. of Illinois Press,
     1973.
     Discusses the origin of attitudes toward women, and the
     role of women in history from antiquity to the present.

674. CUTTER, Irving Samuel, and Henry R. VIETS. A Short History
     of Midwifery. Philadelphia: W. B. Saunders, 1964.
     Discusses the development of clinical midwifery in Great
     Britain, France, Germany, and America since the 13th century.
     Particular attention is given to the development of the
     forceps. Also includes excellent biographical data.

675. DAVIDOFF, Leonore. "Mastered for Life: Servant and Wife
     in Victorian and Edwardian England." Journal of Social
     History, 7 (1974), 406-28.
     Examines how both servants and working-class wives in
     19th-century England were subordinate to masters and hus-
     bands due to paternalistic relationships.

676. HEWITT, Margaret. Wives and Mothers in Victorian Industry.
     London: Rockliff, 1958.
     Analyzes the influence of the factory system on the homes
     and families of married women employed in industry, notably
     age at marriage, mortality, family size, and infant mor-
     tality.

93

677.   MOORE, Katharine. Victorian Wives. New York; St. Martin's
       Press, 1974.
       Discusses notable married women in England and America and
       their sense of purposelessness and uselessness in Victorian
       society.

678.   OREN, Laura. "The Welfare of Women in Laboring Families:
       England, 1860-1950." Clio's Consciousness Raised: New
       Perspectives on the History of Women. Ed. Mary Hartman
       and Lois W. Banner. New York: Harper & Row, 1974,
       pp. 226-44.
       Illustrates how poverty surveys of family budgets reveal
       sexual inequalities in diet, health care, and pocket money
       in working-class families, resulting from pressures on the
       husband's standard of living which women and children had
       to absorb.

679.   OTTO, Patricia Courtney. "Daughters of the British Aris-
       tocracy: Their Marriages in the Eighteenth and Nine-
       teenth Centuries with Particular Reference to the Scot-
       tish Peerage." Diss. Stanford Univ., 1974.
       Demonstrates that a father's rank, birth order, national-
       ity, and time period exerted an influence upon the prob-
       ability of marriage and mate choice among daughters of
       Scottish peers. Although parental control of courtship
       waned through time, most daughters continued to choose
       their husbands from the aristocracy.

680.   PETERSON, M. Jeanne. "The Victorian Governess: Status
       Incongruence in Family and Society." Victorian Studies,
       14 (1970), 7-26.
       Investigates why the governess played such an important
       yet conflicting role in Victorian society, especially
       within the Victorian family.

681.   ROBERTSON, Priscilla. "Some Differences and Contrasts in
       the Structure of Middle-Class Marriages in France and
       England." Paper delivered at the American Historical
       Association, New Orleans, December 1972.
       Discusses how differing financial arrangements, housekeep-
       ing responsibilities, and emotional involvement in mar-
       riage affected the course of the woman's movement in
       France and England.

682.   SCOTT, Joan W., and Louise A. TILLY. "Women's Work and
       the Family in Nineteenth-Century Europe." Comparative
       Studies in Society and History, 17 (1975), 36-64.
       Argues that there is little relationship between women's
       rights and women's work, that large numbers of women worked
       long before they had legal and political rights, and that
       the female labor force increased in size to the early 20th
       century, then declined because of changing work opportunities.

683.   STEARNS, Peter N. "Working-Class Women in Britain, 1890-
       1914." Suffer and Be Still: Women in the Victorian Age.

Ed. Martha Vicinus. Bloomington; Indiana Univ. Press, 1972, pp. 100-20.
Discusses the changes in the conditions of working-class women, the hardships and traumas experienced by the working-class family, and the woman's declining role in the family.

684. TILLY, Louise A. "Industrialization, the Position of Women, and Women's History." Paper delivered at the Round Table on Work and the Status of Women, Paris, June 1975.
Investigates the changing position of peasant and working class women of England and France, especially the link between familial sex roles and productive roles.

685. TILLY, Louise A. "Women at Work in Milan, Italy--1880-World War I." Paper delivered at the American Historical Association, New Orleans, December 1972.
Examines longitudinally the place of women in the labor force of Milan by means of comparative analysis of three censuses. Women worked in relatively few, segregated occupations, mostly in consumer services and garment making. Most women who worked were young and single. With the growth of heavy industry in Milan, women's jobs, based on consumer industry, declined proportionately and absolutely.

686. TILLY, Louise A., et. al. "Women's Work and European Fertility Patterns." Journal of Interdisciplinary History, 6 (1976), 447-76.
Examines Shorter's hypothesis that female emancipation produced increased fertility rates--especially illegitimacy rates--and argues that women of the working classes were not searching for freedom nor experiencing emancipation as a result of work.

687. VAN DE WALLE, Etienne. The Female Population of France in the Nineteenth Century. Princeton: Princeton Univ. Press, 1974.
Explores female age and marital status distribution of 19th-century France, examines the general trends of fertility and nuptiality, and evaluates the existing published statistics.

5. The Post-Modern Family (1945-)

BIRTH CONTROL

688. BLACKER, C. P. "The International Planned Parenthood Federation: Aspects of Its History." Eugenics Review, 56 (1964), 135-42.
Discusses the development of I.P.P.F. and its relation to world events, with emphasis on Britain and the United States.

689. WEBSTER, Ann Adams. "French Women and Politics: The Involvement of Women in the Fight for Contraception Reform,

1953-1968." Diss. Princeton Univ., 1974.
Examines the history of the French family planning movement, the reasons for its failure, and women's involvement in the movement.

CHILDREN

690.   FARID, S. M. "On the Tempo of Childbearing in England and Wales." Population Studies, 28 (1974), 69-83
Shows that marriage cohorts of the years 1951 to 1963 reveal a declining rate in childlessness and an increase in the proporition of marriages with two or more children. Since 1964 there has been a drop in fertility due to increased age at childbearing and decreased completed fertility.

DEMOGRAPHY

691.   GLASS, David Victor. "Fertility Trends in Europe Since the Second World War." Fertility and Family Planning: A World View. Ed. Samuel J. Behrman, et. al. Ann Arbor: Univ. of Michigan Press, 1969, pp. 25-74.
Considers changes in nuptiality which have occurred since the thirties as well as changes in marital fertility to explain oscillations in general fertility.

692.   LIVI-BACCI, Massimo. "Population Policies in Western Europe." Population Studies, 28 (1974), 191-204.
Discusses in general the policies and laws concerning contraception, abortion, and family planning in modern Western Europe, the legislative and social systems favoring procreation, and the problems of mobility.

DOMESTIC LIFE AND CUSTOMS

693.   GEIGER, H. Kent. The Family in Soviet Russia. Cambridge: Harvard Univ. Press, 1968.
Discusses Marxist theory and the family, and considers the impact of communism on the Russian family as revealed in interviews with Soviet refugees.

694.   OAKLEY, Ann. The Sociology of Housework. London: Robertson, 1974.
Investigates women's attitudes toward housework, work conditions and routines of housewives, and the division of labor in modern British families.

695.   OAKLEY, Ann. Woman's Work: The Housewife, Past and Present. New York: Pantheon, 1975.
Examines the organization of work and family life in agricultural societies, the housewife's role in history, and the ideological aspects of women's domesticity.

CHAPTER III:

THE FAMILY IN AMERICAN HISTORY

1. The Colonial Family

GENERAL

696. BAILYN, Bernard. Education in the Forming of American
     Society: Needs and Opportunities for Study. Chapel
     Hill: Univ. of North Carolina Press, 1960.
     Examines the history of early American education, with
     emphasis on the impact of the new world on English ed-
     ucational forms and the importance of family life in
     the educational developments of colonial America.

697. CALHOUN, Arthur Wallace. "The Early American Family."
     Annals of the American Academy of Political and
     Social Science, 160 (1932), 7-12.
     Discusses the bourgeois background of the early American
     family, its Puritan origins, the pioneer family, colon-
     ial women and children, and sexual morality.

698. MILLER, Nathan. "The European Heritage of the American
     Family." Annals of the American Academy of Political
     and Social Science, 160 (1932), 1-6.
     Contends that early Americans brought with them their
     cultural heritage and institutions from Europe, notably
     the subordination of women and the view of marriage as
     a matter of mercenary calculation. But these broke down
     in the American wilderness.

699. ROTHMAN, David J. "A Note on the Study of the Colonial
     Family." William and Mary Quarterly, 23 (1966),
     627-34.
     Analyzes contemporary studies of the colonial family and
     notes their methodological problems, changing attitudes
     toward childhood, and areas for future research.

700. SEWARD, Rudy Ray. "The Colonial Family in America: Toward
     a Socio-Historical Restoration of its Structure."
     Journal of Marriage and the Family, 35 (1973), 58-70.
     Summarizes recent historical research on family size, age
     at marriage, and infant mortality rates as well as notes
     existing methodological problems.

701. VINOVSKIS, Maris. "The Field of Early American Family
     History: A Methodological Critique." Paper delivered
     at the American Studies Association, San Francisco,
     October 1973.
     Argues that demographic historians analyzing the colonial
     family face methodological problems of representativeness,
     the non-consideration of socio-economic development, im-
     proper sample size, and limitations of variables.

CHILDREN

702. BEALES, Ross W. "In Search of the Historical Child:
     Miniature Adulthood and Youth in Colonial New England."
     American Quarterly, 27 (1975), 379-98.
     Concludes that notions of children as miniature adults
     and of the absence of adolescence in colonial New Eng-
     land are, at best, exaggerations of social reality.

703. CHAPMAN, Jimmy Carl. "Changes in the Concepts of Child-
     hood Education in America, 1607-1860." Diss. Univ.
     of Texas, 1972.
     Examines the shifting concepts of childhood in America,
     and argues that as children became accepted as indiv-
     iduals in the early 19th century, education developed
     to provide for their needs.

704. EARLE, Alice Morse. Child Life in Colonial Days. New
     York: Macmillan, 1899.
     Describes infancy, children's dress, school books, chil-
     dren's literature, childrearing modes, and amusements
     in colonial America.

705. FOX, Claire Elizabeth. "Pregnancy, Childbirth, and Early
     Infancy in Anglo-American Culture: 1675-1830." Diss.
     Univ. of Pennsylvania, 1966.
     Describes pregnancy, parturition, post-partum care, and
     care of the newborn in early America as well as discusses
     the concerted efforts by the male medical profession to
     wrest midwifery from women during the 18th century.

706. GAY, Carol. "Cotton Mather and His Children: Some In-
     sights into Puritan Attitudes." Paper delivered at
     the Children's Literature Association, Storrs, Conn.,
     March 1974.

707. GREVEN, Philip J., ed. Child-Rearing Concepts, 1628-1861:
     Historical Sources. Ithasca, Ill.: F. E. Peacock,
     1973.
     An excellent anthology of prominent English and American
     childrearing theorists, revealing the shifting modes of
     childrearing from the early Calvinists to Locke to Bush-
     nell. Emphasis is on the transition from repressive
     methods to independency training.

708. HINER, N. Ray. "Adolescence in Eighteenth-Century America."
     History of Childhood Quarterly, 3 (1975), 253-80.
     Suggests that adolescence, defined as a period of prolonged
     dependence and marginality, was not a development of the
     19th century; it existed and was recognized by adults in
     the early 18th century.

709. ILLICK, Joseph E. "Child-Rearing in Seventeenth-Century
     England and America." The History of Childhood. Ed.
     Lloyd de Mause. New York: Psychohistory Press, 1974,

98

pp. 303-50.
Concludes that colonial childrearing practices were Lockean
in nature, emphasizing internal rather than external discipline. And these practices were closely related to changing demographic and family conditions.

710. MARIETTA, Jack D. "Quaker Family Education in Historical
Perspective." Quaker History, 63 (1974), 3-16.
Examines the importance of family education to colonial
Pennsylvania Quakers, and draws comparisons with the Pur-
itan family.

711. SCHLESINGER, Elizabeth Bancroft. "Cotton Mather and His
Children." William and Mary Quarterly, 10 (1953),
181-9.
Examines the home life, childrearing methods, and peda-
gogical techniques of Cotton Mather as revealed in his
diary.

712. SLATER, Peter Grieg. "Views of Children and of Child
Rearing During the Early National Period: A Study
in the New England Intellect." Diss. Univ. of California at Berkeley, 1970.
Argues that as Puritanism waned, childrearing methods
slowly shifted from Calvinist to Lockean to Romantic
to the teachings of Horace Bushnell. Thus less harsh,
more egalitarian child-training techniques increased
through time.

713. WALZER, John F. "A Period of Ambivalence: Eighteenth
Century American Childhood." The History of Childhood. Ed. Lloyd de Mause. New York: Psychohistory
Press, 1974, pp. 351-82.
Contends that colonial parents harbored an ambivalent
attitude toward their children, rejecting and retaining
their offspring at once. Childrearing practices increasingly stressed individuality and egalitarian relationships.

DEMOGRAPHY

714. CASSEDY, James H. Demography in Early America: Beginnings of the Statistical Mind, 1600-1800. Cambridge:
Harvard Univ. Press, 1969.
Discusses the introduction of vital statistics in early
American history and the role of numbers and statistics
in the religious, secular, and medical affairs of the
colonists.

715. DEMOS, John. "Families in Colonial Bristol, Rhode Island: An Exercise in Historical Demography." William and Mary Quarterly, 25 (1968), 40-57.
Notes that colonial households were small and grew slowly.
By the early 18th-century a loosening of sexual mores occurred as evidenced by an increase in bridal pregnancy.

716. DEMOS, John. "Notes on Life at Plymouth Colony." William
     and Mary Quarterly, 22 (1965), 264-86.
     Examines the fluidity of colonial society with regard to
     mobility and land, and analyzes family structure, age at
     marriage, and household composition of Plymouth Colony.

717. GREVEN, Philip J. "Historical Demography and Colonial
     America." William and Mary Quarterly, 24 (1967),
     438-54.
     Reviews current literature on historical demography,
     methodological problems, sources in colonial history
     for demographic history, problems of integrating demo-
     graphic data with the larger socio-economic context,
     and the necessity for comparative studies.

718. HECHT, Irene W. D. "The Virginia Muster of 1624/5 as
     a Source of Demographic History." William and Mary
     Quarterly, 30 (1973), 65-92.
     Examines the Muster to determine the age profile, racial
     composition, social structure, household size and com-
     position, the extent of servants in households, and the
     sex ratio in 17th-century Virginia.

719. HIGGS, Robert, and H. Louis STETTLER. "Colonial New Eng-
     land Demography: A Sampling Approach." William and
     Mary Quarterly, 27 (1970), 282-94.
     Samples twenty New England towns in the mid-18th century,
     and shows that marriage age was relatively high, maternal
     mortality was one in six, marital fertility was high, and
     the birth rate was high.

720. LOCKRIDGE, Kenneth A. "Monthly Variations in the Level
     of Conceptions as a Tool of Historical Analysis."
     Paper delivered at the Conference on Social History,
     Stony Brook, N.Y., October 1969.
     Examines the monthly variations in conceptions and births
     in colonial America, and finds the major peaks in June
     and lows in September, although the amplitudes varied
     regionally and decreased over time.

721. LOCKRIDGE, Kenneth A. "The Population of Dedham, Massa-
     chusetts, 1636-1736." Economic History Review, 19
     (1966), 318-44.
     Examines population mobility and growth, the relation-
     ship of vital events to each other, the problems of under-
     registration, and compares New England demographic char-
     acteristics with those of Europe.

722. MOLLER, Herbert. "Sex Composition and Correlated Culture:
     Patterns of Colonial America." William and Mary Quar-
     terly, 2 (1945), 113-53.
     Examines passenger lists to determine differential sex
     ratios and their changes through time. Also speculates
     on the impact of colonial sex composition on marriage,
     morality, and racial miscegenation.

723. NORTON, Susan L. "Marital Migration in Essex, County, Massachusetts, in the Colonial and Early Federal Periods." Journal of Marriage and the Family, 35 (1973), 406-18.
Finds that migration at the time of marriage was an important preindustrial social phenomenon. Most moves were short, although a significant proportion involved long-range distances.

724. NORTON, Susan L. "Population Growth in Colonial America: A Study of Ipswich, Massachusetts." Population Studies, 25 (1971), 433-52.
Finds that the rate of natural increase is not attributable to high fertility but to low mortality rates, a product of high nutrition level and the lack of infectious disease.

725. OBERSEIDER, Nancy Lou. "A Socio-Demographic Study of the Family as a Social Unit in Tidewater Virginia, 1660-1776." Diss. Univ. of Maryland, 1975.
Uses family reconstitution to examine 2800 colonial tidewater families. Finds Virginian families smaller than those of New England, while life spans for Virginians were considerably shorter than those in New England. Families were nuclear, mobile, and patriarchal.

726. POTTER, James. "The Growth of Population in America, 1700-1860." Population in History. Ed. David Victor Glass and D. E. C. Eversley. Chicago: Aldine, 1965, pp. 631-88.
Analyzes the deficiencies in early American demographic data and stresses the necessity to focus on particulars rather than aggregates. The rate of growth was uneven both in different colonies/states and over time, but was considerably higher than England. And high agricultural productivity was the key to rapid population growth.

727. RUTMAN, Darrett B., and Anita H. RUTMAN. "'Now-Wives and Sons-in-Law': Parental Death in a Seventeenth Century Virginia County." Paper delivered at the Conference on Early American History, College Park, Md., November 1974.
Examines the extent and social effect of parent loss in a representative tidewater Virginia county.

728. SMITH, Daniel Scott. "The Demographic History of Colonial New England." Journal of Economic History, 32 (1972), 165-83.
Concludes that the rapid growth of colonial New England was more a product of low mortality rates and a high proportion of females who married than of high marital fertility. The relative age of husbands also had an important yet overlooked influence on marital fertility.

729. SMITH, Daniel Scott. "Population, Family and Society in Hingham, Massachusetts, 1635-1880." Diss. Univ. of California at Berkeley, 1973.
Finds that the late 18th-century was a period of transition from the traditional family of orientation to the modern family of procreation; thus, modernization in the family appears to be related more to value changes than economic transformations.

730. SOMERVILLE, James. "A Demographic Profile of the Salem Family, 1660-1770." Paper delivered at the Conference on Social History, Stony Brook, N.Y., October 1969.
Examines Salem families using family reconstitution, and finds that marriage age for both males and females increased from the 17th to the 18th centuries as did the duration of the marriage union. Infant mortality sharply declined by the 18th century.

731. SOMERVILLE, James. "Family Demography and the Published Records: An Analysis of the Vital Statistics of Salem, Massachusetts." Essex Institute Historical Collections, 106 (1970), 243-51.
Explores the Vital Records of the Towns of Massachusetts to 1850 in terms of its format, difficulties and omissions, and importance in family reconstitution.

732. THOMPSON, Roger. "Seventeenth Century English and Colonial Sex Ratios: A Postscript." Population Studies, 28 (1974), 143-65.
Finds that it is difficult to isolate the effects of an unbalanced sex ratio from other variables, yet there are demographic and social factors in colonial American clearly explanable by the sex ratio. This ratio varied greatly between regions and contrasted with England where there was a marked shortage of marriageable men.

733. VINOVSKIS, Maris A. "The 1789 Life Table of Edward Wigglesworth." Journal of Economic History, 31 (1971), 570-90.
Examines the background of Edward Wigleworth's table on longevity, its accuracy, and its methodology.

734. WELLS, Robert Vale. "A Demographic Analysis of Some Middle Colony Quaker Families of the Eighteenth Century." Diss. Princeton Univ., 1969.
Examines the demographic characteristics of 18th-century Quaker families to explain the rapid population growth before 1800 and to ascertain the demographic changes accompanying the American Revolution.

735. WELLS, Robert Vale. "Demographic Change and the Life Cycle of American Families." Journal of Interdisciplinary History, 2 (1971), 273-82.
Compares 18th-century Quaker and modern family cycles, and discovers that families before 1800 were concerned

primarily with childbearing and childrearing while today
the emphasis on the childbearing aspects of marriage has
waned.

736. WELLS, Robert Vale. "Family Size and Fertility Control
      in Eighteenth-Century America: A Study of Quaker
      Families." Population Studies, 25 (1971), 73-82.
      Concludes that few Quakers had large families, that
      age-specific fertility rates declined through time,
      that Quaker fertility patterns differed markedly from
      the larger colonial population.

737. WELLS, Robert Vale. The Population of the British Colonies
      in America Before 1776: A Survey of Census Data. Prince-
      ton: Princeton Univ. Press, 1975.
      Examines census data of 21 colonies before 1776, evaluates
      the validity of these censuses for demographic history, and
      compares population patterns of various colonies.

738. WELLS, Robert Vale. "Quaker Marriage Patterns in a Colonial
      Perspective." William and Mary Quarterly, 29 (1972),
      415-42.
      Concludes that there were striking differences between the
      colonial marriage patterns of men and women, that marriages
      were relatively long, that a large proportion of the pop-
      ulation never married, and that family size was larger than
      European contemporaries although childbearing rates were
      similar.

DIVORCE

739. SPALLETTA, Matteo. "Divorce in Colonial New York." New
      York Historical Society Quarterly, 39 (1955), 422-40.
      Examines the stringent divorce laws and cases of divorce
      under the Dutch and English. Stresses the determination
      of the colonists to break away from a rigid divorce system.

740. WEISBERG, K. Kelly. "'Under Great Temptations Heer':
      Women and Divorce in Puritan Massachusetts." Feminist
      Studies, 2 (1975), 183-94.
      Examines the social conditions affecting 17th-century
      women in Massachusetts and how these conditions broke with
      English legal tradition and influenced the formulation of
      American divorce law.

DOMESTIC ARCHITECTURE

741. CLIFTON, Ronald Dillard. "Forms and Patterns: Room
      Specialization in Maryland, Massachusetts, and Penn-
      sylvania, Family Dwellings: 1725-1834." Diss. Univ.
      of Pennsylvania, 1971.
      Examines the relationship between the use of interior
      architectural space in family dwellings and wealth, oc-
      cupation, family size, geographical location, time of
      living in the dwelling, and home ownership.

742. GARVAN, Anthony N. B. "Architectural Space and Family
      Customs, 1700-1850." Paper delivered at the Social
      Science Research Council Conference on the History
      of the Family, Washington, D. C., October 1967.

DOMESTIC LIFE AND CUSTOMS

743. BISSELL, Linda Auwers. "Family, Friends, and Neighbors:
      Social Interaction in Seventeenth-Century Windsor,
      Connecticut." Diss. Brandies Univ., 1973.
      Analyzes four varieties of social interaction--generational,
      sexual, spatial, and class--in a 17th-century New England
      community, and finds family membership very significant in
      personal relationships as was proper. neighborly actions
      and attitudes.

744. BLAKE, John B. "The Compleat Housewife." Bulletin of the
      History of Medicine, 49 (1975), 30-42.
      Discusses the first cookbook printed in America which com-
      bined cookery, household hints, and medical recipes.

745. BROBECK, Stephen J. "Family Group Portrait Paintings as
      Indices of Family Culture, 1730 to 1855." Paper deliv-
      ered at the Social Science Research Council Conference
      on the History of the Family, Washington, D. C., Octo-
      ber 1967.
      Explores the value and limitations of family group por-
      traits as a source of information about childrearing
      ideals and practices, status differentiation, and family
      types.

746. DEMOS, John. "Demography and Psychology in the Historical
      Study of Family-Life: A Personal Report." Household
      and Family in Past Time. Ed. Peter Laslett and Richard
      Wall. Cambridge: Cambridge Univ. Press, 1972, pp.
      561-70.
      Finds that families in colonial America were nuclear, mod-
      erately large, and crowded in cramped quarters. The re-
      sulting tensions were directed externally at neighbors.
      Moreover, prevalent childrearing practices attempted to
      squelch childhood autonomy and produced guilt and anxiety
      among colonial children.

747. DEMOS, John. A Little Commonwealth: Family Life in Ply-
      mouth Colony. New York: Oxford Univ. Press, 1970.
      Argues that the colonial family was nuclear in composition,
      although children were often bound out for rearing and
      training. Roles and responsibilities within the family
      were similar to modern practices, but the colonial family
      assumed more functions than its contemporary counterpart.

748. DOW, George Francis. Domestic Life in New England in the
      Seventeenth Century. Topsfield, Mass.: Perkins Press,
      1925.
      Describes the clothing and furnishings possessed by 17th

century colonists as well as domestic structures and food.

749. EARLE, Alice Morse. <u>Home Life in Colonial Days</u>. New York:
Macmillan, 1910.
Discusses domestic architecture, diet, clothing, domestic
manufacturing, and pastimes in colonial New England.

750. FARBER, Bernard. <u>Guardians of Virtue: Salem Families in
1800</u>. New York: Basic Books, 1972.
Maintains that the New England family, imbued with the Puritan ethic, was deeply integrated into economic, social
and religious life. Moreover, social class affected the
promotion of capitalism and the socialization process.

751. FROST, Jerry William. <u>The Quaker Family in Colonial America: A Portrait of the Society of Friends</u>. New York:
St. Martin's Press, 1973.
Argues that the family was thoroughly integrated into the
religious and educational aspects of Quaker society, and
that its functions did not decline over time. Quaker childrearing practices produced a personality based on patience,
moderation, and self-control.

752. GOLLIN, Gillian Lindt. "Family Surrogates in Colonial America: The Moravian Experiment." <u>Journal of Marriage and
the Family</u>, 31 (1969), 650-8.
Shows how the Moravian community was rigidly differentiated
by age, sex, and marital status, and how the community developed a choir system to assume former family functions.

753. GREVEN, Philip J. "Family, Mobility, and Revivalism in
Early America: Some Perspectives and Hypotheses."
Paper delivered at the Southern Historical Association,
New Orleans, November 1968.

754. GREVEN, Philip J. <u>Four Generations: Population, Land, and
Family in Colonial Andover, Massachusetts</u>. Ithaca: Cornell Univ. Press, 1970.
Shows how the patriarchal family in which fathers controlled
their mature sons through land distribution slowly gave way
to a loosening of parent-child bonds and to an acceptance of
early independence and autonomy of sons.

755. IRONSIDE, Charles Edward. <u>The Family in Colonial New York:
A Sociological Study</u>. New York: Columbia Univ. Press,
1942.
Examines the static and dynamic aspects of the colonial family in terms of family stability, form and function, familial
roles, and nature of family authority, inheritance customs,
and the institutional setting in colonial New York. Concludes
that family systems in America and Western Europe were markedly similar.

756. JESTER, Annie Lash. <u>Domestic Life in Virginia in the
Seventeenth Century</u>. Williamsburg: Virginia 350th

Anniversary Celebration Corporation, 1957.
Describes the homes, wedding customs, roles of women, servants, furnishings, apparel, and leisure activities of 17th-century Virginians.

757. KTORIDES, Irene. "Marriage Customs in Colonial New England." Historical Journal of Western Massachusetts, 2 (1973), 5-21.
Discusses courtship and marriage patterns in early America with emphasis on bundling, dowries, contracts, and wedding ceremonies.

758. LANTZ, Herman R., et. al. "The American Family in the Preindustrial Period: From Base Lines in History to Change." American Sociological Review, 40 (1975), 21-36.
Finds that antebellum magazines reveal a marked increase in the power of women, the importance of love and personal happiness in mate selection, and a movement toward a more emancipated family with greater choices and options for the group and the individual.

759. LANTZ, Herman R., et. al. "The Preindustrial Family in America: A Further Examination of Early Magazines." American Journal of Sociology, 79 (1973), 566-88.
Concludes that while there was overt male power in the preindustrial family, it was tempered by subtle female power and increased role activities of women. The preindustrial family was influenced by ongoing internal structural changes, settlement conditions, and the changing intellectual climate.

760. LANTZ, Herman R., et. al. "Pre-Industrial Patterns in the Colonial Family in America: A Content Analysis of Colonial Magazines." American Sociological Review, 33 (1968), 413-26.
Argues that colonial magazines reveal that the romantic love complex, the double standard, and the emphasis on personal happiness in mate selection in the preindustrial family. And females exercised subtle power despite the patriarchal pattern of the family.

761. MEYER, Kenneth John. "Social Class and Family Structure: Attitudes Revealed by the Earliest American Novels, 1789-1815." Diss. Univ. of Minnesota, 1965.
Discusses the changing attitudes toward the family in early American novels, with emphasis on mate selection, filial obedience, the role of women, and the determination to maintain lineal ties of patriarchalism.

762. MORGAN, Edmund Sears. The Puritan Family: Religion and Domestic Relations in Seventeenth-Century New England. Rev. ed. New York: Harper & Row, 1966.
Shows that the Puritans, as revealed in literary sources,

viewed marriage in sacred terms, but they were not prudes.
The devoted themselves to the moral training of children,
and had warm, open relationships with their children.
It was the function of the colonial family to maintain
religiosity and preserve the social order.

763. MORGAN, Edmund Sears. Virginians at Home: Family Life
      in the Eighteenth Century. Williamburg: Colonial
      Williamsburg, 1952.
      Surveys briefly the family life of Virginian elites and
      their attitudes toward childrearing, courtship, mar-
      riage, and servants.

764. POWELL, Chilton L. "Marriage in Early New England."
      New England Quarterly, 1 (1928), 323-34.
      Examines civil and common-law marriages in colonial
      New England, their practice in 16th and 17th century
      Europe, and finds little difference between European
      and colonial marriage procedures.

765. ROGERS, Albert Alan. "Family Life in Eighteenth-Cen-
      tury Virginia." Diss. Univ. of Virginia, 1939.
      Uses an institutional approach to the colonial family
      drawn largely from A. W. Calhoun, and describes the
      status of women, courtship, marriage, childrearing,
      and the economic aspects of family life in Virginia.

766. SMITH, Daniel Scott. "Parental Power and Marriage Pat-
      terns: An Analysis of Historical Trends in Hingham,
      Massachusetts." Journal of Marriage and the Family,
      35 (1973), 419-28.
      Discovers changes in the traditional family patterns
      that occurred in the 18th century prior to modernization
      and the decline in marital fertility. These included
      the decline in parental control over marriage.

767. WALSH, Lorena. "Marriage and the Family in Seventeenth
      Century Maryland." Paper delivered at the Confer-
      ence on Early American History, College Park, Md.,
      November 1974.

FAMILY COMPOSITION AND STRUCTURE

768. GREVEN, Philip J. "The Average Size of Families and
      Households in the Province of Massachusetts in 1764
      and in the United States in 1790: An Overview."
      Household and Family in Past Time. Ed. Peter Laslett
      and Richard Wall. Cambridge: Cambridge Univ. Press,
      1972, pp. 545-60.
      Concludes that on the average 18th century American fam-
      ilies were larger than those in Europe, yet colonial
      family size varied greatly regionally, making general-
      izations difficult.

769. GREVEN, Philip J. "Family Structure in Seventeenth

Century Andover, Massachusetts." <u>William and Mary
Quarterly</u>, 23 (1966), 234-56.
Argues that the family structure which developed in
some 17th-century communities was a modified extended
family in which grown children who have married remained economically dependent upon their parents.

770.   GREVEN, Philip J. "An Historical Perspective on Fam-
       ily Structure." Paper delivered at the Social Sci-
       ence Research Council Conference on the History of
       the Family, Washington, D. C., October 1967.

771.   HARDY, John R. "A Cursory Investigation of Household
       Size and Structure in New York State, 1680-1780."
       Undergraduate thesis: Cambridge Univ., 1970.

772.   LOTKA, Alfred James. "The Size of American Families in
       the Eighteenth Century." <u>Journal of the American
       Statistical Association</u>, 22 (1927), 154-70.
       Argues that marital fertility rates in the late colon-
       ial period were very high--about 7.8 children per mar-
       ried woman.

773.   MANK, Russell Walter. "Family Structure in Northampton,
       Massachusetts, 1654-1729." Diss. Univ. of Denver,
       1975.
       Argues that the patterns of family structure which devel-
       oped in Northampton resembled other New England towns,
       notably high birth rates and low mortality rates, with
       moderate-sized and patriarchal families.

774.   SMITH, Daniel Scott. "Changes in the American Family
       Structure Before the Demographic Transition: The
       Case of Hingham, Massachusetts." Paper delivered
       at the Society for the Study of Social Problems,
       New York, August 1973.
       Argues that before the sustained decline of fertility
       in the 19th century, empirically identifiable patterns
       of the traditional or lineal family had weakened. The
       social supports of the traditional system had also
       declined.

775.   WELLS, Robert Vale. "Household Size and Composition
       in the British Colonies in America, 1675-1775."
       <u>Journal of Interdisciplinary History</u>, 4 (1974),
       543-70.
       Compares household size and composition between main-
       land and island British colonies, and finds wide var-
       iation and complexity.

FAMILY LAW AND INHERITANCE

776.   DART, Henry P. "Marriage Contracts of French Colonial
       Louisiana." <u>Louisiana Historical Quarterly</u>, 17
       (1934), 229-41.

Discusses the regulation of marriage contracts by Church
and State, the prevalence of a marital community, and
family law in pre-Spanish Louisiana.

777. KEIM, C. Ray. "Primogeniture and Entail in Colonial
       Virginia." William and Mary Quarterly, 25 (1968),
       545-86.
      Maintains that the customs and law of primogeniture
      and the entailing of estates in Virginia were not sim-
      ilar to England but were altered and sharply decreased
      by demographic, religious, and economic factors of
      colonial society.

778. MORRIS, Richard B. "Primogeniture and Entailed Estates
       in America." Columbia Law Review, 27 (1927), 24-51.
      Contends that primogeniture and entailed estates con-
      flicted with colonial society and legislative trends.
      Shows how the rule of partible descent evolved out of
      the American environment.

779. SMITH, Daniel Scott. "Inheritance and the Position and
       Orientation of Colonial Women." Paper delivered at
       the 2nd Berkshire Conference on the History of Women,
       Cambridge, October 1974.
      Illustrates that colonial men and women had distinct
      testamentary patterns, particularly lineage vs. reci-
      procity orientations toward kin. As land scarcity in-
      creased during the 18th century, men favored their
      sons over their wives.

KINSHIP

780. HECHT, Irene W. D. "Kinship and Migration in 17th Cen-
       tury Virginia." Paper delivered at the Conference
       on the Family, Social Structure and Social Change,
       Worcester, April 1972.

SEXUALITY

781. ADAMS, Charles Francis. "Some Phases of Sexual Morality
       and Church Discipline in Colonial New England." Pro-
       ceedings of the Massachusetts Historical Society, 6
       (1891), 477-519.
      Discusses the Puritan attempts at controlling morality
      and punishing deviance in Suffolk County, Massachusetts,
      and emphasizes civil and religious laws.

782. AURAND, A. Monroe. Little Known Facts About Bundling
       in the New World. Harrisburg: Aurand Press, 1938.
      Examines the history and custom of bundling, especially
      in Pennsylvania.

783. BEALL, Otho T. "Aristotle's Master Piece in America:
       A Landmark in the Folklore of Medicine." William
       and Mary Quarterly, 20 (1963), 207-22.

Shows that the first American sex manuals, drawing from
folklore, the Christian tradition, and medical knowledge,
are an index of popular knowledge and attitudes toward
sex and gynecology in the 18th century.

784. BOTOND-BLAZEK, Joseph Bela. "Puritans and Sex: An In-
         quiry into the Legal Enforcement of Sexual Morality
         in 17th Century Massachusetts." Diss. UCLA, 1962.
      Argues that the Puritans desired to keep temptations
      at a minimum and the community tightly-knit; hence,
      they used punishment as a warning to potential devi-
      ants, but punishment was used with great discrimination
      and selectivity.

785. BULLOUGH, Vern L. "An Early American Sex Manual, Or,
         Aristotle Who?" Early American Literature, 7 (1973),
         236-46.
      Discusses the popularity, impact, sexual theories, and
      biases of the Aristotle manuals in early America, es-
      pecially their emphasis on a more healthy view of sex.

786. FLAHERTY, David H. "Law and the Enforcement of Morals
         in Early America." Perspectives in American History,
         5 (1971), 202-56.
      Examines the changing relationship between law and morals,
      and reveals the success and consequences of colonial
      attempts to legislate morality in the realm of sexual
      offenses.

787. MORGAN, Edmund Sears. "The Puritans and Sex." New
         England Quarterly, 15 (1942), 591-607.
      Maintains that the Puritans, contrary to popular stereo-
      types, were not prudish nor repressive about sexual mat-
      ters. Although there existed moral strictness, offenders
      were treated with tolerance and understanding, and em-
      phasis was on prevention rather than punishment.

788. PARKES, Henry Bamford. "Morals and Law Enforcement in
         Colonial New England." New England Quarterly, 5
         (1932), 431-52.
      Examines the seamier side of colonial New England, in-
      cluding pre-marital fornication, bundling, adultery,
      and divorce. Concludes that colonial New England's
      moral standards were very high.

789. ROTHENBERG, Charles. "Marriage, Morals and the Law in
         Colonial America." New York Law Review, 74 (1940),
         393-8.
      Discusses attitudes toward marriage, community control
      over bachelors, marriage law, and control of morals in
      colonial New England and New Netherlands.

790. STILES, Henry Reed. Bundling: Its Origins, Progress
         and Decline in America. Albany: J. Munsell, 1869.
      Surveys the origin, development, and decline of the

custom of bundling in America, and argues that bundling
was a lower-class custom originating out of necessity.

WOMEN

791. COBBLEDICK, M. Robert. "The Property Rights of Women
      in Puritan New England." Studies in the Science of
      Society. Ed. George Peter Murdock. New Haven:
      Yale Univ. Press, 1937, pp. 107-15.
      Compares the property rights possessed by women in co-
      lonial New England with those in 17th century England.
      Concludes that colonial women had important property
      rights and were better off than their English sisters.

792. FARBER, Bernard. "Women, Marriage, and Illness: Con-
      sumptives in Salem, Massachusetts, 1785-1819."
      Journal of Comparative Family Studies, 4 (1973),
      36-48.
      Examines the meaning of consumption (tuberculosis) for
      Salem women in terms of age at marriage, childbearing,
      birth place, and marital status.

793. KEYSSAR, Alexander. "Widowhood in Eighteenth Century
      Massachusetts: A Problem in the History of the Fam-
      ily." Perspectives in American History, 8 (1974),
      83-122.
      Demonstrates that colonial widows were mature in years
      and generally did not remarry. They often lived with
      or received economic support from their adult children,
      although some widows received state or community relief.
      Widowhood also was related closely to the expansion of
      legal rights for women.

794. SOMERVILLE, James K. "The Salem (Mass.) Woman in the
      Home, 1660-1770." Eighteenth-Century Life, 1 (1974),
      11-4.
      Discusses some of the problems encountered in the study
      of colonial women, and uses wills to reveal the position
      and changing status of Salem women. Concludes that wo-
      men suffered a diminution in their power and authority
      over landed property, a product of the younger gener-
      ation's desire to obtain their landed inheritance before
      parental death.

795. TOMPSETT, Christine H. "A Note on the Economic Status
      of Widows in Colonial New York." New York History,
      55 (1974), 319-32.
      Examines the socio-economic status of colonial widows,
      as reflected in the value of their property.

2. The Modern Family (1800-1945)

GENERAL

796. BARDIS, Panos D. "Changes in the Colonial and Modern
      American Family Systems." Social Science, 38 (1963),
      103-14.
      Contrasts courtship, women's status, family size, fam-
      ily functions, and childrearing patterns between the
      colonial and modern American family.

797. CALHOUN, Arthur Wallace. Social History of the American
      Family. 3 vols. New York: Barnes & Noble, 1917.
      Examines the forces that have shaped marriage, control-
      led fertility and sexual morality, determined status and
      roles of family members, and influenced family formation.
      The traditional survey of American family history.

798. DEMOS, John. "The American Family in Past Time." Amer-
      ican Scholar, 43 (1974), 422-46.
      Offers an excellent interpretative essay of the basic
      themes and changes in American family history, conclud-
      ing that there was no golden age of the family and that
      the family, despite attempts to modify it, possesses a
      markedly reactive character.

799. FILENE, Peter Gabriel. Him/Her/Self: Sex Roles in
      Modern America. New York: Harcourt Brace Jovan-
      ovich, 1975.
      Analyzes how middle-class men and women defined them-
      selves from the late Victorian Era on, why these def-
      initions changed, and the psychological and intellectual
      dilemmas encountered as men and women sought satisfac-
      tory roles.

800. HANDLIN, Oscar, and Mary F. HANDLIN. Facing Life:
      Youth and the Family in American History. Boston:
      Little, Brown & Co., 1971.
      Describes the youthful wish to be free as reflected in
      the developing ways of leaving home: the family, the
      economic system, and the educational system.

801. LASLETT, Barbara. "The Family as a Public and Private
      Institution: An Historical Perspective." Journal
      of Marriage and the Family, 35 (1973), 480-94.
      Maintains that the private family--an institution of
      limited access and greater control over the audience
      of potential observers--is a modern development and
      the consequence of the separation of work and family
      activities.

802. MCPHARLIN, Paul. Love and Courtship in America. New
      York: Hastings House, 1946.
      Offers a popular and pictorial account of courting cus-
      toms in American history.

803. PRENTICE, Allison. "Education and the Metaphor of the
     Family: The Upper Canadian Example." History of
     Education Quarterly, 12 (1972), 281-303.
     Shows that some Canadian educators, envisioning the
     family as the antidote to social ills, wanted education-
     al institutions to imitate the family model; others did
     not. This dialogue is important because it reflects
     the changing conceptions of the ideal family.

BIRTH CONTROL

804. BARTLESON, Henrietta Lorraine. "The American Birth Con-
     trol Movement: A Study in Collective Behavior with
     Especial Reference to N. Smelser's Model of Norm-Or-
     iented Movements." Diss. Syracuse Univ., 1974.
     Examines the background of contraceptive practices,
     early origins of birth control agitation, legal restric-
     tions and religious controls, and the institutional
     acceptance of birth control—all within the context of
     Smelser's model of collective behavior.

805. BROOKS, Carol Flora. "The Early History of Anticontra-
     ception Laws in Massachusetts and Connecticut."
     American Quarterly, 18 (1966), 3-23.
     Demonstrates that the passage of anticontraceptive laws
     was not the result of religious or moral controversy
     but was part of the attempt to prohibit the circulation
     of obscene literature. Opposition to the laws came
     from sex radicals and civil libertarians.

806. CHESLER, Ellen. "Feminism, Sexuality, and Birth Control:
     A Closer Look at the Birth Control Clinic, 1923-1945."
     Paper delivered at the 2nd Berkshire Conference on
     the History of Women, Cambridge, October 1974.
     Examines the records of the Birth Control Clinical Re-
     search Bureau, founded in 1923 in New York by Margaret
     Sanger, and suggests that pioneer women in the birth
     control movement established medical facilities where
     contraception was offered to women as a dimension of a
     broader program of marriage hygiene intended to affirm
     the dignity of the female sexual role as well as to
     promote fertility decline.

807. CIRILLO, Vincent J. "Birth Control in Nineteenth Century
     America: A View from Three Contemporaries." Yale
     Journal of Biology and Medicine, 47 (1974), 260-7.
     Examines the social, philosophical, and technical aspects
     of birth control as revealed by John Humphrey Noyes,
     Anthony Comstock, and Edward Bliss Foote.

808. CIRILLO, Vincent J. "Edward Foote's Medical Common Sense:
     An Early American Comment on Birth Control." Journal
     of the History of Medicine, 25 (1970), 341-5.
     Examines New York physician Edward Foote's book advocating
     birth control in the mid-19th century.

809. GORDON, Linda. "The Politics of Birth Control, 1920-
      1940: The Impact of Professionals." International
      Journal of Health Services, 5 (1975), 253-77.
      Discusses the transformation of the birth control move-
      ment from a concern with women's rights and sexual free-
      dom to a respectable, reform cause concerned with med-
      ical health and population control as well as holding
      back the spread of birth control information. This
      transition was the product of professionalization, es-
      pecially the takeover by doctors and academic eugenists.

810. GORDON, Linda. "The Politics of Population: Birth Con-
      trol and the Eugenics Movement." Radical America,
      8 (1974), 61-97.
      Discusses the influence of eugenics, especially its
      racism and elitism, on the birth control movement and
      its implications for women's reproductive self-deter-
      mination.

811. GORDON, Linda. "Voluntary Motherhood: The Beginnings
      of Feminist Birth Control Ideas in the United States."
      Clio's Consciousness Raised: New Perspectives on the
      History of Women. Ed. Mary Hartman and Lois W. Ban-
      ner. New York: Harper & Row, 1974, pp. 54-71.
      Shows that the advocates of voluntary motherhood, although
      comprised of three diverse types--suffragists, moral re-
      formers, and Free Lovers, all agreed that modernization
      was disintegrating the family and loosening sexual moral-
      ity. Birth control was viewed not only as a means of
      emancipating women, but as an answer to larger social
      problems.

812. GORDON, Linda. Woman's Body, Woman's Right: A Social
      History of Birth Control in America. New York:
      Viking, 1976.
      Examines the American birth control movement from the
      early 19th century to the present, especially its social
      context, professionalization, and the impact on the lives
      of women.

813. JOHNSON, R. Christian. "The Interaction of Biomedical
      Scientists with the American Birth Control Movement,
      1900-1960." Paper delivered to the American Histor-
      ical Association, New Orleans, December 1972.

814. KENNEDY, Anne. "History of the Development of Contra-
      ceptive Materials in the United States." American
      Medicine, 41 (1935), 159-61.
      Discusses the development and manufacturing of the
      diaphragm and vaginal jelly from 1925 to 1935.

815. KENNEDY, David M. Birth Control in America: The Career
      of Margaret Sanger. New Haven: Yale Univ. Press,
      1970.
      Examines the public career of Margaret Sanger and her

relationship with the birth control movement between
1912 and WWII. An excellent study of the changing at-
titudal and institutional responses to attempts at
birth limitation.

816. LADER, Lawrence. The Margaret Sanger Story, and the
Fight for Birth Control. New York: Doubleday,
1955.
Discusses the life of birth control advocate Margaret
Sanger and her crusade to make birth control socially
acceptable.

817. MCCORMICK, C. O. "The History of Birth Control in America." Journal of the Indiana Medical Association,
27 (1934), 385-91.
Traces the origins, extent, and legislative impact of
the voluntary parenthood movement in America, with
special emphasis on Margaret Sanger and the differences
between the conservative and radical flanks. Also examines the institutional manifestations of the movement.

818. REED, James W. "Birth Control and the Americans, 1830-
1970." Diss. Harvard Univ., 1974.
Explains American efforts at contraception and population
limitation since the mid-19th century, including the
major figures, development of contraceptive research,
and controversies of the movement. Considerable attention is given to the social context in which the
movement developed.

819. RIEGEL, Robert E. "Dr. Knowlton: American Pioneer in
the Birth Control Movement." New England Quarterly,
6 (1933), 470-90.
Describes the life, ideas, and activities of Charles
Knowlton, a Massachusetts physician who pioneered the
American birth control movement.

CHILDREN

820. ANDERSON, John E. "Child Development: An Historical
Perspective." Child Development, 27 (1956), 181-96.
Surveys the history of the child development movement
from late 19th-century studies of the child to the growth
of scientific literature about children.

821. BAKAN, David. "Adolescence in America: From Idea to
Social Fact." Daedalus, 100 (1971), 979-95.
Contends that the term "adolescence" is a product of
modern urban-industrial life. It was invented to ful-
fill the exigencies of the emerging social order, i.e.
to prolong the childhood years.

822. BERNERT, Eleanor H. America's Children. New York:
Wiley, 1958.
Discusses the changing trends from 1900 to 1950 in the

115

size and distribution of child and youth population,
living and family arrangements, childhood dependency,
school attendance, and youth at work.

823. BLOOM, Lynn Zimmerman. "It's All for Your Own Good:
      Parent-Child Relationships in Popular American Child
      Rearing Literature, 1820-1970." Paper delivered at
      the Popular Culture Association, Milwaukee, May
      1974.

824. BREMNER, Robert, et. al., eds. Children and Youth in
      America: A Documentary History. 3 vols. Cambridge:
      Harvard Univ. Press, 1970-74.
      A good anthology of the history of public policy toward
      children and youth. Argues that the history of the
      child is one of optimism and increasing liberty and
      freedom.

825. BRIM, Orville G. "A History of Education for Child
      Rearing." Education for Child Rearing. New York:
      Russell Sage Foundation, 1959, pp. 321-49.
      Presents an overview of the development of organized
      parent education programs in America, and describes
      contemporary activities of these programs.

826. CABLE, Mary. The Little Darlings: A History of Child
      Rearing in America. New York: Charles Scribner's
      Sons, 1975.
      Surveys childrearing literature in America, and argues
      that attitudes toward children have shifted from the
      Calvinist belief that children were born evil to the
      modern conviction that children have potential goodness.

827. COHN, Jan Kadetsky. "Growing Up Good: Popular Attitudes
      Toward House and Family in America." Paper delivered
      at the Popular Culture Association, Milwaukee, May
      1974.
      Argues that in the last hundred years, a combination of
      Victorian sentimentalism, democratic idealism and the
      business ethic reshaped American ideas about child-rear-
      ing. Because the same values came to define the American
      house, both as property and as a home, popular ideas
      about home-ownership and child-rearing developed a cur-
      ious and powerful interdependency.

828. DAMIS, Elaine V. "The History of Child-Rearing Advice
      in America from 1800-1940." Honor's Thesis, Rad-
      cliffe College, 1960.
      Reviews childrearing literature in America from the
      diminution of Calvinism to the more scientific approach
      to children.

829. DAVIS, Helen Holmes. "Conceptions of Child Nature and
      Training from 1825 to 1880: A Study in the History
      of American Educational Theory." Master's Thesis,

116

Univ. of Cincinnati, 1936.
Traces the changing attitudes toward children by American educators--notably Bronson Alcott--from harsh Puritanism to a more humane attitude where children were regarded as children and no longer considered unregenerate and depraved.

830. DEMOS, John, and Virginia DEMOS. "Adolescence in Historical Perspective." Journal of Marriage and the Family, 31 (1969), 632-8.
Contends that adolescence as a concept is closely related to the rural to urban transition which removed economic functions from the child, separated adult and child social roles, and allowed a "youth culture" to emerge.

831. FRANK, Lawrence K. "The Beginning of Child Development and Family Education in the Twentieth Century." Merrill-Palmer Quarterly, 8 (1962), 207-27.
Discusses the new interest in the study of children and the desire to develop new patterns in child rearing and parental education in early 20th century America.

832. FRISCH, John Richard. "Youth Culture in America, 1790-1865." Diss. Univ. of Missouri, 1970.
Argues that 19th-century adolescence was not a stormy, problem-filled stage of life, nor was there a generational gap. Youth exhibited Victorian sexual standards and married for sound personal qualities. Nor were young people more interested in religion than with other institutions.

833. GRAFF, Harvey J. "Patterns of Dependency and Child Development in the Mid-Nineteenth Century City: A Sample from Boston, 1860." History of Education Quarterly, 13 (1973), 129-44.
Finds that urban adolescent experiences were increasingly graded by age, notably the ages for leaving school and commencing work. Although male youth resided at home in a stage of semi-dependency until age twenty, females were dependent on the family until their early twenties.

834. HASSAN, Ihab Habib. "The Idea of Adolescence in American Fiction." American Fiction." American Quarterly, 10 (1958), 312-24.
Examines the complex image of youth in American fiction, its relationship to the American experience, and its change through time.

835. KATZ, Michael B. "Growing Up in the Nineteenth Century: Relations Between Home, Work, School, and Marriage, Hamilton, Ontario, 1851 and 1861." Canadian Social History Project, Interim Report, 4 (1972), 50-101.
Suggests that the children of the past did not leave home as independent persons in one giant step, but most

spent some time living in a semi-dependent state in some-
one else's household.

836. KETT, Joseph F. "Adolescence and Youth in Nineteenth
         Century America." Journal of Interdisciplinary His-
         tory, 2 (1971), 283-98.
      Argues that colonial Americans did not see youth as a
      concept, but in the 19th century as juvenile innocence
      was stressed and life envisioned as a cycle of seasons,
      adolescence as a stage of life became slowly defined.
      This concept was augmented by the emphasis on teenage
      religious conversion and increased age-grading of soci-
      ety.

837. KETT, Joseph F. "Growing Up in Rural New England, 1800-
         1840." Anonymous Americans: Explorations in Nine-
         teenth Century Social History. Ed. Tamara K. Hareven.
         Englewood Cliffs: Prentice-Hall, 1971, pp. 1-17.
      Analyzes the period of semidependency, the impact of
      schooling and discipline on young people, religious
      instruction and conversion of adolescents, and the tur-
      bulence of youth in rural New England.

838. KUHN, Anne Louise. The Mother's Role in Childhood Ed-
         ucation: New England Concepts, 1830-1860. New Haven:
         Yale Univ. Press, 1947.
      Portrays the educational role of the mother in New Eng-
      land families as revealed in the writings of clergymen,
      physicians, educators, and social reformers.

839. MCLOUGHLIN, William G. "Evangelical Child-Rearing in
         the Age of Jackson: Francis Wayland's View on When
         and How to Subdue the Wilfulness of Children." Jour-
         nal of Social History, 9 (1975), 21-39.
      Discusses Francis Wayland's method of subduing the stub-
      born will of his infant son and the social implications
      of Wayland's childrearing techniques.

840. MAYER, Henry. "From Young Man to Adolescent: Social
         Control and the Concept of Adolescence, 1880-1905."
         Paper delivered at the American Historical Association,
         New York, December 1971.

841. MEADOWS, Iris Culver. "Concepts of Child Nature in Amer-
         ican Life and Education, 1800-1900." Diss. Univ. of
         Missouri, 1951.
      Examines the ideas relative to child nature from Puritan-
      ism to the beginning of the child study movement as re-
      vealed in the writings of major theorists, teacher
      training textbooks, school books, and other educational
      literature.

842. MECHLING, Jay Edmund. "A Role-Learning Model for the
         Study of Historical Change in Parent Behavior; With
         a Test of the Model on the Behavior of American

Parents in the Great Depression." Diss. Univ. of
Pennsylvania, 1971.
Develops a role-learning model of parent behavior con-
structed around role-learning processes and the process of intra-role conflict resolution, and tests this
model on parental behavior during the Great Depression
of the 1930s.

843. RAPSON, Richard L. "The American Child as Seen by British
      Travelers, 1845-1935." American Quarterly, 17 (1965),
      520-34.
      Illustrates how British travelers in America were appal-
      led at the precocity of American children, an observation
      indicating that traditional parent-child relationships
      were changing under the impact of democratic ideals and
      that these changes occurred in America before they took
      place in England.

844. RYERSON, Alice Judson. "Medical Advice on Child Rearing,
      1550-1900." Harvard Educational Review, 31 (1961),
      302-23.
      Maintains that prior to 1750, the turning point in child-
      rearing, childrearing manuals emphasized childhood de-
      pendency and obedience. But from 1750 to 1900, there
      was a shift toward permissiveness and independency.
      These changes reflect the personality needs of an in-
      dustrial society.

845. RYERSON, Alice Judson. "Medical Advice on Childrearing
      Practices, 1550-1900." Diss. Harvard Univ., 1960.
      Traces the shift in childrearing practices from depen-
      dency to permissiveness as revealed in American and Eng-
      lish medical writings, identifies periods of change in
      childrearing, relates these changes to personality de-
      velopment, and finds a dramatic shift in childrearing
      in the 18th century.

846. SEARS, Barbara Anne. "An Historical Study of Selected
      Popular Beliefs and Practices Pertaining to Pregnancy
      and Childbirth in the State of Texas from 1845 Through
      1968." Diss. Texas Woman's Univ., 1972.

847. SENN, Milton J. E. "Changing Concepts on Child Care: A
      Historical Review." New York Academy of Medicine.
      The March of Medicine, No. 17. New York: Inter-
      national Univ. Press, 1955, pp. 83-103.
      Surveys medical attitudes toward child care and dis-
      cusses briefly the history of pediatrics.

848. STEERE, Geoffrey Hazard. "Changing Values in Child
      Socialization: A Study of United States Child-Rear-
      ing Literature, 1865-1929." Diss. Univ. of Penn-
      sylvania, 1964.
      Argues that there was a change in American childrearing
      literature from 1865 to 1929 from an intuitive-religious

119

orientation to a scientific-relativistic orientation
of certain recommended patterns of child socialization,
a change which illustrates wider changes in American
values.

849. STEERE, Geoffrey Hazard. "Child-Rearing Literature and
      Modernization Theory." Paper delivered at the Amer-
      ican Studies Association, San Francisco, October
      1973.
      Notes that American childrearing literature did not
      fully modernize until the 1920s with respect to for-
      mat, authorship, and content; but the pace of modern-
      ization remains vague.

850. STEERE, Geoffrey Hazard. "Freudianism and Child-Rear-
      ing in the Twenties." American Quarterly, 20 (1968),
      759-67.
      Contends that despite Freud's influence on the intel-
      lectuals of the 1920s, there were few discussions of
      Freudianism in the popular childrearing manuals of the
      period, indicating that Freud had a minimal impact on
      the middle class.

851. STENDLER, Celia B. "Sixty Years of Child Training
      Practices: Revolution in the Nursery." Journal
      of Pediatrics, 36 (1950), 122-34.
      Examines articles on child training found in popular
      women's magazines from 1890 to 1950, and documents a
      shift from a sentimental approach to childrearing to
      an emphasis on self-regulation.

852. STRICKLAND, Charles. "A Transcendental Father: The
      Child-Rearing Practices of Bronson Alcott." His-
      tory of Childhood Quarterly, 1 (1973), 4-51.
      Shows that Bronson Alcott, rejecting the harsh child-
      rearing theories of his day, experimented in a roman-
      tic mode of childrearing which strove for moral per-
      fection, self-control, and freedom.

853. SUNLEY, Robert. "Early Nineteenth-Century American
      Literature on Child-Rearing." Childhood in Contem-
      porary Cultures. Ed. Margaret Mead and Martha Wolf-
      enstein. Chicago: Univ. of Chicago Press, 1955,
      pp. 150-67.
      Argues that from 1820 to 1860 Americans became increas-
      ingly interested in children and their problems. The
      childrearing literature of this period de-emphasized
      corporal punishment and stressed moral independence,
      but was in disagreement over the nature of the child.

854. TAYLOR, William R. "The Nurture of Children in Early
      Nineteenth-Century America." Paper delivered at
      the American Historical Association, New York,
      December 1966.

855. WILSON, Elizabeth Andrews. "Hygienic Care and Management
         of the Child in the American Family Prior to 1860."
         Master's Thesis, Duke Univ., 1940.
      Reviews the characteristics of the American family before
      1860, including evidence of infant mortality, the use of
      midwives and nurses, infant diet and health, exercise and
      recreations of children, and children's clothing.

856. WISHY, Bernard W. The Child and the Republic: The Dawn
         of American Child Nurture. Philadelphia: Univ. of
         Pennsylvania Press, 1968.
      Illustrates that 19th century American attitudes toward
      child nurture, home care, and religious and moral life
      were filled with contradictions about authority versus
      freedom.

857. WITHAM, W. Tasker. The Adolescent in the American Novel,
         1920-1960. New York: Frederick Ungar, 1964.
      Examines the American novel of adolescence and the prob-
      lems--sex, family, education, community, and career--faced
      by adolescents of these novels.

858. WOLFENSTEIN, Martha. "Fun Morality: An Analysis of
         Recent American Child-Training Literature." Childhood
         in Contemporary Cultures. Ed. Margaret Mead and Martha
         Wolfenstein. Chicago: Univ. of Chicago Press, 1955,
         pp. 168-78.
      Demonstrates that recent American childrearing methods
      reject the Puritan ethic and stress play, amusement,
      freedom, and exploration on the part of the child. These
      trends reflect larger attitudinal changes toward work and
      play.

859. ZAND, Helen Stankiewicz. "Polish American Childways."
         Polish American Studies, 16 (1959), 74-9.
      Discusses oldwives' tales and immigrant customs of child-
      rearing by Polish-Americans as well as modern modes of
      child-training.

DEMOGRAPHY

860. BASH, Wendell H. "Changing Birth Rates in Developing
         America: New York State, 1840-1875." Milbank Memor-
         ial Quarterly, 41 (1963), 161-82.
      Explores rural-urban differentials and compares fertil-
      ity ratios between cities, counties, and the state to
      indicate the degree of urbanization.

861. BASH, Wendell H. "Differential Fertility in Madison
         County, New York, 1865." Milbank Memorial Quarterly,
         33 (1955), 161-86.
      Examines fertility in terms of geography, nativity,
      occupation, value of dwelling, and cash value of farm.
      Finds that the "J" hypothesis of the relationship be-
      tween social status and birth rates is not correct for

mid-19th century New York State.

862. BOUVIER, Leon Francis. "The Spacing of Births Among
      French Canadian Families: A Historical Approach."
      Canadian Review of Sociology and Anthropology, 5
      (1968), 17-26.
      Uses the genealogy of one family to determine and com-
      pare birth intervals in the Canadian and U.S. branches
      of the family between 1650 and 1950.

863. CALMES, Alan. "Residential Patterns in Nineteenth Cen-
      tury Fincastle, Virginia." Paper delivered at the
      Historical Urbanization in North America Confer-
      ence, Toronto, January 1973.
      Illustrates how the methods of family reconstitution
      and demographic history, as utilized in the Roanoke
      19th-Century Family History Project, are useful in map-
      ping migratory and residential patterns of whites and
      blacks.

864. CARTER, Gregg Lee. "Social Demography of the Chinese
      in Nevada: 1870-1880." Nevada Historical Society
      Quarterly, 18 (1975), 73-89.
      Discusses the highly unbalanced sex ratio of Nevada's
      Chinese and its disruptive effect on Chinese family
      life.

865. CIOCCO, Antonio. "The Trend of Age at Marriage in
      Washington County, Maryland, From 1897 to 1938."
      Human Biology, 12 (1940), 59-76.
      Concludes that there is an association between late
      marriages and socio-economic level. Also shows that
      the median age at marriage of males and females exhib-
      ited a slight decline, especially between 1897 and
      1914.

866. DENTON, Frank T., and Peter J. GEORGE. "The Influence
      of Socio-Economic Variables on Family Size in Went-
      worth County, Ontario, 1871: A Statistical Analysis
      of Historical Micro-Data." Canadian Review of Socio-
      logy and Anthropology, 10 (1973), 334-45.
      Examines the effect of age, place of birth, religion,
      ethnic origin, employment, and rural/urban residence
      on family size in mid-19th century Canada.

867. DENTON, Frank T., and Peter J. GEORGE. "Socio-Economic
      Characteristics of Families in Wentworth County,
      1871: Some Further Results." Social History, 7
      (1974), 103-10.
      Finds that wife's birthplace was the strongest indicator
      of the number of children in Canadian families, and that
      the differences in family size between rural and urban
      families were not due to socio-economic differences.

868. EASTERLIN, Richard Ainley. The American Baby Boom in

Historical Perspective. New York: National Bureau of Economic Research, 1962.
Examines the causes of population change and patterns in terms of the Kuznets-cycle conception of economic change. Concludes that the modern baby boom is a break with historical experience.

869. EASTERLIN, Richard Ainley. "Does Human Fertility Adjust to the Environment?" American Economic Review, 61 (1971), 399-407.
Contends that the secular decline in American fertility from 1810 on was a voluntary response to changing environmental conditions, especially the rural to urban transition.

870. EASTERLIN, Richard Ainley, et. al. "Farms and Farm Families in Old and New Areas: The Northern States in 1860." Demographic Processes and Family Organization in Nineteenth-Century American Society. Ed. Tamara K. Hareven and Maris A. Vinovskis. Princeton: Princeton Univ. Press, forthcoming.
Analyzes the factors contributing to the 19th-century fertility decline in rural America. Special attention is given to parents' desire to "establish" their children.

871. EBLEN, Jack E. "An Analysis of Nineteenth-Century Frontier Populations." Demography, 2 (1965), 399-413.
Notes that the frontier was short-lived, with the population having more children under age ten, a higher sex ratio, and fewer adults over forty than the national average. The family unit, not the single individual, was the norm on the frontier.

872. ELDER, Glen H. Children of the Great Depression: Social Change in Life Experience. Chicago: Univ. of Chicago Press, 1974.
Examines the Depression experience on the lives of Oakland (California) individuals and the implications of sharp socio-economic change for family change and intergenerational relations.

873. FORSTER, Colin, and G.S.L. TUCKER. Economic Opportunity and White American Fertility Ratios: 1800-1860. New Haven: Yale Univ. Press, 1972.
Examines critically Yasuba's thesis that the availability of new land, not urbanization, was the major determinant of fertility in the early 19th century. Concludes that the thesis is essentially correct.

874. GLICK, Paul C. "Family Trends in the United States, 1890-1940." American Sociological Review, 7 (1942), 505-14.
Describes declining family size and decreasing number of children in the family since 1890, the distribution of

families by region and race, and the average size
family by region, place, and race.

875. GRABILL, Wilson H., et. al. The Fertility of American
      Women. New York: John Wiley, 1958.
      Examines reproductive trends in America since 1790 as
      well as the impact of residence, race, nativity, age,
      and socio-economic variables on fertility rates.

876. HALL, Peter Dobkin. "Family Structure and Class Con-
      solidation Among the Boston Brahmins." Diss. State
      Univ. of New York at Stony Brook, 1973.
      Examines the relationship between Boston merchant fam-
      ilies, the problems of technological innovation, and
      institutional development.

877. HALL, Peter Dobkin. "Family Structure and Economic
      Origin: Massachusetts Merchants, 1700-1900."
      Paper delivered at the American Sociological Assoc-
      iation, Montreal, August 1974.
      Analyzes marriage patterns, wealth transmission, busi-
      ness organization, and career patterns of eastern mer-
      chant families and how family structure varied with
      economic demands.

878. HAREVEN, Tamara K., and Maris A. VINOVSKIS. "Marital
      Fertility, Ethnicity, and Occupation in Urban Fam-
      ilies: An Analysis of South Boston and the South
      End in 1880." Journal of Social History, 8 (1975),
      69-93.
      Examines the relationship between fertility, ethnicity,
      and occupation in Boston, using the child-woman ratio
      as an estimate of fertility. Argues that ethnicity was
      a major determinant of fertility differentials at the
      household level.

879. HASTINGS, Donald W., and J. Gregory ROBINSON. "Incidence
      of Childlessness for United States Women, Cohorts
      Born 1891-1945." Social Biology, 21 (1974), 178-84.
      Uses cohort-specific age-specific estimates to examine
      the incidence of childlessness among all women and
      ever-married women over time.

880. JAFFE, A. J. "Differential Fertility in the White Pop-
      ulation in Early America." Journal of Heredity, 31
      (1940), 407-11.
      Analyzes fertility differentials in America from 1800
      to 1840, and finds wide variations in the birth rate
      geographically, economically, and by urban-rural res-
      idency.

881. KENNEDY, Ruby Jo Reeves. "Single or Triple Melting-Pot?
      Intermarriage Trends in New Haven, 1870-1940."
      American Journal of Sociology, 49 (1944), 331-9.
      Argues that a triple-religious cleavage rather than a

multilinear nationality cleavage characterizes American
society.

882. KENNEDY, Ruby Jo Reeves. "Single or Triple Melting-Pot?
      Intermarriage in New Haven, 1870-1950." American
      Journal of Sociology, 58 (1952), 56-9.
      Concludes that a "triple-melting-pot" type of assimilation
      is taking place with high in-marriage rates among Catholics,
      Protestants, and Jews.

883. LEET, Don R. "Population Pressure and Human Fertility
      Response: Ohio, 1810-1860." Journal of Economic
      History, 34 (1974), 286-8.
      Examines fertility differentials in antebellum Ohio
      and argues that land availability in relation to the
      number of potential young farmers explains fertility
      differentials better than origin, urbanization, liter-
      acy, or man-land population density.

884. MIDDLETON, Russell. "Fertility Values in American Maga-
      zine Fiction, 1916-1956." Public Opinion Quarterly,
      24 (1960), 139-43.
      Analyzes popular magazine fiction in 1916, 1936, and
      1956 to determine whether changes in fertility values
      paralleled changes in fertility behavior, and finds the
      existence of such a pattern.

885. MODELL, John. "Family and Fertility on the Indiana
      Frontier, 1820." American Quarterly, 23 (1971),
      615-34.
      Argues that on the frontier, nuclear families provided
      the basic social unit, that high fertility was closely
      related to the frontier's complex social system rather
      than population density, and that fertility varied with
      the degree of "urbanization" on the frontier.

886. MODELL, John. "Patterns of Consumption, Acculturation,
      and Family Income Strategy in Late 19th-Century Amer-
      ica." Demographic Processes and Family Organization
      in Nineteenth-Century American Society. Ed. Tamara
      K. Hareven and Maris A. Vinovskis. Princeton: Prince-
      ton Univ. Press, forthcoming.
      Notes that Irish working-class families first emulated
      the consumption patterns of native families before
      heads' income approached native levels. High fertility
      and child labor, consistent with this initial pattern,
      were reduced over time as heads' income more nearly
      resembled that of natives.

887. MONAHAN, Thomas Patrick. "One Hundred Years of Marriages
      in Massachusetts." American Journal of Sociology, 56
      (1951), 534-45.
      Notes that there has been no significant long-term change
      in age at marriage since 1890, and argues that the cul-
      tural heritage of a group determines age at marriage.

888. MONAHAN, Thomas Patrick. The Pattern of Age at Marriage in the United States. 2 vols. Philadelphia: Stephenson-Brothers, 1951.
Examines the long term trend in the average age at marriage as well as the marriage rate, percentage who marry, remarriage, child marriage, and marriage restrictions. Finds little change over time in the proportion married, and discovers wide geographical and cultural variations in age at first marriage. Concludes that youthful marriages were not prevalent in the colonial period.

889. MOTT, Frank L. "Portrait of an American Mill Town: Demographic Response in Mid-Nineteenth Century Warren, Rhode Island." Population Studies, 26 (1972), 147-57.
Illustrates how industrialization fostered grave demographic consequences in some communities, resulting in low fertility rates, high proportions of unmarried, unbalanced sex rations, and high age at marriage.

890. NOTESTEIN, Frank W. "The Decrease in the Size of Families from 1890 to 1910." Milbank Memorial Fund Quarterly Bulletin, 9 (1931), 181-88.
Illustrates that the declining birth rate is related to a decrease in the proportion of very large families rather than an increase in childless and one-child families.

891. POTTER, James. "American Population in the Early National Period." Population and Economics: Proceedings of Section V of the Fourth Congress of the International Economic History Association, 1968. Winnipeg: Univ. of Manitoba Press, 1970, pp. 55-69.
Shows that the population of colonial America grew at a fast rate with fastest growth in the newest settlements and slower growth in the older areas. Also illustrates that the rate of natural increase declined from 1790 to 1860 but varied significantly between regions with lowest fertility ratios in urbanized states and counties. Explanations given include the health in towns, age and sex structure, and family limitation.

892. RAPHAEL, Marc Lee. "European Jewish and Non-Jewish Marital Patterns in Los Angeles, 1910-1913." Western States Jewish Historical Quarterly, 6 (1974), 100-6.
Argues that Los Anegles marriage licenses between 1910 and 1913 reveal that ethnic, national, and religious attachments were greater than generally suspected, despite the lack of residential propinquity.

893. RATHEE, Rajpal Singh. "Case Studies in Family Structure and Decision Process." Diss. Univ. of Wisconsin, 1966.
Examines the ways in which the goals, values, and resources of Wisconsin farm families influence the farm

126

enterprise, with emphasis on family life cycle, economic factors, and neighborhood and community relations.

894. RYDER, Norman B. "The Emergence of a Modern Fertility
Pattern: United States, 1917-66." Fertility and
Family Planning: A World View. Ed. Samuel J. Behrman, et. al. Ann Arbor: Univ. of Michigan Press:,
1969, pp. 99-123.
Analyzes the age-specific order-specific birth rates,
and the age-specific marriage rates, for cohorts of
women born 1891-1945 to determine the trend in fertility.

895. SOUTH, John B. "Age of Marriage and Completed Family
Size." Intermountain Economic Review, 3 (1972),
53-60.

896. TEMKIN-GREENER, Helena. "Marital Migration in Historic
Shelburne, Massachusetts, 1770-1849." Paper delivered at the Conference on Historical and Anthropological Approaches to the Community and the Family,
Deerfield, Mass., March 1975.
Analyzes marriage records of Shelburne in order to assess
the frequency and the extent of migration at marriage.
Observes an increase in the overall rate of exogamous
marriages. The distribution of the migration distances
appears to have a characteristic leptokurtic shape.
The average marital distance for the total time period
was 8.41 miles, and the median was 8.5 miles.

897. TEMKIN-GREENER, Helena, and Alan C. SWEDLUND. "Fertility
Transition in the Connecticut Valley: 1740-1850."
Unpublished paper, 1975.
Analyzes fertility trends in historical communities of
the Connecticut River Valley and shows that the decline
in fertility began as early as the 1780s. This decline
appears to be the result of at least some effort at
conscious family limitation, as indicated by changes
in the mean and variance of family size.

898. TEPPERMAN, Lorne. "Ethnic Variations in Marriage and
Fertility: Canada 1871." Canadian Review of Sociology and Anthropology, 11 (1974), 324-43.
Argues that ethnic identity strongly influenced fertility
and to a lesser degree nuptiality, especially through
customs of land distribution.

899. T'IEN, H. Yuan. "A Demographic Aspect of Interstate
Variation in American Fertility, 1800-1860." Milbank Memorial Fund Quarterly, 37 (1959), 49-59.
Argues that sex ratio differences account for fertility
differentials and trends in the ante-bellum period.

900. VINOVSKIS, Maris A. "Demographic Changes in America From
the Revolution to the Civil War: An Analysis of the

Socio-Economic Determinants of Fertility Differentials
and Trends in Massachusetts from 1765 to 1860." Diss.
Harvard Univ., 1975.

901. VINOVSKIS, Maris A. "A Multivariate Regression Analysis
      of Fertility Differentials among Massachusetts Towns
      and Regions in 1860." Paper delivered at the Confer-
      ence on Early Industrialization, Shifts in Fertility,
      and Changes in Family Structure, Princeton, June 1972.

902. VINOVSKIS, Maris A. "Socioeconomic Determinants of Fer-
      tility Differentials in Essex County, Massachusetts."
      Paper delivered at the American Historical Association,
      Chicago, December 1974.

903. VINOVSKIS, Maris A. "Socioeconomic Determinants of Inter-
      state Fertility Differentials in the United States in
      1850 and 1860." Journal of Interdisciplinary History,
      6 (1976), 375-96.
      Examines the hypothesis that the relative availability of
      farm land accounted for fertility differentials and trends.
      Concludes that the best predictor of fertility different-
      ials was the percentage of illiterate white adults.

904. WILLIAMS, Blaine T. "Demographic Characteristics of the
      Pioneer Family in a North Central Texas Area of 1850."
      Proceedings of the Southwest Sociological Association,
      15 (1965), 80-88.
      Examines marriage patterns, age differences between spouses,
      divorce, literacy, and migration patterns of frontier fam-
      ilies in Texas in 1850.

905. WILLIAMS, Blaine T. "The Frontier Family: Demographic
      Fact and Historical Myth." Essays on the American
      West. Ed. Harold M. Hollingsworth and Sandra L. Myers.
      Austin: Univ. of Texas Press, 1969, pp. 40-65.
      Describes the characteristics of pioneer families who
      lived in north central Texas in 1850, their migration
      patterns, family structure and composition, age at mar-
      riage, and the status of women.

906. YASUBA, Yasukichi. Birth Rates of the White Population in
      the United States, 1800-1860. Baltimore: Johns Hopkins
      Univ. Press, 1962.
      Discusses why the birth rate in the United States started
      to fall before European rates, and argues that there was
      a close correlation between the availability of easily
      accessible land and the refined birth rate in the early
      decades of the 19th century, but industrialization-urban-
      ization became the primary determinant of fertility by
      the mid-19th century.

DIVORCE

907. BARNETT, James Harwood. Divorce and the American Divorce

128

Novel, 1858-1937. New York: Russell & Russell, 1968.
Compares the development of divorce legislation with an analysis of the plots and material of American divorce novels to determine the interrelations of literature and society, and to reveal the changing attitudes toward divorce in America.

908. BARNETT, James Harwood, and Rhoda GRUEN. "Recent American Divorce Novels, 1938-1945: A Study in the Sociology of Literature." Social Forces, 26 (1948), 322-7.
Studies literary reflections of social attitudes and practices relevant to divorce in modern America as revealed in 25 divorce novels.

909. BLAKE, Nelson Manfred. The Road to Reno: A History of Divorce in the United States. New York: Macmillan, 1962.
Studies the evolution of American divorce legislation from colonial times to the present, with emphasis on developments in New York State.

910. GOODMAN, Elizabeth Scarborough. "The History of Marriage Counseling Research: A Quantitative Study." Diss. Univ. of New Hampshire, 1972.
Analyzes trends in marriage counseling research from 1929 to 1968, its relationship to social conditions, and its development as a quasi-scientific field.

911. LASCH, Christopher. "Divorce and the Family in America." Atlantic Monthly, November 1966, pp. 57-61.
Notes that divorce reform came about because women were portrayed as victims, not equals, in need of special protection. Argues that easier divorce has helped to preserve the family, not threaten it.

912. MAY, Elaine Tyler. "The Pursuit of Domestic Perfection: Marriage and Divorce in Los Angeles, 1890-1920." Diss. UCLA, 1975.
Contends that divorce did not stem from a dissatisfaction with marriage itself or a desire by women for economic independence or sexual freedom. Rather, it originated from the inability of married life to meet the expectations of happiness and fulfillment sought by the participants.

913. O'NEILL, William L. "Divorce as a Moral Issue: A Hundred Years of Controversy." 'Remember the Ladies': New Perspectives on Women in American History. Ed. Carol V.R. George. Syracuse: Syracuse Univ. Press, 1975, pp. 127-43.
Reviews the trends and striking features regarding the history of divorce, attitudes toward divorce, and scientific studies on divorce.

129

914. O'NEILL, William L. "Divorce in the Progressive Era."
       American Quarterly, 17 (1965), 203-17.
       Argues that the precipitate rise in the divorce rate
       during the Progressive Era fostered both an antidivorce
       movement which feared that the family was decaying and
       prodivorce sentiments which saw divorce as socially
       therapeutic. Yet both groups, by making divorce a dis-
       cussable issue, made divorce more tolerable and ac-
       ceptable.

915. O'NEILL, William L. *Divorce in the Progressive Era*.
       New Haven: Yale Univ. Press, 1967.
       Illustrates how mass divorce was an adjustment of the
       Victorian family and the Protestant sexual ethic to
       the demands of modern society. Increased divorce did
       not foster a revolution in morals nor a decrease in
       family cohesion.

916. WIRES, Richard. *The Divorce Issue and Reform in Nine-
       teenth-Century Indiana*. Muncie: Ball State Univ.
       Press, 1967.
       Examines the legal and legislative aspects of divorce
       and reform in Indiana where liberal divorce laws ex-
       isted in the mid-19th century.

DOMESTIC ARCHITECTURE

917. BUNKLE, Phillida E. "The Gothic Revival and Domestic
       Piety: The Architecture of the Sentimental Family,
       1830-1860." Paper delivered at the Australian and
       New Zealand American Studies Association, New South
       Wales, August 1974.
       Shows that the ideology of domestic piety, which flour-
       ished in the Northern United States after 1830, was re-
       flected in the domestic architecture of the Gothic
       Revival. The landscape architect, Downing, popularized
       and disseminated the ideal of the sentimental family in
       designs which emphasized the separation of the home
       from the world of work and the essentially emotional
       function of family life.

918. DUBOVIK, Paul N. "Housing in Holyoke and Its Effects
       on Family Life, 1860-1910." *Historical Journal of
       Western Massachusetts*, 4 (1975), 40-50.
       Discusses planned company housing in Holyoke, its de-
       terioration, and the effects of inadequate and unsan-
       itary housing on family life.

919. GIEDION, Siegfried. *Mechanization Takes Command: A
       Contribution to Anonymous History*. New York: Oxford
       Univ. Press, 1948.
       Contains a good discussion of the mechanization of the
       household, notably organization of the work process,
       the introduction of machinery in cooking and cleaning,
       and their social impact on women's roles.

920. LYNES, Russell. The Domesticated Americans. New York: Harper & Row, 1963.
Discusses American manners, domestic technology, and domestic architecture in an historical perspective.

921. ROTSCH, Melvin M. "The Home Environment." Technology in Western Civilization. Ed. Melvin Kranzberg and Carroll W. Pursell. New York: Oxford Univ. Press, 1967, II, pp. 217-33.
Discusses the problems and progress in developing facilities in the home for sanitation, lighting, heating, and air conditioning.

922. TWOMBLY, Robert C. "Saving the Family: Middle Class Attraction to Wright's Prairie House, 1901-1909." American Quarterly, 27 (1975), 57-72.
Maintains that architect Frank Lloyd Wright, through his prairie houses, tried to protect the middle-class family from the uncertainties resulting from a rapidly changing urban environment.

DOMESTIC LIFE AND CUSTOMS

923. ANGELL, Robert Cooley. The Family Encounters the Depression. New York: Charles Scribner's Sons, 1936.
Attempts to discern the impact of the depression on family life and the interrelationships among family members by studying the families of 50 sociology students.

924. BOWIE, Lucy L. "Young Men in Love, 1795 and 1823." Maryland Historical Magazine, 41 (1946), 219-34.
Examines a group of love letters written by Annapolis young men, and reveals courting and marriage customs of Federalist America.

925. BRIDGES, William E. "Family Patterns and Social Values in America, 1825-1875." American Quarterly, 17 (1965), 3-11.
Argues that 19th-century acculturation practices were designed to produce impersonality and emotional non-dependence. Notes that tne home ironically served increasingly as a counterweight to the effects of these values.

926. CANNING, Ray Russell. "Changing Patterns and Problems of Family Life in Provo, Utah, 1905-1955." Diss. Univ. of Utah, 1956.
Examines selected couples married between 1905-10, 1925-30, and 1945-50 and finds a shift from the authoritarian family to a more democratic type, but such change was not so great among Mormon families.

927. CHUDACOFF, Howard P. "Newlyweds and Family Extension:

The First Stage of the Family Cycle in Providence,
Rhode Island, 1864-1865 and 1879-1880." Paper delivered at the Conference on the Family in the Process of Urbanization, Williams College, July 1974.
Concludes that newlywed couples sacrificed independence
and privacy for potential assistance from parents by
residing close to or in their parents' household.

928. CONNOR, Paul. "Patriarchy: Old World and New." American Quarterly, 17 (1965), 48-62.
Discusses the Southern infatuation with the patriarchal
ideal in the antebellum era, and compares the patriarchal
theory of George Fitzhigh and Sir. Robert Filmer.

929. COSGROVE, William Emmett. "Marriage and the Family in
Some Nineteenth-Century American Novels." Diss.
Univ. of Iowa, 1972.
Discusses the clash between the individual desire for
freedom and family responsibilities in selected roman-
tic, realistic, and naturalistic American fiction.

930. CULBERT, David H. "World War II: The Southern Experience." FDR's America. Ed. David E. Kyvig. St.
Charles, Mo.: Forum Press, 1976, pp. 113-30.
Uses excerpts from family history projects written at
LSU to show the diversity of experience in the South
between 1939 and 1945, especially as reflected in the
family and local community.

931. FURSTENBERG, Frank F. "Industrialization and the American Family: A Look Backward." American Sociological Review, 31 (1966), 326-38.
Examines accounts of antebellum foreign travelers on the
family, and concludes that mate selection, marital relationships, and parent-child relations in the preindustrial family were strikingly similar to the modern family.

932. GOODSELL, Willystine. "The American Family in the Nineteenth Century." Annals of the American Academy of
Political and Social Science, 160 (1932), 13-22.
Discusses the waning of the patriarchal family under the
impact of the frontier, democratic ideas, industrialization, and the decline of religion.

933. GORDON, Michael. "The Ideal Husband as Depicted in the
Nineteenth-Century Marriage Manual." Family Coordinator, 18 (1969), 226-31.
Deals with the image of the ideal husband and his role
as found in marriage manuals.

934. GORDON, Michael, and M. Charles BERNSTEIN. "Mate Choice
and Domestic Life in the Nineteenth-Century Marriage
Manual." Journal of Marriage and the Family, 32
(1970), 665-74.
Discusses marriage manuals, their criteria for mate

selection, and their depiction of ideal domestic relations.

935.   HAREVEN, Tamara K. "Family Time and Industrial Time:
       Family and Work in a Planned Corporation Town, 1900-
       1924." Journal of Urban History, 1 (1975), 365-89.
       Discusses the role of the family in the adaptation of
       workers to industrial life and the interaction of family
       time and the demands of industrial capitalism.

936.   HAREVEN, Tamara K. "The Laborers of Manchester, New
       Hampshire, 1912-1922: The Role of Family and Eth-
       nicity in Adjustment to Industrial Life." Labor
       History, 16 (1975), 249-65.
       Examines how Manchester textile workers shaped the in-
       dustrial system to fit their wants and traditions, and
       shows the role of the family in modifying preindustrial
       customs to fit new conditions.

937.   HERMAN, Sondra R. "Loving Courtship or the Marriage
       Market? The Ideal and Its Critics, 1871-1911."
       American Quarterly, 25 (1973), 235-54.
       Examines the late 19th-century feminist debate over
       courtship as love-seeking or as a marriage market.
       While marital advisers defended the status quo, critics
       charged that the family was overly-materialistic and
       perpetuated sexual discrimination.

938.   HINTON, Jane Lee. "'Out of All Times of Trouble': The
       Family in the Fiction of Eudora Welty." Diss. Van-
       derbilt Univ., 1974.
       Discusses the role and function of the family in the
       writings of novelist, Eudora Welty. Contends that the
       family becomes Welty's most important metaphor for all
       human relationships.

939.   JEFFREY, Kirk. "The Family as a Utopian Retreat from the
       City: The Nineteenth Century." Soundings, 55 (1972),
       21-41.
       Shows that the home was idealized as an Edenic retreat
       from urban life and the loneliness of democratic society,
       yet this ideal conflicted with the demands of domestic
       life and the desire for individual freedom.

940.   JEFFREY, Kirk. "Family History: The Middle-Class Amer-
       ican Family in the Urban Context, 1830-1870." Diss.
       Stanford Univ., 1972.
       Argues that the portrayal of the "home" as a separate
       sphere from the "world" was a negative reaction to the
       city and a response which militated against kin and social
       ties. This resulted in strains within the family.

941.   JOHNSON, Guion Griffis. "Courtship and Marriage Customs
       in Antebellum North Carolina." North Carolina His-
       torical Review, 8 (1931), 384-402.
       Discusses parental consent for courtship, courtship

customs, the coquette, illegitimacy, the engagement, and the marriage ceremony in the antebellum South.

942. KANTER, Rosabeth Moss. "Urban Communes and Family History." Paper delivered at the Organization of American Historians, Denver, April 1974.

943. KATZ, Michael B. The People of Hamilton, Canada West: Family and Class in a Mid-Nineteenth-Century City. Cambridge: Cambridge Univ. Press, 1976. Analyzes the social structure, life cycle, household structure, mobility, and ethnicity in Hamilton, Ontario. Argues that structural rigidity and individual transiency characterized life in Hamilton.

944. KEPHART, William M. "Experimental Family Organization: An Historico-Cultural Report on the Oneida Community." Marriage and Family Living, 25 (1963), 261-71. Describes the family functions, sexual practices, eugenics program, and the leadership of Noyes in the Oneida (New York) community of the 19th century.

945. KOMAROVSKY, Mirra. The Unemployed Man and His Family. New York: Dryden Press, 1940. Discusses the impact of unemployment on the head of household, and analyzes the relation between the man's role as economic provider and his authority in the family.

946. LASCH, Christopher. "'Selfish Women': The Campaign to Save the American Family, 1880-1920." Columbia Forum, 4 (1975), 24-31. Discusses popular apprehension about the future of the family, stemming from increased divorce, declining fertility, changing status of women, and criticism of traditional morality. Reveals the ironies in the movement to revive domesticity and domestic virtues.

947. LEFF, Mark H. "Consensus for Reform: The Mothers' Pension Movement in the Progressive Era." Social Service Review, 47 (1973), 397-417. Discusses the origins, goals, and activities of the mothers'-pension movement to mitigate the hardship to widowed mothers resulting from child-labor laws and compulsory education.

948. LEYBURN, James Graham. "The Frontier Family." Diss. Yale Univ., 1927. Argues that frontier society is a child-society undergoing evolution and notes that there is more freedom in frontier marriage and the family, that the woman's position is higher, and that children on the frontier are more economic assets than in civilized society.

949. LYMAN, Stanford M. "Marriage and the Family Among Chinese Immigrants to America, 1850-1960." Phylon,

29 (1968), 321-30.
Discusses the ways in which the Chinese responded to the
shortage of women through the services of community or-
ganizations and secret societies.

950. MCGLONE, Robert Elno. "Suffer the Children: The Emergence of Modern Middle-Class Family Life in America,
1820-1870." Diss. UCLA, 1971.
Describes changing parent-child relations and childrearing practices in the mid-19th century to identify
changing conditions of personality formation and to
outline the issues in 19th-century family history.

951. MCGOVERN, James R. "Yankee Family: A Generational
Study." Paper delivered at the American Historical
Association, New Orleans, December 1972.
Discusses the changes in psychological types, childrearing, and value orientation of the members of one
family traced over three centuries. Argues that the
family shifted from an emphasis on "consensual affiliation" to "sacred technology," from other-relatedness
to individuality.

952. MCKINLEY, Blaine Edward. "'The Stranger in the Gates':
Employer Reactions Toward Domestic Servants in America, 1825-1875." Diss. Michigan State Univ., 1969.
Examines the attitudes and responses of Northern em-
ployers towards their servants to understand the class
consciousness of the upper and middle levels of society
and to ascertain the impact of Jacksonian egalitarian-
ism on American social relations.

953. MCLAUGHLIN, Virginia Yans. "A Flexible Tradition:
South Italian Immigrants Confront a New Work Experience." Journal of Social History, 7 (1974),
429-45.
Maintains that despite economic and social deprivation,
the South Italian immigrant family was relatively stable,
cohesive, and adapted readily to the forces of modernization.

954. MCLAUGHLIN, Virginia Yans. "Like the Fingers of the
Hand: The Family and Community Life of First-Gen-
eration Italian-Americans in Buffalo, New York,
1880-1930." Diss. State Univ. of New York at Buffalo, 1970.
Argues that immigration, urbanization, and industrialization did not disorganize ethnic family life as great
as social scientists have formerly believed. Kinship
and the extended family were more important in an urban
setting.

955. MARTIN, Edeen. "Frontier Marriage and the Status Quo."
Westport Historical Quarterly, 10 (1975), 99-108.
Argues that choosing a mate on the frontier was a matter

of economic necessity rather than individual whim. The
most desired criteria were good health and perseverance.
Abandonment and desertion were also real problems in
frontier society.

956. MILDEN, James Wallace. "The Sacred Sanctuary: Family
Life in Nineteenth-Century America." Diss. Univ.
of Maryland, 1974.
Discusses the tensions, ironies, and contradictions of
19th-century family life as depicted by marital advice
literature, particularly the interaction between family
and society.

957. MORGAN, Winona Louise. The Family Meets the Depression.
Minneapolis: Univ. of Minnesota Press, 1939.
Discusses the effects of time and the depression on
normal family life and how stability and satisfaction
in family life was maintained.

958. MUSTO, David F. "The Appalachian Family." Paper delivered at the American Historical Association, Boston,
December 1970.

959. NAFZIGER, John Marvin. "The Development of the Twentieth Century American Mennonite Family as Reflected
in Mennonite Writings." Diss. New York Univ., 1972.
Examines and delineates the changes in the 20th-century
American Memmonite family, their relation to changes
in general American family life, and the implications
of these changes for Mennonite education.

960. NELSON, Anne K., and Hart M. NELSON. "Family Articles
in Frontier Newspapers: An Examination of One Aspect of Turner's Frontier Thesis." Journal of Marriage and the Family, 31 (1969), 644-50.
Argues that frontier newspapers tried to preserve the
values of the seaboard and were not responsive to the
changing character of the community.

961. PARTRIDGE, Bellamy, and Otto BETTMANN. As We Were,
Family Life, 1850-1900. New York: McGraw-Hill,
1946.
Portrays informally the domestic scene in America in
the late 19th century and includes an excellent selection of contemporary prints.

962. PESSEN, Edward. "The Marital Theory and Practices of
the Antebellum Urban Elite." New York History, 53
(1972), 389-410.
Argues that the urban rich in antebellum America, con-
tinuing the practices of the colonial elites, married
into families of similar wealth and status and thus
perpetuated an exclusive social world.

963. RYAN, Mary Patricia. "American Society and the Cult

of Domesticity, 1830-1860." Diss. Univ. of California
at Santa Barbara, 1971.
Explores the interdependent development of industrial society and modern family organization, notably the rise of
a cult of domesticity and the emergence of the modern
family ideal.

964. SHULL, Martha Irene Smith. "The Novels of Louisa May
Alcott as Commentary on the American Family." Diss.
Bowling Green State Univ., 1975.
Shows that Alcott's novels reveal how the matriarchal
family was a response to social change, but this family
pattern was essentially conservative, despite Alcott's
emphasis on the liberties and education of women.

965. STOUFFER, Samuel A., and Paul F. LAZARSFELD. The Family
in the Depression. New York: Social Science Research
Council, 1937.
Investigates the relationship of economic depression to
marriage and the family, husband-wife relationships, and
sex mores.

966. SWICORD, Elizabeth Reid. "Boarding Houses: An American
Institution, 1800-1860." Master's Thesis, Univ. of
Maryland, 1966.
Surveys the origins of boarding houses in America, their
location and occupants, and their functional role in
urban society as revealed in the observations of foreign travelers.

967. TAYLOR, Donald Lavor. "Courtship as a Social Institution
in the United States, 1930 to 1945." Diss. Duke Univ.
1945.
Uses a functional approach to discover the desires that
courtship attempts to satisfy, and examines rating and
dating patterns and patterns of selection and engagement
in the United States.

968. TAYLOR, William R. "Domesticity in England and America,
1770-1840." Paper delivered at the Symposium on the
Role of Education in Nineteenth-Century America,
Chatham, Mass., June 1964.

969. TAYLOR, William R., and Christopher LASCH. "Two 'Kindred
Spirits': Sorority and Family in New England, 1839-
1846." New England Quarterly, 36 (1963), 23-41.
Argues that excessive mobility and the family's disintegration as a source of affection and understanding led
many men and women to seek solace in voluntary associations
and in the society of kindred spirits.

970. WALTERS, Ronald G. "The Family and Ante-Bellum Reform:
An Interpretation." Societas, 3 (1973), 221-32.
Contends that the family, not the individual, was the
pervasive concern of antebellum social reformers who,

fearing the consequences of modernization, wished to
regulate the family and use it to redeem society and
curb sexual proclivities.

FAMILY COMPOSITION AND STRUCTURE

971. BATEMAN, Fred, and James D. FOUST. "A Sample of Rural
          Households Selected from the 1860 Manuscript Cen-
          suses." Agricultural History, 48 (1974), 75-93.
      Discusses the completion of a sample of northern rural
      households from the 1860 manuscript censuses, its con-
      tents, and the results of various tests of represent-
      ativeness.

972. BLOOMBERG, Susan Hirsch. "The Household and the Fam-
          ily: The Effects of Industrialization on Skilled
          Workers in Newark, 1840-1860." Paper delivered at
          the Organization of American Historians, Denver,
          April 1974.
      Argues that industrialization did not affect signifi-
      cantly the economic interrelationships in artisans'
      households because the male remained the sole bread-
      winner, but apprenticeship and boarding by teenage
      boys declined as these boys began increasingly to
      live with and depend on their parents.

973. BLOOMBERG, Susan Hirsch, et. al. "A Census Probe Into
          Nineteenth-Century Family History: Southern Mich-
          igan, 1850-1880." Journal of Social History, 5
          (1971), 26-45.
      Concludes that household size, especially in rural areas,
      was diminishing, that the number of children per family
      was decreasing and that children were more closely spaced,
      and that occupation and place of birth have an unclear
      relationship to household size.

974. BLUMIN, Stuart M. "Rip Van Winkle's Grandchildren:
          Family and Household in the Hudson Valley, 1800-
          1860." Journal of Urban History, 1 (1975), 293-315.
      Discusses the influence of cities on the formation of
      rural families, the changes in family structure and
      differential fertility rates, and changes in family
      composition in the early 19th century.

975. DEL CASTILLO, Richard Griswold. "La Familia Chicano:
          Social Changes in the Chicano Family of Los Angeles,
          1850-1880." Journal of Ethnic Studies, 3 (1975),
          41-58.
      Illustrates that Chicano family structure was not af-
      fected by industrialization, and speculates that the
      extended Chicano family may have been more adaptable
      to the demands of urban life, although these families
      became less common by 1880.

976. DEL CASTILLO, Richard Griswold. "Preliminary Comparison

138

of Chicano, Immigrant, and Native-Born Family Structures, 1850-1880." Aztlan, 6 (1975), 87-96.

977. FARBER, Bernard. "Shifting Sands: Tuscon Elite Families in 1870." Paper delivered at the Pacific
Sociological Association, Scottsdale, Arizona, May
1973.

978. GAGAN, David, and Herbert MAYS. "Historical Demography
and Canadian Social History: Families and Land in
Peel County, Ontario." Canadian Historical Review,
54 (1973), 27-47.
Discusses how rural mid-Victorian Ontario was a transient society with the mobile being the youthful, the
unskilled, and small families. Typical rural families
were nuclear, but many contained the young itinerants
and hence served an important yet ignored function in
the transition from dependency to independency.

979. GLASCO, Laurence Admiral. "Ethnicity and Social Structure: Irish, Germans, and Native-Born of Buffalo,
N.Y., 1850-1860." Diss. State Univ. of New York at
Buffalo, 1973.
Examines Irish, Germans, and native-born in 1855 Buffalo,
and compares their demographic, economic, and family
structures. Demographic and family patterns aided in
ethnic adjustment and social stability.

980. GLASCO, Laurence Admiral. "The Life Cycles and Household Structure of American Ethnic Groups: Irish,
Germans, and Native-born Whites in Buffalo, New York,
1855." Journal of Urban History, 1 (1975), 339-64.
Discusses the relationship between life cycle and economic
behavior and household organization, and examines how age
and sex are related to the processes of ethnic stratification and acculturation.

981. HAREVEN, Tamara K. "The Family and Social Organization
in 19th-Century Boston." Paper delivered at the Conference on the Family, Social Structure, and Social
Change, Worcester, April 1972.

982. HAREVEN, Tamara K. "Family Structure and Social Change
in Boston." Paper delivered at the Organization of
American Historians, Washington, D.C., April 1972.

983. KATZ, Michael B. "Some Changes in Household Structure,
1851-1861." Canadian Social History Project, Interim
Report, 4 (1972), 1-9.
Finds that increased immigration and economic pressures
in Hamilton, Ontario, caused a reduction in household
size, but not a decline in the number of children per
family.

984. LASLETT, Barbara. "Family Structure on an American

Frontier: Los Angeles, California, in 1850." American Journal of Sociology, 81 (1975), 109-28.
Notes that the nuclear family predominated in preindustrial Los Angeles, but observes that the occupation of
and the value of the land owned by the household head
were related to household types.

985. LIPMAN-BLUMEN, Jean. "Crisis Framework Applied to Micro-
sociological Family Changes: Marriage, Divorce, and
Occupational Trends Associated With World War II."
Journal of Marriage and the Family, 37 (1975), 889-902.
Proposes a framework for analyzing role change as a
system response to crisis, and applies this model to
macro-changes in family structure as a result of World
War II.

986. MATTIS, Mary Catherine. "The Irish Family in Buffalo,
New York, 1855-1875: A Socio-Historical Analysis."
Diss. Washington Univ., 1975.
Describes the employment structure of Buffalo, the
changes and continuities of family organizational patterns among the Irish, and the interaction of the opportunity structure and the family, especially the importance of the family in faciliating social mobility.

987. MODELL, John, and Tamara K. HAREVEN. "Urbanization and
the Malleable Household: An Examination of Boarding
and Lodging in American Families." Journal of Marriage and the Family, 35 (1973), 467-79.
Shows that changes in attitudes toward privacy and fear
of family disintegration under the impact of boarding,
prompted the institution of boarding to disappear grad-
ually. But boarding was not destructive to the family
and indeed cushioned the shock of urban life for the
newly-arrived.

988. O'CONNER, Peter. "Varying Types of Extended Family Structures in Stockton, California, in 1880." Paper delivered at the Pacific Sociological Association,
Scottsdale, Arizona, May 1973.

989. PI-SUNYER, Mary Jane Richards. "Households in a Nineteenth-Century Town: A Historical Demographic Study
of Household and Family Size and Composition in Am-
herst, Massachusetts, 1850-1880." Diss. Univ. of
Massachusetts, 1973.
Examines the interfaces of family structure and economic
change in a small town, the relationship between occupation and household size, and the impact of industrialization on vital events.

990. PRYOR, Edward Thomas. "Family Structure and Change:
Rhode Island, 1875 and 1960." Diss. Brown Univ., 1966.
Attempts to reconstruct the demographic history and to
measure specific structural changes in organization

within the Rhode Island family between 1875 and 1960.
Concludes that the small, nuclear family is not some-
thing new nor a product of industrialization.

991. PRYOR, Edward Thomas. "Rhode Island Family Structure,
        1875 and 1960." Household and Family in Past Time.
        Ed. Peter Laslett and Richard Wall. Cambridge:
        Cambridge Univ. Press, 1972, pp. 571-89.
      Reveals that between 1875 and the present there has
      been little change in Rhode Island family structure,
      the entire period being dominated by the small family.
      But notes that there is a shift toward smaller and
      one-person households and the inclusion of fewer non-
      relatives in households.

992. SENNETT, Richard. Families Against the City: Middle
        Class Homes of Industrial Chicago, 1872-1890. Cam-
        bridge: Harvard Univ. Press, 1970.
      Believes that the nuclear family, as an unsuccessful
      adaptation to urban life, sacrificed sociability for
      privacy and sheltered sons from the hostilities of mod-
      ern industrial life. It limited social mobility and
      did not prepare children to cope with urban society.

993. SENNETT, Richard. "Middle-Class Families and Urban
        Violence: The Experience of a Chicago Community in
        the Nineteenth Century." Nineteenth-Century Cities:
        Essays in the New Urban History. Ed. Stephan Thern-
        strom and Richard Sennett. New Haven: Yale Univ.
        Press, 1969, pp. 386-420.
      Contends that family experience and structure explain
      the overreaction of middle-class families to social
      disorder. The small, intensive nuclear family inhib-
      ited social mobility, sheltered children from the lar-
      ger world, and produced a dread of the unknown.

994. SEWARD, Rudy Ray. "The American Family: A Study of
        Structural Trends From the Colonial Period to the
        Present." Diss. Southern Illinois Univ., 1974.
      Demonstrates that American family structure has varied
      much less over time than previously assumed, and that
      the majority of family units at any given time in the
      American past were nuclear in structure. Also argues
      that the decrease in family size is due to marital fer-
      tility decline, not structural shifts or modernization.

995. SEWARD, Rudy Ray. "Family Structure in the United States
        for 1850: Pre-Industrial or Transitional." Paper
        delivered at the Society for the Study of Social
        Problems, New York, August 1973.
      Compares family structure for the U.S. in 1850 with 1960
      census data, and finds that a majority of 1850 families
      were similar in structure to contemporary families. This
      calls into question the impact of modernization on family
      structure.

996. SEWARD, Rudy Ray. "Nineteenth Century American Family
       Structure: Establishing Historical Baselines."
       Paper delivered at the American Sociological Assoc-
       iation, San Francisco, August 1975.
       Presents structural data for the American family during
       the late 19th century to provide baselines for the per-
       iod of rapid industrial and urban development. Detailed
       information available on manuscript census schedules from
       1850 to 1880 supplied the source of this data. The
       findings suggest that, structurally, the family changed
       very little throughout the sample period and that the
       incidences for the various structural aspects tended to
       be very similar to those occurring in the contemporary
       American family.

997. SILVERMAN, Julius. "Patterns of Working Class Family
       and Community Life: The Irish in New York City,
       1845-1865." Master's Thesis, Columbia Univ., 1973.

998. STAPLES, Robert. "The Mexican-American Family: Its
       Modification Over Time and Space." Phylon, 32 (1971),
       179-92.
       Analyzes the history and development of the Mexican-
       American family, and shows the prevalence of extended
       family organization and its importance in Chicano cul-
       ture.

FAMILY LAW AND INHERITANCE

999. BOUSHY, Theodore F. "The Historical Development of the
       Domestic Relations Court." Diss. Univ. of Oklahoma,
       1950.
       Traces the development and extension of the domestic
       relations or family court in the United States, from
       its origins in the juvenile court to development of
       the modern family court system.

1000. CLARKE, Helen I. Social Legislation: American Laws
       Dealing with the Family, Child, and Dependent. New
       York: D. Appleton-Century, 1940.
       Examines American legislation pertaining to the family
       and child in an historical perspective, including dis-
       cussions of parental rights, adoption, illegitimacy,
       and marriage law.

1001. FARBER, Bernard. "Historical Trends in American Family
       Law, as a Reflection of Changing Family Patterns."
       Paper delivered at the Conference on the Family, So-
       cial Structure, and Social Change, Worcester, April
       1972.

1002. FOWLER, David H. "Northern Attitudes toward Interracial
       Marriages: A Study of Legislation and Public Opinion
       in the Middle Atlantic States and the States of the
       old Northwest." Diss. Yale Univ., 1963.

Studies intermarriage laws since the colonial era, their
enactment and repeal, their uses as a form of legal dis-
crimination, and their relationship to the larger social
context.

1003. FRIEDMAN, Lawrence M. "Patterns of Testation in the Nine-
          teenth Century: A Study of Essex County (New Jersey)
          Wills." American Journal of Legal History, 8 (1964),
          34-53.
       Analyzes wills from late 19th-century New Jersey to de-
       termine the identity of the testator, age of will, drafts-
       menship, testamentary patterns, and types of gifts.

1004. SCHMITT, Robert C., and Rose C. STROMBEL. "Marriage and
          Divorce in Hawaii Before 1870." Hawaii Historical
          Review, 2 (1966), 267-71.
       Describes the effects of Christian missionaries on Hawaiian
       marriage customs and the resultant marriage and divorce
       laws which were eventually liberalized in 1870.

1005. STEIN, Stuart J. "Common-Law Marriage: Its History and
          Certain Contemporary Problems." Journal of Family
          Law, 9 (1970), 271-99.
       Discusses the historical development and acceptance of
       common-law marriages as well as examines contemporary
       legal presuppositions and problems.

KINSHIP

1006. BIEDER, Robert E. "Kinship as a Factor in Migration."
          Journal of Marriage and the Family, 35 (1973), 429-39.
       Illustrates how kinship contributed to the settlement
       patterns of 19th-century frontier communities as well
       as retarded out-migration from these communities.

1007. GRIFFEN, Clyde, and Sally GRIFFEN. "Family and Business
          in a Small City: Poughkeepsie, New York, 1850-1880."
          Journal of Urban History, 1 (1975), 316-38.
       Studies business arrangements between relatives, and
       concludes that the extended family played a significant
       role in business entrepreneurship.

SEXUALITY

1008. ABERLE, Sophie, and George W. CORNER. Twenty-Five Years
          of Sex Research: History of the National Research
          Council Committee for Research in Problems of Sex,
          1922-1947. Philadelphia: W.B. Saunders, 1953.
       Describes the history of the Committee, its administra-
       tive problems, and scientific contributions to sex bio-
       logy and behavior.

1009. BARKER-BENFIELD, Benjamin. "The Spermatic Economy: A
          Nineteenth-Century View of Sexuality." Feminist
          Studies, 1 (1972), 45-74.

Contends that male physicians harbored deep anxieties over female sexuality. The rise of gynecology represents an attempt by males to control or curb female sexual expression.

1010. BLISS, Michael. "'Pur Books on Avoided Subjects': Pre-Freudian Sexual Ideas in Canada." Canadian Historical Association. Historical Papers, 1970. Ottawa: CHA, 1970, pp. 89-108.
Outlines the fundamental ideas expressed in Canadian sex manuals between 1900 and 1915, and attempts to place these ideas in North American medical and popular thought.

1011. BURNHAM, John C. "The Progressive Era Revolution in American Attitudes Toward Sex." Journal of American History, 59 (1973), 885-908.
Notes that the social hygiene movement, despite its attacks on the double standard and the conspiracy of silence, was conservative, moralistic, and attempted to mold behavior and attitudes from above. Yet it succeeded in changing American attitudes toward sex.

1012. CANNON, Charles A. "The Awesome Power of Sex: The Polemical Campaign Against Mormon Polygamy." Pacific Historical Review, 43 (1974), 61-82.
Examines the reactions to Mormon polygamy and how Mormon polygamists came to be excluded from the cult of domesticity.

1013. DEGLER, Carl N. "What Ought to Be and What Was: Women's Sexuality in the Nineteenth Century." American Historical Review, 79 (1974), 1467-1490.
Argues that Victorian medical writers were concerned with prescribing rather than describing, and their sexual ideology is not reflective of social realities. Most people did not follow the prescriptions of the advice manuals, nor were they hostile to sexual feelings and desires.

1014. DITZION, Sidney Herbert. Marriage, Morals, and Sex in America: A History of Ideas. New York: Bookman Associates, 1953.
Surveys the ideas, not social realities, about marriage, sexual equality, courtship, sexuality, sex radicalism, and those movements or thinkers who molded significantly American attitudes toward marriage.

1015. DWYER, William M., ed. What Everyone Knew About Sex: Explained in the Words of Orson Squire Fowler and Other Victorian Moralists. London: MacDonald & Janes, 1973.
Presents the beliefs and writings of some fifty Victorians on sex, abortion, courtship, venereal disease, and female disorders.

1016. GORDON, Michael. "From an Unfortunate Necessity to a
      Cult of Mutual Orgasm: Sex in American Marital Ed-
      ucation Literature, 1830-1940." Studies in the
      Sociology of Sex. Ed. James M. Henslin. New York:
      Appleton-Century-Crofts, 1971, pp. 53-77.
      Examines selected marriage manuals to determine their
      view of female sexuality, the role of sex in marriage,
      and contraceptive advice.

1017. HALLER, John S. "From Maidenhood to Menopause: Sex
      Education for Women in Victorian America." Journal
      of Popular Culture, 6 (1972), 49-69.
      Shows that sex, portrayed in Victorian marriage man-
      uals, was a base human tendency at variance with fem-
      inine virtue and modesty. And Victorian sexual atti-
      tudes reflected middle-class prejudices, aspirations,
      and pretentions of respectibility.

1018. HALLER, John S., and Robin M. HALLER. The Physician
      and Sexuality in Victorian America. Urbana: Univ.
      of Illinois Press, 1974.
      Examines Victorian sexuality, sex roles, and the phy-
      sians who dealt with sexual fears and problems. Argues
      that Victorian women sought sexual freedom by restrict-
      ing their sexual role in marriage.

1019. HALLER, Mark Hughlin. Eugenics: Hereditarian Attitudes
      in American Thought. New Brunswick: Rutgers Univ.
      Press, 1963.
      Discusses the history of the American eugenics movement
      and the social consequences of hereditarian viewpoints.

1020. HIRSH, Joseph. "Sex Attitudes and Venereology in New
      York City One Hundred Years Ago." Journal of Social
      Hygiene, 38 (1952), 212-9.
      Examines attitudes of the medical community toward
      patients with syphilis and gonorrhea. Also presents
      examples from the case book of Mount Sinai Hospital.

1021. JONES, James Howard. "Progressives and Scientists:
      The Development of Scientific Research on Sex in
      the United States, 1920-1963." Paper delivered at
      the American Historical Association, New Orleans,
      December 1972.

1022. LASCH, Christopher. "Ideology of Sexual Emancipation
      and Its Domestication, 1900-1935." Katallagete,
      5 (1975), 19-24.
      Discusses the reformers who proposed a new code of sex-
      ual ethics based on a scientific study of sex, but
      critical of the prevailing morality, especially roman-
      tic love.

1023. MAW, Wallace H. "Fifty Years of Sex Education in the
      Public Schools of the United States (1900-1950):

A History of Ideas." Diss. Univ. of Cincinnati, 1953.
Examines the ideas expressed in educational literature regarding sex education to determine the extent to which these ideas changed and the intellectual and social setting in which sex education developed in the public schools.

1024. MUNCY, Raymond Lee. <u>Sex and Marriage in Utopian Communities: 19th Century America</u>. Bloomington: Indiana Univ. Press, 1973.
Discusses the difficulty with which 19th-century utopians encountered and dealt with monogamous marriage and the family.

1025. NISSENBAUM, Stephen Willner. "Careful Love: Sylvester Graham and the Emergence of Victorian Sexual Theory in the United States, 1830-1840." Diss. Univ. of Wisconsin, 1968.
Examines the sexual theory of Sylvester Graham, his intellectual mileau, and his abandonment of previous ideas about the regulation of sexual activity.

1026. NISSENBAUM, Stephen Willner. "Sex, Reform, and Social Change, 1830-1860." Paper delivered at the Organization of American Historians, Washington, D.C., April 1972.
Describes the new attitudes toward sexuality that emerged shortly after 1830, compares them with older attitudes, and points toward a description of the urbanized constituency to which they appealed.

1027. O'NEILL, William L., ed. <u>The American Sexual Dilemma</u>. New York: Holt, Rinehart & Winston, 1972.
Contains articles dealing with changing American sex norms in the 20th century, notably advances in sex research and the so-called sexual revolution.

1028. PERRY, Lewis C. "The Neurosis of an Antebellum Reformer: Henry Clarke Wright." Paper delivered at the Organization of American Historians, Denver, April 1974.
Uses psychoanalytic techniques to analyze the life and though of an influential American physician and sex reformer.

1029. PICKENS, Donald K. <u>Eugenics and the Progressives</u>. Nashville: Vanderbilt Univ. Press, 1968.
Examines American eugenists from 1860 to 1930 in terms of their intellectual context and their attempts to use science to control and reform society, including sterilization and birth control.

1030. PIVAR, David J. <u>The Purity Crusade: Sexual Morality and Social Control, 1868-1900</u>. Westport, Conn.: Greenwood Press, 1973.

Argues that purity leaders, fearful of uncontrolled
social change, hoped to transform urban America and
create a new social character for urban man by imple-
menting a variety of sex reforms to regulate vice,
venereal disease, prostitution, and sex education.

1031. ROBINSON, Paul A. The Modernization of Sex. New York:
      Harper & Row, 1976.
      Examines the ideas and assumptions of Havelock Ellis,
      Kinsey, and Masters and Johnson. Argues that these
      sexual modernists revolted against Victorianism and
      advocated sexual democracy.

1032. ROSENBERG, Charles E. "Sexuality, Class and Role in
      19th-Century America." American Quarterly, 25 (1973),
      131-53.
      Argues that sexual hygiene literature addressed to the
      middle class was characterized by ambiguity, an emphasis
      on aggressive masculinity, and increasing repressiveness.
      The literature, moreover, shaped and mirrored class and
      gender roles.

1033. RUGOFF, Milton Allan. Prudery and Passion. New York:
      G.P. Putnam's Sons, 1971.
      Examines 19th-century attitudes and anxieties about sex
      and the attitudes and fate of those who rebelled against
      traditional moral standards.

1034. SAGARIN, Edward. "Sex Research and Sociology: Retro-
      spective and Prospective." Studies in the Sociology
      of Sex. Ed. James M. Henslin. New York: Appleton-
      Century-Crofts, 1971, pp. 377-408.
      Examines past efforts and the present status of sex re-
      search in sociology.

1035. SAUER, R. "Attitudes to Abortion in America, 1800-1973."
      Population Studies, 28 (1974), 53-67.
      Argues that attitudes toward abortion, as revealed in
      popular and professional literature, have increasingly
      liberalized, perhaps a product of low-fertility values
      embraced by industrial society.

1036. SCOTT, Clifford Haley. "American Views of Sex in the
      Gilded Age." Paper delivered at the American His-
      torical Association, Washington, D.C., December 1969.

1037. SEARS, Hal D. "The Sex Radicals in High Victorian Amer-
      ica." Virginia Quarterly Review, 48 (1972), 377-92.
      Argues that sex radicalism was not merely an adjunct of
      the feminist movement, but was a separate movement which
      stressed libertarian principles, free love, full sexual
      equality, and birth control.

1038. SMIGEL, Edwin O., and Rita SEIDEN. "The Decline and
      Fall of the Double Standard." Annals of the American

Academy of Political and Social Science, 376 (1968),
6-17.
Argues that the shifts in sexual behavior which occurred
in the 1920s have changed only slightly in the 1960s.
Concludes that the double standard is declining, but has
not yet fallen.

1039. SMITH, Daniel Scott. "The Dating of the American Sexual
Revolution: Evidence and Interpretation." _The American Family in Social-Historical Perspective_. Ed.
Michael Gordon. New York: St. Martin's Press, 1973,
pp. 321-35.
Shows that the so-called sexual revolution, when measured
by pre-marital pregnancy rates, dates not from the 1920s
but from the late 19th century. Nor has the liberalization
of sexual behavior been continuous or the same for all
social groups at a given point in history.

1040. SMITH, Daniel Scott, and Michael S. HINDUS. "Premarital
Pregnancy in America, 1640-1971: An Overview and
Interpretation." _Journal of Interdisciplinary His-
tory_, 5 (1975), 537-70.
Demonstrates that premarital pregnancy in American history occurs in a cyclical pattern, with such pregnancy
increasing in periods of social disorder, of ambiguous
intergenerational relationships, and of weakening social
control over sexual behavior.

1041. STRONG, Floyd Brian. "Ideas of the Early Sex Education
Movement in America, 1890-1920." _History of Education
Quarterly_, 12 (1972), 129-61.
Notes that as sex became openly discussed and attitudes
shifted from sex for procreation to sex for pleasure,
moral conservatives sought new ways to socialize the
young sexually and turned to sexual instruction, but
such instruction tried to preserve the old morality
rather than encourage discussions of sexuality and sexual adjustment.

1042. STRONG, Floyd Brian. "Sex, Character, and Reform in
America, 1830-1920: A Psychological Inquiry into
American History." Diss. Stanford Univ., 1972.
Studies the interaction between personality and sexual
attitudes in America and the attempt by educators to
preserve older moral standards through sex education
in the public schools. Concludes that Victorian sexual anxieties were related to certain patterns of family relations.

1043. STRONG, Floyd Brian. "Toward a History of the Exper-
iential Family: Sex and Incest in the Nineteenth
Century Family." _Journal of Marriage and the Fam-
ily_, 35 (1973), 457-66.
Contends that latent incestuous attachments were en-
couraged between mothers and sons in 19th-century

148

America, and that these in turn prompted men to experience sexual anxieties and to separate women into "good" and "bad" according to whether they were sexual.

1044. VERTINSKY, Patricia Anne. "Education for Sexual Morality: Moral Reform and the Regulation of American Sexual Behavior in the Nineteenth Century." Diss. Univ. of British Columbia, 1975.
Contends that 19th-century moral reformers endeavored to preserve a traditional morality in the face of rapidly changing social conditions and a perceived increase in sexual deviancy, especially prostitution. Though their initial efforts were directed at the family, reformers by the late 19th century, convinced that parents were inadequately performing their sex education duties, turned to the school as the agency of sexual instruction.

1045. WALTERS, Ronald G., ed. Primers for Prudery: Sexual Advice to Victorian America. Englewood Cliffs: Prentice-Hall, 1974.
An excellent anthology of 19th-century sex manuals and their advice on prostitution, birth control, masturbation, intercourse, and sex roles in the context of Victorian social and cultural forces.

1046. WASSERSTROM, William. Heiress of all the Ages: Sex and Sentiment in the Genteel Tradition. Minneapolis: Univ. of Minnesota Press, 1959.
Examines ideas about sex and sentiment in Victorian America, especially the belief in the restorative power of love.

1047. WOLKOFF, Regina Lois. "The Ethics of Sex: Individuality and the Social Order in Early Twentieth-Century American Sexual Advice Literature." Diss. Univ. of Michigan, 1974.
Shows that between 1890 and 1920 there was a move towards more freer sexual expression which reversed previously held beliefs about the subordination of individual desires to the requirements of civilized society.

WOMEN

1048. ANDREWS, William D., and Deborah C. ANDREWS. "Technology and the Housewife in Nineteenth-Century America." Women's Studies, 2 (1974), 309-28.
Shows that the home was envisaged as the antidote to technology, yet the campaign to professionalize housekeeping ironically embraced technology as a liberating force and as a means of elevating the woman's status. Linked to technology, the housewife became a new social type.

1049. BACON, Elizabeth Mickle. "The Growth of Household Conviences in the United States from 1865 to 1900."

Diss. Radcliffe College, 1944.
Examines women's magazines, cook books, and domestic
manuals to learn the impact of the development of household conveniences on the emancipation of middle-class
women. Emphasizes changes in heating and lighting,
food preparation, appliances, and cleaning. Argues
that women increasingly became employed outside the
home as homemaking was simplified and took less time.

1050. BARKER-BENFIELD, Benjamin. The Horrors of the Half-
Known Life: Male Attitudes Toward Women and Sexuality in Nineteenth-Century America. New York:
Harper & Row, 1975.
Examines the roots of gynecology in America and its
hostility toward women and its attempt to control
and repress female sexuality.

1051. BUNKLE, Phillida E. "Sentimental Womanhood and Domestic Education, 1830-1870." History of Education
Quarterly, 14 (1974), 13-30.
Argues that the ascription of women with dependent and
spiritual characteristics occurred not because females
lost former economic functions but because evangelical
Protestantism defined women in terms of their powers
of redemption.

1052. COWAN, Ruth Schwartz. "A Case Study of Technological
and Social Change: The Washing Machine and the
Working Wife." Clio's Consciousness Raised: New
Perspectives on the History of Women. Ed. Mary
Hartman and Lois W. Banner. New York: Harper &
Row, 1974, pp. 245-53.
Calls for a reexamination of the assumption that machine
technology liberated women from household tasks. Argues
that functions and tasks of women may have actually increased with technological innovation, and that the en-
trance of married women into the labor force may have
little relationship to the growth of household technology.

1053. COWAN, Ruth Schwartz. "The 'Industrial Revolution' in
the Home: Household Technology and Social Change in
the 20th Century." Technology and Culture, 17 (1976),
1-23.
Debates prevailing sociological theory about the impact
of modern technology on family life. Shows that under
industrialization the functions of the housewife actually
increased and the housewife remained unspecialized. Nor
has technology destroyed family life.

1054. DALSIMER, Marlyn Hartzell. "Women and Family in the
Oneida Community, 1837-1881." Diss. New York Univ.,
1975.
Examines the social history of women and familial relations in the Oneida Community, especially the extent
and content of female emancipation.

1055.   DONEGAN, Jane Bauer.   "Man-Midwifery and the Delicacy
        of the Sexes."   'Remember the Ladies':   New Perspec-
        tives on Women in American History.   Ed. Carol V.R.
        George.   Syracuse: Syracuse Univ. Press, 1975,
        pp. 90-109.
        Discusses male physicians' tenuous hold upon the prac-
        tice of midwifery in the 19th century and their attempts
        to control obstetrics despite opposing public opinion.

1056.   DONEGAN, Jane Bauer.   "Midwifery in America, 1760-1860:
        A Study in Medicine and Morality."   Diss. Syracuse
        Univ., 1972.
        Investigates obstetrical practices in urban America,
        and traces the transition of obstetrics from untrained
        midwives to professional male physicians, notably how
        males obtained the monopoly and its social impact.

1057.   FASS, Paula.   "Marriage and Women in the Twenties."
        Paper delivered at the Berkshire Conference of Women
        Historians, New Brunswick, March 1973.

1058.   FRITSCHNER, Linda Marie.   "The Rise and Fall of Home
        Economics: A Study with Implications for Women,
        Education, and Change."   Diss. Univ. of California
        at Davis, 1973.
        Illustrates that the founders of the home economics
        movement felt their lifestyle threatened by social
        change and sought to preserve a passing order and con-
        trol change.   But federal subsidies to the movement
        contributed to family fragmentation and to the economic
        rationalization of the feminine role.

1059.   HARTMANN, Heidi Irmgard.   "Capitalism and Women's Work
        in the Home, 1900-1930."   Diss. Yale Univ., 1974.
        Argues that changes in housework were influenced by the
        requirements of capitalist production and the patri-
        archal family system.   Notes that these systems rein-
        forced domesticity and did not significantly decrease
        the time spent on household chores.

1060.   JENSEN, Richard.   "Family, Career, and Reform: Women
        Leaders of the Progressive Era."   The American Family
        in Social-Historical Perspective.   Ed. Michael Gor-
        don.   New York: St. Martin's Press, 1973, pp. 267-80.
        Discovers that locally or nationally prominent women who
        supported suffrage did not differ markedly from those
        opposed suffrage, with the exception that the former
        were more likely to be mothers who were active in civic
        and political affairs.

1061.   KLEINBERG, Susan J.   "Technology and Women's Work: The
        Lives of Working-Class Women in Pittsburgh, 1870-1900."
        Labor History, 17 (1976), 58-72.
        Examines the lives and work of women in their homes and
        the impact of domestic and municipal technology on

working class women.

1062. KLEINBERG, Susan J. "Technology's Stepdaughters: The
       Impact of Industrialization Upon Working Class Women,
       Pittsburgh, 1865-1890." Diss. Univ. of Pittsburgh,
       1973.
       Analyzes the impact of industrialization, technological
       diffusion, and urban growth on working class women and
       their families. Also examines how sex roles were in-
       fluenced by class, ethnicity, and economic structure,
       notably how the Pittsburgh economy reinforced women's
       traditional economic and social roles.

1063. KOBRIN, Frances E. "The American Midwife Controversy:
       A Crisis of Professionalization." Bulletin of the
       History of Medicine, 40 (1966), 350-63.
       Discusses the debate between the obstetrical specialist
       and his adversary, the midwife, in the early 20th cen-
       tury and the eventual triumph of obstetricians over mid-
       wives.

1064. MCGOVERN, James R. "The American Woman's Pre-World War
       I Freedom in Manners and Morals." Journal of Amer-
       ican History, 55 (1968), 315-33.
       Believes that the revolution in morals and manners,
       traditionally traced to the 1920s, actually occurred
       prior to WWI when individualization and the social
       changes accompanying urbanization resulted in a marked
       shift in woman's sex role and an identification with
       more "masculine" norms.

1065. MCLAUGHLIN, Virginia Yans. "Patterns of Work and Fam-
       ily Organization: Buffalo's Italians." Journal of
       Interdisciplinary History, 2 (1971), 299-314.
       Notes that contrary to the traditional belief that the
       movement of females into the work force led to disruptive
       family life, the assumption of new economic roles by
       Italian women did not significantly alter traditional
       familial arrangements.

1066. MULLIGAN, Jane Silverman. "The Madonna and Child in
       American Culture, 1830-1916." Diss. UCLA, 1975.
       Examines the cultural concept of motherhood in America,
       and the rise and institutionalization of the belief in
       the woman and child as redeemers of the secularized
       and urbanized society.

1067. ROEMER, Kenneth M. "Sex Roles, Utopia and Change: The
       Family in Late Nineteenth-Century Utopian Literature."
       American Studies, 13 (1972), 33-48.
       Discusses the descriptions of present and future love
       affairs and family life found in utopian literature in
       terms of American attitudes about sex roles.

1068. SKLAR, Kathryn Kish. Catharine Beecher: A Study in

152

American Domesticity. New Haven: Yale Univ. Press, 1973.
Surveys the life of educator and social philosopher, Catharine Beecher, and her attempt to increase women's power in the home.

1069. SMITH, Daniel Scott. "Family Limitation, Sexual Control, and Domestic Feminism in Victorian America." Clio's Consciousness Raised: New Perspectives on the History of Women. Ed. Mary Hartman and Lois W. Banner. New York: Harper & Row, 1974, pp. 119-36.
Contends that during the late 19th century women experienced a marked increase in power and a sense of autonomy within the family as evidenced by the decline in marital fertility. This movement of "domestic feminism" was an important phase in the history of women.

1070. SMITH-ROSENBERG, Carroll. "Puberty to Menopause: The Cycle of Femininity in Nineteenth-Century America." Clio's Consciousness Raised: New Perspectives on the History of Women. Ed. Mary Hartman and Lois W. Banner. New York: Harper & Row, 1974, pp. 23-37.
Maintains that physicians' attitudes toward and explanations of puberty and menopause helped to shape socially defined sex roles, assisted physicians in acting out their professional role as healers, and served as a means through which ambivalence toward sexuality could be expressed.

1071. SMITH-ROSENBERG, Carroll, and Charles E. ROSENBERG. "The Female Animal: Medical and Biological Views of Woman and Her Role in Nineteenth-Century America." Journal of American History, 60 (1973), 332-56.
Illustrates that when the number of roles for females expanded, medical and biological arguments were employed by men to preserve traditional sex roles and thwart demands by women for higher education and family limitation.

1072. STRASSER, Susan. "Household Technology and Women's Roles: The Nineteenth Century Background." Paper delivered at the Smithsonian Institution, Washington, D.C. March 1974.
Argues that despite its promise to revolutionize society, technology did not alter significantly woman's domestic role. Innovations that relieved women's household chores in the areas of clothing, food preparation, cleaning, and utilities did not disintegrate sex stereotypes.

1073. UHLENBERG, Peter R. "A Study of Cohort Life Cycles: Cohorts of Native Born Massachusetts Women, 1830-1920." Population Studies, 23 (1968), 407-20.
Applies life cycle analysis to several female cohorts of native-born Massachusetts women.

153

1074. VANEK, Joan. "Keeping Busy: Time Spent in Housework,
       United States, 1920-1970." Diss. Univ. of Michigan,
       1973.
       Argues that time spent in household chores by nonemployed
       American women has remained constant despite enormous
       changes in the household, but that of employed women has
       markedly decreased. Socioeconomic status is not a major
       factor in time spent in household work, although the
       upper levels initially began the reduction of household
       work.

1075. VANEK, Joan. "Social Class Variations in Time Spent in
       Housework, 1920-1970." Paper delivered at the 2nd
       Berkshire Conference on the History of Women, Cambridge,
       October 1974.
       Notes that data on time patterns in homemaking reveal a
       shift in the way class affects life style. In 1930,
       homemaking showed a variation by class which is no longer
       in evidence today. Technological and economic factors
       provided a force for the diffusion to all strata of pat-
       terns once appropriate only to an elite.

1076. WALKOWITZ, Daniel J. "Working-Class Women in the Gilded
       Age: Factory, Community and Family Life among Cohoes,
       New York, Cotton Workers." _Journal of Social History_,
       5 (1972), 464-90.
       Examines the needs and values that influenced working
       class women's behavior, the impact of industrialization
       on the postion of women, and the relationship between
       factory, community, and family life.

1077. WARBASSE, Elizabeth Bowles. "The Changing Legal Rights
       of Married Women, 1800-1861." Diss. Radcliffe Col-
       lege, 1960.
       Traces the development of the married woman's status in
       common law from a legal nonentity, with few rights to
       her property, earnings, and children, to an individual
       recognized by law. Notes that married women's legis-
       lation ironically originated in the antebellum South,
       a region generally resistant to reform, but rapidly
       spread northward thereafter.

1078. WEIGLEY, Emma Seifrit. "It Might Have Been Euthenics:
       The Lake Placid Conferences and the Home Economics
       Movement." _American Quarterly_, 26 (1974), 79-96.
       Shows how the home economics movement, stressing the
       centrality of the family, tried to apply the principles
       of science to improve the quality of family life. The
       movement did not reject the traditional concept of the
       woman as mother and housekeeper.

1079. WEIN, Roberta. "Educated Women and the Limits of Do-
       mesticity, 1830-1918." Diss. New York Univ., 1974.
       Examines the relationship between domestic values and
       the educated woman's response to these values over time

at selected women's colleges.

1080. WEIN, Roberta. "Women's Colleges and Domesticity,
          1875-1918." History of Education Quarterly, 14
          (1974), 31-48.
       Explains that late 19th century female colleges faced
       an important issue: whether women's colleges should
       perpetuate domesticity or prepare women for careerism.
       By WWI, after debate and experimentation, female col-
       leges and their graduates had not challenged the do-
       mesticity cult nor beliefs in female subservience.

1081. WELTER, Barbara. "The Cult of True Womanhood: 1820-
          1860." American Quarterly, 18 (1966), 151-74.
       Notes that the cult of true womanhood, revolving around
       the attributes of piety, purity, submissiveness, and
       domesticity, promised its adherents happiness and power.
       But it ironically told women to play an active role in
       redeeming external society.

1082. WERTZ, Dorothy C., and Richard W. WERTZ. "Midwives and
          Man-Midwives in Nineteenth-Century America." Paper
          delivered at the 2nd Berkshire Conference on the His-
          tory of Women, Cambridge, October 1974.
       Argues that male doctors supplanted midwives because of
       new birth technologies, changes in women's status, the
       entrepreneureal character of American medicine, and in-
       creased attention to the abnormal, rather than the nor-
       mal, birth.

1083. WHITE, Barbara Anne. "Growing Up Female: Adolescent
          Girlhood in American Literature." Diss. Univ. of
          Wisconsin, 1974.
       Discusses novels of adolescence by women, and finds that
       protagonists generally rejected traditional concepts of
       womanhood but were hampered in their rebellion by social
       institutions and female upbringing. Adolescence, in short,
       becomes a trap.

                3. The Post-Modern Family (1945-)

GENERAL

1084. WINCH, Robert F. "Permanence and Change in the History of
          the American Family and Some Speculations as to Its
          Future." Journal of Marriage and the Family, 32 (1970),
          6-15.
       Notes changes in the American family since 1790 such as
       declining household size and familial functions, and
       speculates on changing family structure.

BIRTH CONTROL

1085. HELLMAN, Louis M. "Family Planning Comes of Age."

American Journal of Obstetrics and Gynecology, 109 (1971), 214-24.
Discusses the shift in policy by federal and local governments toward birth control and the mobilization of public opinion in favor of tax-supported contraception as well as shifting attitudes and policy toward abortion since 1950.

1086. JAFFE, Frederick S. "Knowledge, Perception, and Change: Notes on a Fragment of Social History." Mt. Sinai Journal of Medicine, 42 (1975), 286-99.
Describes the changes in the assumptions of the Planned Parenthood movement in the 1950s and how these changes contributed to the movement's success in the 1960s.

1087. RAINWATER, Lee, and Karol Kane WEINSTEIN. And the Poor Get Children: Sex, Contraception, and Family Planning in the Working Class. Chicago: Quadrangle, 1960.
Investigates the problems beset by Planned Parenthood in their working with the lower classes, and discusses the psychological factors involved in fertility control.

CHILDREN

1088. BIGNER, Jerry J. "Parent Education in Popular Literature: 1950-1970." Family Coordinator, 21 (1972), 313-19.
Examines popular women's magazines via content analysis to determine changes in childrearing advice, and finds a shift toward rearing children to become self-actualizing individuals.

1089. BORSTELMANN, L. J. "Dr. Locke and Dr. Spock: Continuity and Change in American Conceptions of Childrearing." Paper delivered at the Southeastern Regional Meeting of the Society for Research in Child Development, Chapel Hill, N.C., March 1974.
Compares the ideas of Locke and Spock on childrearing goals and methods, parental authority, discipline, and the concept of play.

1090. COLEMAN, James S., et. al. Youth: Transition to Adulthood. Chicago: Univ. of Chicago Press, 1974.
Presents the background of youth culture in contemporary America, including the history of age grouping and the demography of youth, and proposes alternative directions for change.

1091. SULMAN, A. Michael. "The Humanization of the American Child: Benjamin Spock as a Popularizer of Psychoanalytic Thought." Journal of the History of the Behavioral Sciences, 9 (1973), 258-65.
Discusses how Spock broke with the childrearing traditions of the 1920s and 1930s by popularizing psychoanalytic ideas.

1092. ZUCKERMAN, Michael. "Dr. Spock: The Confidence Man."
       The Family in History. Ed. Charles E. Rosenberg.
       Philadelphia: Univ. of Pennsylvania Press, 1975,
       pp. 179-207.
       Examines the social ideals and success of Benjamin
       Spock, and relates his admonitions to the emerging
       corporate social order.

DEMOGRAPHY

1093. COBB, Nancy Hendrix. "The Effect of Spatial, Social,
          and Racial Distance and Marriageable Population on
          Inter-area Marriage Rates in Nashville, Tennessee,
          1940-1970." Diss. Vanderbilt Univ., 1974.
       Argues that marriage rates between residential areas
       of a city vary inversely with the spatial, social, and
       racial distance of the pairs from each other, but the
       relationship between marriageable population and inter-
       area marriage rates depends largely on area size.

1094. CUTRIGHT, Phillips. "Components of Change in the Num-
          ber of Female Family Heads Aged 15-44: United
          States, 1940-1970." Journal of Marriage and the
          Family, 36 (1974), 714-21.
       Discusses the statuses through which a woman passes
       to become a female head of family to explain the
       large increase in female family heads between 1940
       and 1970.

1095. GLICK, Paul C. American Families. New York: John
          Wiley and Sons, 1957.
       Presents a demographic analysis of American families
       based on the 1950 census, with emphasis on family
       life cycle and household composition.

1096. GLICK, Paul C. "A Demographer Looks at American Fam-
          ilies." Journal of Marriage and the Family, 37 (1975),
          15-26.
       Surveys excellently the recent demographic changes in
       marriage and fertility, delay in marriage, singleness
       among middle-age women, divorce by socio-economic group-
       ing, living arrangements, and kinship networks.

1097. KOBRIN, Frances E. "Household Headship and Its Changes
          in the United States, 1940-1960, 1970." Journal of
          the American Statistical Association, 68 (1973),
          793-800.
       Discusses household headship as a demographic variable,
       and describes changes in the likelihood of an adult
       being a household head and the type of head.

1098. ROSENWAIKE, Ira. "Two Generations of Italians in Amer-
          ica (1940-1960): Their Fertility Experience." Inter-
          national Migration Review, 7 (1973), 271-80.
       Uses the Italian fertility experience to illustrate that

the level of fertility is a key indicator of integration
into mainstream American society.

DIVORCE

1099. STETSON, Dorothy M., and Gerald C. WRIGHT.   "The Effects
       of Laws on Divorce in American States." Journal of
       Marriage and the Family, 37 (1975), 537-47.
       Explores the impact of state divorce laws on divorce
       rates, and concludes that a strong relationship exists
       between the permissiveness of divorce laws and divorce
       rates.

DOMESTIC LIFE AND CUSTOMS

1100. ADAMS, Bert N. The American Family: A Sociological
       Interpretation. Chicago: Markham Publishing, 1971.
       Uses historical and comparative analysis to discuss
       current marriage and family patterns, love and mate
       selection, aging, and the family's response to change.

1101. BERNARD, Jessie. The Future of Marriage. New York:
       World Publishing, 1972.
       Argues that marriage consists of two marriages--his and
       hers--with his marriage being good while her marriage
       being damaging.

1102. BLACKABY, James. "Family Structure in the Comics, or
       Who is Baby Minnie?" Paper delivered at the Popular
       Culture Association, Milwaukee, May 1974.

1103. BUCCI, Jerry Michael. "Love, Marriage, and Family Life
       Themes in the Popular Song: A Comparison of the
       Years 1940 and 1965." Diss. Columbia Univ., 1968.
       Examines the popular songs of 1940 and 1965 for themes
       of love, marriage, family life, and boy-girl relation-
       ships.

1104. CONNOR, John. "Acculturation and Family Continuities
       in Three Generations of Japanese Americans." Journal
       of Marriage and the Family, 36 (1974), 159-65.
       Examines the extent to which the Japanese-American fam-
       ily has abandoned traditional Japanese characteristics
       and become assimilated into American society.

1105. ELKIN, Frederick. The Family in Canada: An Account of
       Present Knowledge and Gaps in Knowledge About Canadian
       Families. Ottawa: Canadian Conference on the Family,
       1964.
       Reviews the general trends of the contemporary Canadian
       family, including demographic changes, variations among
       families, familial roles, and the deviant family.

1106. GORDON, Michael, ed. The Nuclear Family in Crisis: The
       Search for Alternatives. New York: Harper & Row,

1972.
Contains articles dealing with the Moravians and the
Oneida community, the kibbutz, the Soviet family, com-
munes, and group marriage.

1107. HOEBER, Daniel Robert. "The Many Marriages of Robert
       Frost: An Analysis of the Marriage Group in Frost's
       Poetry." Diss. Southern Illinois Univ., 1975.
       Shows that Frost was concerned not only with marriage
       as a theme, but also with the conflicts of marriage
       and their causes.

1108. KELLER, Suzanne Infeld. The American Lower Class Fam-
       ily. Albany: Division for Youth, 1968.
       Discusses the demographic characteristics, types, and
       cultural values of lower class families. Also deals
       with the childrearing, sex roles, and social problems
       of these families.

1109. KOMAROVSKY, Mirra. Blue-Collar Marriage. New York:
       Random House, 1964.
       Discusses socialization into conjugal roles by the
       working class, and analyzes the daily activities and
       relationships of blue-collar marriages.

1110. LEWIS, Oscar. La Vida: A Puerto Rican Family in the
       Culture of Poverty, San Juan and New York. New
       York: Random House, 1966.
       Interviews several generations of a Puerto Rican fam-
       ily to reveal their story, and documents the squalor
       and violence of their lives.

1111. MODELL, John. "Japanese American Family: A Perspec-
       tive for Future Investigations." Pacific Histor-
       ical Review, 37 (1968), 67-81.
       Argues that the many-generational family served as an
       anchor for values and an important agent in assisting
       Japanese-Americans in coping with their new environ-
       ment.

1112. MOORE, Barrington. "Thoughts on the Future of the Fam-
       ily." Political Power and Social Theory. Cambridge:
       Harvard Univ. Press, 1958, pp. 160-78.
       Assesses current sociological research on the family,
       and suggests that the family may become obsolete as
       its economic functions disappear.

1113. NAPP, Ralph von Tresckow. "Individual Freedom or Auto-
       nomy at Work in the American Family." Paper deliver-
       ed at the Popular Culture Association in the South,
       Birmingham, October 1974.
       Argues that freedom in the family is only possible in
       the attainment of individual freedom, and that auto-
       nomy cannot work for any individual in an environment
       where there is no reciprocity.

1114. PLAGMAN, Linda Marie. "The Modern Pilgrims: Marriage
       and the Self in the Work of John Updike." Diss.
       Marquette Univ., 1974.
       Observes that marriage and its problems are one of
       Updike's major concerns. He draws his ideas of love
       from Karl Barth and the Christian love tradition of
       self-sacrifice.

1115. ROTH, David Sidney. "The Strongest Link: A Study of
       the Family in the Fiction of Three Major Jewish-
       American Novelists: 1945-1970." Diss. Kent State
       Univ., 1974.
       Discusses the treatment of the family in the writings
       of Roth, Malamud, and Bellow. Emphasizes the theme
       of increased pressures on the family and consequential
       familial disruption.

1116. SKOLNICK, Arlene S., and Jerome H. SKOLNICK. Family
       in Transition: Rethinking Marriage, Sexuality,
       Child Rearing and Family Organization. Boston:
       Little, Brown, 1971.
       Questions the survival of the contemporary family, and
       argues that the social problems of the nuclear family
       are inherent to its structure.

1117. STOCKBURGER, Walker N. "The Effects of the Second
       World War on Marriage and the Family in the United
       States." Diss. Southern Baptist Theological Seminary,
       1952.

1118. THAMM, Robert. Beyond Marriage and the Nuclear Family.
       San Francisco: Canfield Press, 1975.
       Proposes an alternative kind of family--the communal
       family--which offers structure and flexibility, sta-
       bility and versatility, privacy and sociability.

FAMILY LAW AND INHERITANCE

1119. FARBER, Bernard. Family and Kinship in Modern Society.
       Glenview, Ill.: Scott, Foresman, 1973.
       Contends that the family model as revealed in popular
       behavior and family law has changed from the adherence
       to the sacrosanct conjugal unit ("natural state") to
       a "legal" paradigm where the government has steadily
       intervened in family relations.

1120. PARKER, Stanley. "The New Marriage Contract: Theory
       and Practice." Paper delivered at the Popular Cul-
       ture Association, Milwaukee, May 1974.

KINSHIP

1121. ADAMS, Bert N. "Isolation, Function, and Beyond: Amer-
       ican Kinship in the 1960s." Journal of Marriage and
       the Family, 32 (1970), 575-97.

Reviews recent sociological studies of kinship, and notes
the increasing emphasis on system interrelations, comparative analysis, and identification of variables affecting
kinship.

SEXUALITY

1122. BRECHER, Edward. The Sex Researchers. Boston: Little,
       Brown, 1969.
       Provides the historical context of sex researchers and
       describes the conclusions of scientific studies of sex
       published in the United States and Europe.

1123. GAGNON, John H. "Sex Research and Social Change."
       Archives of Sexual Behavior, 4 (1975), 111-42.
       Discusses the history of scientific sex research and
       changes in its models and methodologies, from Freud
       and Ellis to Masters and Johnson.

1124. JONES, James Howard. "The Origins of the Institute
       for Sex Research: A History." Diss. Indiana Univ.,
       1973.
       Surveys the origins, intellectual underpinnings, in-
       stitutional support and problems, and critics of Al-
       fred C. Kinsey's Institute for Sex Research.

1125. POMEROY, Wardell Baxter. Dr. Kinsey and the Institute
       for Sex Research. New York: Harper & Row, 1972.
       Discusses uncritically the life of Alfred Kinsey, his
       research in sexual behavior, and his relations with
       the press.

1126. REISS, Ira L. "The Sexual Renaissance: A Summary and
       Analysis." Journal of Social Issues, 22 (1966),
       123-37.
       Notes that a permissive premarital sexual tradition
       has taken root in contemporary America, but its mean-
       ing is different for various segments of the population.
       It also has led to generational conflict.

                    4. The Black Family

GENERAL

1127. CLARKE, John Henrik. "The Black Family in Historical
       Perspective." Journal of Afro-American Issues, 3
       (1975), 336-42.
       Argues that the central achievement of the black family
       is its survival. Also reviews the main features of the
       black family in Africa and their transformation under
       slavery.

1128. DAVIS, Lenwood G. The Black Family in Urban Areas in
       the United States. 2nd ed. Monticello, Ill.:

Council of Planning Librarians, 1975.
A useful reference guide and bibliography of the black
family, its childrearing modes, and parent-child relationships. Also includes citations on the history
of the black family.

1129. INDIANA UNIVERSITY LIBRARY. The Black Family and the
Black Woman: A Bibliography. Bloomington: Indiana
Univ. Bookstore, 1972.

1130. STAPLES, Robert. "Towards a Sociology of the Black
Family: A Theoretical and Methodological Assessment." Journal of Marriage and the Family, 33 (1971),
119-30.
Summarizes current research and theories of black families. Concludes that many studies suffer from precon-
ceived assumptions about the pathological character of
the black family and from the use of normative social
science models.

CHILDREN

1131. FRAZIER, Edward Franklin. Negro Youth at the Crossroads:
Their Personality Development in the Middle States.
Washington: American Council on Education, 1940.
Investigates the limitations placed on urban black youth
in the 1930s, and analyzes the effects of family, school,
and church on their personalities.

1132. JOHNSON, Charles S. Growing Up in the Black Belt: Negro
Youth in the Rural South. Washington: American
Council on Education, 1941.
Attempts to ascertain what the effect of being black has
upon personality development of rural black youth.

DEMOGRAPHY

1133. COALE, Ansley, and Norfleet W. RIVES. "A Statistical
Reconstruction of the Black Population of the United
States, 1880-1970: Estimates of True Numbers by Age
and Sex, Birth Rates, and Total Fertility." Population Index, 39 (1973), 3-36.
Attempts to reconstruct the black population, distributed by age and sex, from 1880 to 1970, and compares
black and white fertility trends since the early 19th
century.

1134. FARLEY, Reynolds. "The Demographic Rates and Social
Institutions of the Nineteenth Century Negro Population: A Stable Population Analysis." Demography,
2 (1965), 386-98.
Uses quasi-stable population techniques to estimate
birth and death rates. Concludes that black fertility
rates remained high while mortality rates increased
during the second half of the century.

1135. FOGEL, Robert, and Stanley ENGERMAN. Time on the Cross:
       The Economics of American Negro Slavery. Boston:
       Little, Brown, 1974.
       Discusses the functions assigned to the slave family, the
       attempts to promote the stability of slave families, the
       extent of slave breeding and promiscuity, family com-
       position and structure, and division of labor within the
       slave family.

1136. ZELNIK, Melvin. "The Fertility of the American Negro in
          1830 and 1850." Population Studies, 20 (1966), 77-83.
       Estimates the black birth rate in the mid-19th century
       using stable population techniques.

DOMESTIC LIFE AND CUSTOMS

1137. ABZUG, Robert H. "The Black Family during Reconstruction."
       Key Issues in the Afro-American Experience. Ed. Nathan
       Huggins, et. al. New York: Harcourt Brace Jovanovich,
       1971, II, pp. 26-41.
       Argues that blacks had a moral and emotional commitment
       to family life and that the black family was stabilizing
       and functioning positively in the South during Recon-
       struction.

1138. BERNARD, Jessie. Marriage and Family Among Negroes.
       Englewood Cliffs: Prentice-Hall, 1966.
       Studies changes in the black family since 1940 with
       emphasis on sex roles, socialization, and structural
       shifts.

1139. BILLINGSLEY, Andrew. Black Families in White America.
       Englewood Cliffs: Prentice-Hall, 1968.
       Argues that the black family, faced with the crippling
       effects of poverty and racism, has survived amasingly
       well and is not disintegrating in the urban ghetto.
       Notes that the black family must be viewed as a sub-
       system of the larger society.

1140. BILLINGSLEY, Andrew, and Amy Tate BILLINGSLEY. "Negro
       Family Life in America." Social Service Review,
       39 (1965), 310-19.
       Deals with the historical and modern forces that have
       shaped black family life, and examines the distinctive
       features of black family life.

1141. BILLINGSLEY, Andrew, and Marilyn GREENE. "The Black
       Family." Paper delivered at the 2nd Berkshire Con-
       ference on the History of Women, Cambridge, October
       1974.

1142. BLASSINGAME, John. The Slave Community: Plantation
       Life in the Antebellum South. New York: Oxford
       Univ. Press, 1972.
       Describes how the monogamous family was an important

163

survival mechanism for slaves despite its weakness and
dependency on the master for strength.

1143. BROUWER, Merle G. "Marriage and Family Life Among Blacks
in Colonial Pennsylvania." Pennsylvania Magazine of
History and Biography, 99 (1975), 368-72.
Notes that although the marriages of blacks had no legal
standing in colonial Pennsylvania and masters frequently
split slave families, slaves did contract marriages but
maintained only tenuous marital relationships.

1144. COMER, James P. "The Black Family in America." Paper
delivered at the American Historical Association,
Boston, December 1970.

1145. DUBOIS, William Edward Burghardt, ed. The Negro American
Family. 1919; rpt. Cambridge: MIT Press, 1970.
Argues that the history of the black family is one of
increasing disorganization, a characteristic fostered
by slavery, emancipation, and urbanization. A good
analysis of urban black family life in the early 1900s.

1146. FRAZIER, Edward Franklin. The Negro Family in the
United States. Rev. ed. Chicago: Univ. of Chicago Press, 1948.
Contends that slavery destroyed African familial forms,
but a relatively stable black family emerged under
slavery. Emancipation and the rural-to-urban migration
were also destructive to black family life, but a stable
black family has again developed.

1147. FRAZIER, Edward Franklin. "The Negro Slave Family."
Journal of Negro History, 15 (1930), 198-259.
Examines slave biographies and autobiographies to determine the extent to which the black family developed
as an independent cultural group and the extent to
which a family consciousness was developed.

1148. GENOVESE, Eugene D. Roll, Jordan, Roll: The World
the Slaves Made. New York: Pantheon, 1974.
Argues that the slaves created impressive norms of family life--especially the nuclear norm--and that black
families were relatively stable and functioned reason-
ably well within the larger white-dominated society.

1149. GUILLORY, Barbara Marie. "The Black Family: A Case
For Change and Survival in White America." Diss.
Tulane Univ., 1974.
Examines the role of the black family in terms of its
historical functions in the satisfaction of sexual
desires, security and protection of family members,
and socialization of children. Also discusses the impact of general socio-economic conditions on the black
family.

1150. HEISS, Jerold. The Case of the Black Family: A Socio-
      logical Inquiry. New York: Columbia Univ. Press,
      1975.
      Uses National Opinion Research Center data to examine
      and compare the characteristics of black families with
      those of white families. Also analyzes the effects of
      these characteristics within the black group.

1151. JONES, Bobby Frank. "A Cultural Middle Passage: Slave
      Marriage and Family in the Ante-Bellum South." Diss.
      Univ. of North Carolina, 1965.
      Discusses how the slave family was established by the
      master culture as a disciplinary measure to regulate
      male sex drive, and shows how family strength depended
      on individual commitment and support from the master.
      Slave families had a higher degree of illegitimacy,
      were more loosely organized, and emphasized the female's
      role more than white families.

1152. LABINJOH, Justin. "The Sexual Life of the Oppressed:
      An Examination of the Family Life of Ante-Bellum
      Slaves." Phylon, 35 (1974), 375-97.
      Suggests that slaves had fairly stable families and
      that antebellum planters recognized and improved
      slave familial relationships.

1153. MEBANE, Mary Elizabeth. "The Family in the Works of
      Charles W. Chesnut and Selected Works of Richard
      Wright." Diss. Univ. of North Carolina, 1973.
      Discusses the ideal black bourgeois family upheld by
      Chesnut and Wright's portrayal of the Southern black
      peasant family and the Northern urban black family.

1154. RAWICK, George. From Sundown to Sunup: The Making
      of the Black Community. New York: Greenwood Press,
      1972.
      Maintains that stable, male-headed kinship units that
      adopted to the conditions of slavery were common among
      slaves, although the entire slave community acted as
      an extended kinship network.

1155. RIPLEY, C. Peter. "The Black Family in Transition:
      Louisana, 1860-1865." Journal of Southern His-
      tory, 41 (1975), 369-80.
      Examines the impact of the Civil War, the military, and
      the changing role of the master-turned-employer on the
      black family in Louisana.

1156. RUCHAMES, Louis. "Race, Marriage and Abolition in Mass-
      achusetts." Journal of Negro History, 40 (1955),
      250-73.
      Describes the movement by Massachusetts abolitionists
      to eliminate segregation and guarantee equality of
      status for blacks in marriage law.

1157.   SCHWENINGER, Loren. "A Slave Family in the Ante Bellum
         South." Journal of Negro History, 60 (1975), 29-44.
         Examines the Thomas-Rapier family to shed light on the
         family experiences of antebellum slaves. Concludes that
         separation of family members and sexual exploitation led
         to family loyalty and unity, not familial disintegration.

1158.   SHOWERS, Susan. "A Weddin' and a Buryin' in the Black
         Belt." The Negro and His Folklore in Nineteenth
         Century Periodicals. Ed. Bruce Jackson. Austin:
         Univ. of Texas Press, 1967, pp. 293-301.
         Describes wedding customs in the late 19th century
         rural South.

1159.   SIDES, Sudie Duncan. "Slave Weddings and Religion:
         Plantation Life in the Southern States Before
         the American Civil War." History Today, 24 (1974),
         77-88.
         Discusses the role of religion in the lives of slaves
         and the cultural significance of slave weddings.

1160.   STAPLES, Robert, ed. The Black Family: Essays and
         Studies. Belmont, Cal.: Wadsworth, 1971.
         An anthology aimed at understanding the psychosocial
         dimensions of black family life, including its his-
         torical background and the controversy over the Moyn-
         ihan Report.

1161.   WHITE, John. "Whatever Happened to the Slave Family
         in the Old South?" Journal of American Studies,
         8 (1974), 383-90.
         Reviews the argument that slavery resulted in the de-
         struction of the black family, and concludes that the
         black family survived under and adapted to enslavement.

1162.   WILLIE, Charles Vert, ed. The Family Life of Black
         People. Columbus: Charles E. Merrill, 1970.
         An anthology which examines social factors and black
         family life, the stability of the black family, family
         structure, and the disintegration of the black family.

FAMILY COMPOSITION AND STRUCTURE

1163.   BABCHUCK, Nicholas, and John A. BALLWEG. "Black Family
         Structure and Primary Relations." Phylon, 33 (1972),
         334-47.
         Analyzes the primary relations of lower, working, and
         middle-class black couples. Concludes the middle-class
         blacks and whites have similar values and behavior and
         that working-class blacks have mutual primary-group
         resources.

1164.   FURSTENBERG, Frank F., et. al. "The Origins of the
         Female-Headed Black Family: The Impact of the Urban
         Experience." Journal of Interdisciplinary History,

6 (1975), 211-33.
Demonstrates that household structure varied little
between urban racial and ethnic groups in Philadelphia
between 1850 and 1880, but economic status did have a
major effect on black family structure. The matrifocal black family, thus, is a product not of slavery
but of the urban experience with its poverty and dis-
crimination.

1165. GOLIBER, Thomas J. "Cuyahoga Blacks: A Social and
     Demographic Study, 1850-1880." Master's Thesis,
     Kent State Univ., 1972.
Examines geographical mobility, the origins and social
characteristics, and household and residential patterns
of Cleveland blacks. Concludes that the urban black
household was male-headed and becoming smaller over
time and that single household dwellings decreased
while the number of blacks living in multiple units
increased.

1166. GUTMAN, Herbert G. "Persistent Myths About the Afro-
     American Family." Journal of Interdisciplinary
     History, 6 (1975), 181-210.
Argues that one should not assume that contemporary
black family disorganization is a product of slavery
and racism. Presents demographic evidence to prove
that most 19th-century free blacks, North and South,
lived in two-parent households as did most poor
blacks, rural and urban.

1167. GUTMAN, Herbert G. "The Buffalo, New York, Negro
     1855-1875: A Study of the Family Structure of
     Free Negroes and Some of Its Implications." Paper
     delivered at the Wisconsin Conference on the His-
     tory of American Political and Social Behavior,
     Madison, May 1968.
Illustrates that the family structure of Northern free
blacks before 1863 and Southern blacks after emancipation was nuclear and similar in structure to lower-
class whites. The matriarchal family was not a by-
product of slavery or emancipation.

1168. GUTMAN, Herbert G, and Laurence A. GLASCO. "The Negro
     Family, Household, and Occupational Structure,
     1855-1925, with special emphasis on Buffalo, New
     York, but including Comparative Data from New
     York, New York, Brooklyn, New York, Mobile, Ala-
     bama, and Adams County, Mississippi." Paper
     delivered at the Yale Conference on Nineteenth
     Century Cities, New Haven, November 1968.
Shows that family structure among free blacks was
not disorganized, but rather most households contained a husband and wife. Nor did income and occupation alone determine black family structure.

1169. HERSHBERG, Theodore. "Free Blacks in Ante-Bellum Phila-
           delphia: A Study of Ex-Slaves, Free-Born and Socio-
           Economic Decline." Journal of Social History, 5
           (1971-72), 183-209.
       Illustrates how the Philadelphia free black community
       suffered from an unbalanced sex ratio, weak family struc-
       ture (although households were generally two-parent),
       and residential segregation. Ex-slaves, however, were
       generally better off than free-born blacks.

1170. HERZOG, Elizabeth. "Is There a 'Breakdown' of the
           Negro Family?" Social Work, 11 (1966), 3-10.
       Reviews the controversy surrounding the 'breakdown' of
       black family life. Concludes that there has been no
       substantial change in family structure but instead a
       growing white recognition of a long-standing situation.

1171. HYMAN, Herbert H., and John Stelton REED. "'Black Matri-
           archy' Reconsidered: Evidence From Secondary Analysis
           of Sample Surveys." Public Opinion Quarterly, 33
           (1969), 346-54.
       Examines the proportion of female-headed households and
       the notion of female predominance over family affairs in
       black families. Argues that "black matriarchy" is an
       illusion.

1172. LAMMERMEIER, Paul J. "The Urban Black Family of the 19th
           Century: A Study of Black Family Structure in the
           Ohio Valley, 1850-1880." Journal of Marriage and the
           Family, 35 (1973), 440-56.
       Demonstrates that urban black family structure in the
       Ohio Valley was not based on female-headship but was
       two-parent and male-headed. It showed few effects of
       the slavery matriarchy; rather most black families were
       patriarchal. But there was a slow increase in female-
       headed families and residential segregation.

1173. MOYNIHAN, Daniel Patrick. "The Negro Family: The Case
           for National Action." The Moynihan Report and the
           Politics of Controversy. Ed. Lee Rainwater and Wil-
           liam L. Yancey. Cambridge: MIT Press, 1967, pp.
           41-124.
       Documents the debilitating effects of poverty and dis-
       crimination on black families--especially declining male
       headship--and notes that these problems are more acute
       in urban areas.

1174. OBLINGER, Carl D. "Vestiges of Poverty: Black Families
           and Fragments of Black Families in Southeastern Penn-
           sylvania, 1830-1860." Family in Historical Perspectives
           Newsletter, No. 4 (Summer 1973), pp. 9-14.
       Describes the family patterns of the mid-19th-century
       black poor in Southeastern Pennsylvania and the methods
       used to reconstruct the transient black population.

1175.   PLECK, Elizabeth H.   "The Two-Parent Household: Black
        Family Structure in Late Nineteenth-Century Boston."
        Journal of Social History, 6 (1972), 3-31.
        Emphasizes that despite the lack of employment opportu-
        nities, a high death rate, and much transiency, the
        typical black family in Boston consisted of two-parents,
        and family organization was relatively stable. But
        subtle differences existed between the household com-
        position of rural and urban-born heads of household,
        between migrants and native Bostonians.

1176.   RAINWATER, Lee.   "Crucible of Identity: The Negro Lower
        Class Family." Daedalus, 95 (1966), 172-216.
        Describes and analyzes lower-class black family patterns
        and their role in the "tangle of pathology" which char-
        acterizes the ghetto.

1177.   SHIFFLET, Crandall A.   "The Household Composition of
        Rural Black Families: Louisa County, Virginia, 1880."
        Journal of Interdisciplinary History, 6 (1975),
        235-60.
        Shows that family cycle reveals significant alterations
        in black household composition because of the burden of
        poverty and consequential reliance on kinship networks.

KINSHIP

1178.   SMITH, Raymond T.   "The Nuclear Family in Afro-American
        Kinship." Journal of Comparative Family Studies, 1
        (1970-1), 55-70.
        Argues that although most blacks live in nuclear families
        and define kinship in terms of the nuclear family, they
        do not share middle class beliefs in an independent nu-
        clear family system, especially in terms of sex-role dif-
        ferentiation.

WOMEN

1179.   DAVIS, Angela.   "Reflections on the Black Woman's Role
        in the Community of Slaves." Black Scholar, December
        1971, pp. 2-16.
        Discusses the black woman as she interacted with her
        people and her oppressive environment during slavery,
        and debunks the myth of the matriarchal black woman.

1180.   GUTMAN, Herbert G.   "Black Women in the Family Since 1865."
        Paper delivered at the Berkshire Conference of Women
        Historians, New Brunswick, March 1973.

1181.   JACKSON, Jacquelyne J.   "But Where are the Men?" Black
        Scholar, December 1971, pp. 30-41.
        Examines the myths which assert that black women have
        advantages over black men with regard to education, oc-
        cupation, employment, and income.

1182. PARKHURST, Jessie Wragg. "Role of the Black Mammy in
the Plantation Household." Journal of Negro History,
23 (1938), 349-69.
Explains how the role of the "Mammy" stemmed from the
slaves' position on the plantation. Also discusses
her position in the white household, her relations with
the children, and the relations between the Mammy and
the mistress.

CHAPTER IV:

THE FAMILY IN NON-WESTERN HISTORY

1. The Latin American Family

CHILDREN

1183. CARSCH, H. "The Family, Child-Rearing and Social Con-
      trols Among the Aztecs." International Anthropo-
      logical and Linguistic Review, 3 (1958), 8-21.
      Discusses the relationship between childrearing, the
      family, and transmission of culture among the Aztec
      society prior to Spanish annihilation.

1184. ROBERTS, Robert E. "Modernization and Infant Mortality
      in Mexico." Economic Development and Cultural Change,
      21 (1973), 655-69.
      Demonstrates that as Mexico modernized between 1930 and
      1960, the infant mortality rate waned. Also speculates
      that this decline should now be followed by a decline
      in fertility.

DEMOGRAPHY

1185. COUSINS, Winifred M. "Slave Family Life in the British
      Colonies: 1800-1834." Sociological Review, 27 (1935),
      35-55.
      Discusses the conditions of family life among slaves in
      the British West Indies, including sex ratio, birthrates,
      slave marriages, and family size and composition.

1186. DUNN, Richard S. "The Barbados Census of 1680: Profile
      of the Richest Colony in English America." William
      and Mary Quarterly, 26 (1969), 3-30.
      Examines 1680 census records to determine household size
      and composition, property distribution, and migration
      patterns.

1187. HATT, Paul K. Backgrounds of Human Fertility in Puerto
      Rico: A Sociological Survey. Princeton: Princeton
      Univ. Press, 1952.
      Examines the attitude patterns, life conditions, and
      cultural factors which influence fertility levels in
      Puerto Rico.

1188. HIGMAN, Barry W. "Household Structure and Fertility on
      Jamaican Slave Plantations: A Nineteenth Century
      Example." Population Studies, 27 (1973), 527-50.
      Discusses the differences between household types of
      Africans and Creoles. Concludes that family instability
      and casual mating patterns depressed slave fertility.

1189. MERRICK, Thomas W. "Interregional Differences in Fertility

171

in Brazil, 1950-1970." Demography, 11 (1974), 423-40.
Examines interregional fertility differences in Brazil
between 1950 and 1970. Concludes that substantial interregional migration contributed to the widening differences.

1190. MOLEN, Patricia. "Population and Social Patterns in
Barbados in the Early Eighteenth Century." William
and Mary Quarterly, 28 (1971), 287-300.
Examines the age structure and sex ratio of Barbados
as well as family structure and proportion married.

DOMESTIC LIFE AND CUSTOMS

1191. CLARKE, Edith. My Mother Who Fathered Me: A Study of
the Family in Three Selected Communities in Jamaica.
London: George Allen & Unwin, 1966.
Examines three rural Jamaican communities to show how
different ways of life influence family patterns, the
relationship between family members, and household
composition.

1192. GERBER, Stanford N., ed. The Family in the Caribbean.
Puerto Rico: Institute of Caribbean Studies, 1968.
An anthology of essays dealing with the Caribbean fam-
ily as a whole and in specific areas.

1193. MACDONALD, John Stuart, and Leatrice D. MACDONALD.
"Transformation of African and Indian Family Traditions
in the Southern Caribbean." Comparative Studies in
Society and History, 15 (1973), 171-98.
Argues that there was little pressure for blacks to adopt
a solidary family and household after slavery, but that
East Indian family solidarity continued as an escape from
the agro-factory.

FAMILY COMPOSITION AND STRUCTURE

1194. HIGMAN, Barry W. "The Slave Family and Household in the
British West Indies, 1800-1834." Journal of Interdisciplinary History, 6 (1975), 261-87.
Shows that West Indian slave families were nuclear in
structure, although this does not imply the lack of
familial disorganization. Nor does it imply that the
nuclear family was the social model.

1195. RAMOS, Donald. "Marriage and the Family in Colonial Vila
Rica." Hispanic American Historical Review, 55 (1975),
200-25.
Argues that in early 19th-century Brazil there were few
patriarchal, extended families, that a wide variety of
family types existed with nuclear and matrifocal families
predominating, and that marriage segmented the population.

1196. SMITH, Michael Garfield. West Indian Family Structure.
Seattle: Univ. of Washington Press, 1962.

Analyzes and compares the domestic organization and mating practice of selected West Indian societies to determine the principles of family structure.

1197. SMITH, Raymond Thomas. Negro Family in British Guiana: Family Structure and Social Status in the Villages. London: Routledge & Paul, 1956.
Uses the developmental cycle to examine the black West Indian family and how it fulfills the task of child rearing despite its matriarchal structure.

SEXUALITY

1198. DIGGS, Irene. "Colonial Sexual Behavior." Negro History Bulletin, 37 (1974), 214-6.
Discusses concubinage and polygamy among Spanish colonists and conquerors as well as the family life of slaves.

1199. MARTINEZ-ALIER, Verena. "Elopement and Seduction in Nineteenth-Century Cuba." Past & Present, 55 (1972), 91-129.
Argues that elopement and seduction were deviations in a highly stratified society, with elopement often stemming from socio-economic inequality of partners. With the end of colonialism came unstable matrimonial unions and the matrifocal family.

1200. MARTINEZ-ALIER, Verena. Marriage, Class and Colour in Nineteenth-Century Cuba: A Study of Racial Attitudes and Sexual Values in a Slave Society. London: Cambridge Univ. Press, 1974.
Examines deviations from the normative marriage behavior in 19th-century Cuba, notably parental opposition to a given marriage and elopement and interracial marriage.

WOMEN

1201. COUTURIER, Edith B. "Women in a Noble Family: The Mexican Reglas, 1756-1828." Paper delivered at the Berkshire Conference of Women Historicans, New Brunswick, March 1973.
Studies eight women who influenced their family history as administrators of property, as consumers of the patrimony, and as mothers.

2. The Asian/African Family

GENERAL

1202. FRUIN, Mark. "Sources for the Study of Population in Premodern Japan." The Family in Historical Perspectives Newsletter, No. 7 (Winter 1974), pp. 11-14.
Shows that the Japanese attempts to register people by Buddhist temple affiliation provide excellent sources for the demographic analysis of the Tokugawa period.

1203. GUPTA, Kuntesh. "Structure and Organization of the
          Indian Family: The Emerging Patterns." International
          Journal of Contemporary Sociology, 10 (1973), 163-82.
       Reviews Indian family studies since 1955 and their class-
       ification of the structure and organization of Indian
       families into several patterns of family living.

1204. PATTERSON, Maureen L. P. "Chitpavan Brahman Family His-
          tories: Sources for a Study of Social Structure and
          Social Change in Maharashtra." Structure and Change
          in Indian Society. Ed. Milton Singer and Bernard S.
          Cohn. Chicago: Aldine Publishing Co., 1968, pp.
          397-411.
       Examines family histories published between 1914 and
       1963 in Maharshtra to determine their validity as in-
       dices of social change and the dynamics of the Chit-
       pavan caste.

1205. SHAH, A. M. "Basic Terms and Concepts in the Study of
          the Family in India." Indian Economic and Social
          History Review, 1 (1964), 1-36.
       Examines basic Indian concepts and terms--family, extend-
       ed family, lineage, and so on--as used by various scholars
       in their studies of the family in India.

BIRTH CONTROL

1206. MUSALLAM, Basim Fuad. "Sex and Society in Islam: The
          Sanction and Medieval Techniques of Birth Control."
          Diss. Harvard Univ., 1973.
       Examines the extent of contraception and abortion in
       the medieval Arab Middle East as revealed in Islamic
       jurisprudence, fatawa, medicine, erotics, and materia
       medica. Deals with both legal and religious attitudes
       as well as techniques of birth control.

1207. THAPAR, Savitri. "Family Planning in India." Population
          Studies, 17 (1963), 4-19.
       Discusses the history of Indian family planning from the
       early writings of S.P.K. Wattel to the acceptance of pop-
       ulation control by the 1935 Indian National Congress.

CHILDREN

1208. GOODY, Jack R. "Adoption in Cross-Cultural Perspective."
          Comparative Studies in Society and History, 11 (1969),
          55-78.
       Examines the reasons for the uneven distribution of
       adoption between Eurasian and African societies, and
       analyzes the functions of adoption, notably its relation
       to the rise of vertical inheritance.

1209. MEAD, Margaret. Coming of Age in Samoa. New York:
          W. Morrow and Co., 1928.
       Questions the inevitability of the difficulties and

conflicts of adolescence, and argues that behavior and
personality are culture bound.

1210.   RADDOCK, David M. "Growing Up in New China: A Twist
        in the Circle of Filial Piety." History of Child-
        hood Quarterly, 2 (1974), 201-20.
        Shows that modern Chinese youth are not authority-de-
        pendent and impassive. Although filiality is upheld,
        the present move toward horizontal parent-child relation-
        ships encourages youthful rebellion.

1211.   VATSA, Rajendra Singh. "The Movement Against Infant-Mar-
        riages in India, 1860-1914." Journal of Indian His-
        tory, 49 (1971), 289-303.
        Illustrates how English and Indian reformers succeeded
        in raising the age of consummation of marriage for girls
        from 10 to 14, despite rigid Hindu opposition.

1212.   YOKOE, Katsumi. "Historical Trends in Home Discipline."
        Families in East and West. Ed. Reuben Hill and Rene
        Konig. Paris: Mouton, 1970, pp. 175-86.
        Examines historical trends in the family life of the
        Japanese, including parent-child relations, childrearing,
        and schooling.

DEMOGRAPHY

1213.   BASAVARAJAPPA, K. G. "The Influence of Fluctuations in
        Economic Conditions on Fertility and Marriage Rates,
        Australia 1920-21 to 1937-38 and 1946-47 to 1966-67."
        Population Studies, 25 (1971), 39-54.
        Demonstrates that economic factors had a noticeable neg-
        ative influence on Australian marriage and confinement
        rates during the years 1920 to 1938, but a much lesser
        effect on post-war rates.

1214.   BASAVARAJAPPA, K. G. "Pre-Marital Pregnancies and
        Ex-Nuptial Births in Australia, 1911-66." Austra-
        lian and New Zealand Journal of Sociology, 4 (1968),
        126-45.
        Illustrates that Australian pre-marital pregnancies
        declined from 1911 to 1914, peaked in 1928-33, fell to
        their lowest level in 1945, and then rose slightly after
        1945 in the younger age cohorts. Ex-nuptial births de-
        clined from 1911 to 1950, followed by a rapid rise after
        1950.

1215.   ENG, Robert Y., and Thomas C. SMITH. "Peasant Families
        and Population Control in Eighteenth-Century Japan."
        Journal of Interdisciplinary History, 6 (1976), 417-45.
        Analyzes why marital fertility was low in 18th century
        Japan despite an expanding economy. Concludes that in-
        fanticide was widely practiced as a means of population
        control.

175

1216. HANLEY, Susan B. "Fertility, Mortality, and Life Expec-
       tancy in Pre-Modern Japan." Population Studies, 28
       (1974), 127-42.
       Concludes that fertility and mortality rates in 18th
       century Japanese villages were relatively low, and that
       life expectancy was similar to pre-1850 Europe. Thus,
       industrialization had a minimal effect on Japanese demo-
       graphic patterns.

1217. HANLEY, Susan B. "Toward an Analysis of Demographic
       and Economic Development in Tokugawa Japan: A Vil-
       lage Study." Journal of Asian Studies, 31-3 (1972),
       515-38.
       Argues that pre-modern Japanese villages controlled
       population through various birth limitation practices
       such as short childbearing cycles, infanticide, and
       abortion.

1218. HAYAMI, Akira. "The Demographic Analysis of a Village
       in Tokugawa Japan: Kando-Shinden of Owari Province,
       1778-1971." Keio Economic Studies, 5 (1968), 50-88.
       Discusses the problems of census materials in Tokugawa
       Japan, and uses family reconstitution methods to reveal
       changes in population, family size, age composition,
       and vital rates in a Japanese village.

1219. HAYAMI, Akira. "The Demographic Aspects of a Village
       in Tokugawa Japan." Population and Economics: Pro-
       ceedings of Section V of the Fourth Congress of the
       International Economic History Association, 1968.
       Ed. Paul Deprez. Winnipeg: Univ. of Manitoba Press,
       1970, pp. 109-25.
       Uses traditional population analysis and family recon-
       stitution to examine the demographic aspects of a Japanese
       village from 1691 to 1871, including household size, age
       at marriage, fertility rates, and infant mortality.

1220. RELE, J. R. "Some Aspects of Family and Fertility in
       India." Population Studies, 15 (1962), 267-78.
       Analyzes rural households in modern India in terms of
       fertility, age at marriage, birth intervals, and child-
       lessness.

1221. ROSS, Robert. "The 'White' Population of South Africa
       in the Eighteenth Century." Population Studies, 29
       (1975), 217-30.
       Examines population growth of the Afrikaners with data
       on fertility, family size, age at marriage, and nuptial-
       ity.

1222. TAEUBER, Irene B. "Japan's Demographic Transition Re-
       Examined." Population Studies, 14 (1960), 28-39.
       Argues that the concept of demographic transition pre-
       sents major research problems, especially the inter-
       relation of demographic change and cultural and social

factors.

DIVORCE

1223. ANDERSON, J. N. D. "Reforms in the Law of Divorce in the Muslin World." Studia Islamica, 31 (1970), 41-52.
Notes that divorce law legislation in the Muslin world began in the early 20th century. As a result, most Moslem wives can now obtain a divorce on several grounds.

1224. SARMA, R. Naga Raja. "Ethics of Divorce in Ancient India." International Journal of Ethics, 41 (1931), 329-42.
Cites ancient authors of the Smriti texts to show that Hindu law has permitted divorce. Also criticizes contemporary Indian legislators for their failure at divorce law reform.

DOMESTIC LIFE AND CUSTOMS

1225. AQUINA, Mary. "A Note on Missionary Influence on Shona Marriage." Rhodes-Livingstone Journal, 33 (1963), 68-79.
Shows that Jesuit influence significantly altered Southern Rhodesian marriage patterns, especially parental control over mate selection.

1226. BIGGERSTAFF, Knight. "The Peasant Family: The Chinese Large-Family, Its Role and Recent Trends." The Cultural Approach to History. Ed. Caroline Farrar Ware. New York: Columbia Univ. Press, 1940, pp. 109-24.
Discusses the importance of the large-family in Chinese life, its strengths and weaknesses, and investigates the factors which have been threatening the large-family.

1227. CHANDA, Sudhendu. "Ancient Marriage in India." Social Welfare, May 1971, pp. 15, 22.
Discusses the eight kinds of marriage mentioned in ancient Indian literature and the rites associated with each.

1228. CHANG, Dae Hong. "The Historical Development of the Korean Socio-Family System Since 1392--A Legalistic Interpretation." University of Manila Journal of East Asiatic Studies, 11 (1967), 1-124.
Discusses the changing structure and function of Korean family systems as well as rules and customs governing matrimony from 1392 to the present.

1229. DARDESS, John W. "The Cheng Communal Family Social Organization and Neo-Confucianism in Yuan and Early Ming China." Harvard Journal of Asiatic Studies, 34 (1974), 7-52.
Investigates the history and organization of a family

commune--the Cheng family--and examines how Neo-Con-
fuscian writers in the Yuan and Early Ming periods
sought to uphold the communal family as a social model.

1230.   EBERHARD, Wolfram. "The Upperclass Family in Traditional
        China." The Family in History. Ed. Charles E. Rosen-
        berg. Philadelphia: Univ. of Pennsylvania Press,
        1975, pp. 59-94.
        Examines the traditional Chinese family as a need-ful-
        filling institution, how it changed, and how it oper-
        ated in the political realities of history.

1231.   FREEDMAN, Maurice. "Chinese Kinship and Marriage in
        Early Singapore." Journal of Southeast Asian His-
        tory, 3 (1962), 65-73.
        Shows that kinship and marriage customs in 19th-century
        Singapore differed significantly among Baba and non-Baba
        Chinese with the former emphasizing strong kinship ties.

1232.   FREEDMAN, Maurice. "The Family in China, Past and Pre-
        sent." Pacific Affairs, 34 (1961-62), 323-36.
        Examines the relationship between the pre-modern Chinese
        family, kinship, and the state. Also discusses tensions
        inherent in the family and the impact of communism on
        the contemporary Chinese family.

1233.   FREEDMAN, Maurice, ed. Family and Kinship in Chinese
        Society. Stanford: Stanford Univ. Press, 1970.
        An anthology which examines the Chinese family, marriage,
        and kinship, including childrearing, the family in modern
        Chinese fiction, land and lineage, and Chinese genealogy.

1234.   GOODY, Jack R. "Class and Marriage in Asia and Eurasia."
        American Journal of Sociology, 76 (1971), 585-603.
        Argues that out-marriage and bridewealth are character-
        istic of African states and that they tend to strengthen
        social and cultural ties within a society.

1235.   INDEN, Richard B. Marriage and Rank in Bengali Culture:
        A History of Caste and Clan in Middle-Period Bengal.
        Berkeley: Univ. of California Press, 1975.
        Examines Hindu and Kaystha castes from 1500 to 1850, and
        explains how clans were graded within a caste and how
        marriages were arranged between and within grades.

1236.   KAPADIA, Kanailal M. Marriage and Family in India. 3rd
        ed. New York: Oxford Univ. Press, 1966.
        Studies Hindu marriage law, age at marriage, mate choice,
        status of women, and the joint-family.

1237.   KATRAK, Jamshed Cawasji. Marriage in Ancient Iran.
        Bombay: n.p., 1965.
        Argues that ancient Iranians practiced monogamy, strictly
        regulated divorce and inter-marriages, and prohibited
        consanguineous marriages.

1238. KHATRI, A. A. "Analysis of Fiction for Comparative Study
       of Family Systems." Paper delivered at the Society
       for the Study of Social Problems, San Francisco, Au-
       gust 1975.
       Surveys Indian social novels during three time periods to
       study their portrayal of marriage and family relationships,
       and discusses a methodological approach for the analysis
       of fiction.

1239. LEVY, Marion Joseph. The Family Revolution in Modern
       China. Cambridge: Harvard Univ. Press, 1949.
       Describes the traditional and ideal family structure
       of China and the transition away from traditional kin-
       ship grouping.

1240. MCCULLOUGH, William H. "Japanese Marriage Institutions
       in the Heian Period." Harvard Journal of Asiatic
       Studies, 27 (1967), 103-67.

1241. MADAN, Triloki Nath. Family and Kinship: A Study of
       the Pandits of Rural Kashmir. London: Asia Publish-
       ing House, 1965.
       Discusses the kinship patterns, marriage, and homesteads
       of Brahman villagers. Contends that the disruption of
       large households is not a sign of familial decay, but
       the conclusion of individual family cycles.

1242. MEHTA, Aban B. The Domestic Servant Class. Bombay:
       Popular Book Depot, 1960.
       Examines the working and social conditions of servants
       in Bombay, India.

1243. MEYER, Johann Jakob. "Marriage Ceremonies in Ancient
       India, As Portrayed in Her Epic Literature." Open
       Court, 31 (1917), 203-7.
       Uses ancient Indian marriage rituals to determine views
       about marriage, courtship, and love.

1244. MITRA, Veda. Happy Married Life in Ancient India. New
       Delhi: Arya Book Depot, 1965.
       Deals with three aspects of life in ancient India--edu-
       cation, the family, and the status of women--and argues
       that egalitarian relationships were prevalent in ancient
       Indian society as was the joint family system.

1245. SHARMA, Ram Sharon. "Caste and Marriage in Ancient In-
       dia (c. 600 B.C.-c. 500 A.D.)." Journal of the Bihar
       Research Society, 40 (1954), 38-54.
       Discusses the influence of caste upon approved and dis-
       couraged forms of marriage, divorce, and polygamy. Also
       discusses inter-caste unions and their implications.

1246. SINGER, Milton. "The Indian Joint Family in Modern In-
       dustry." Structure and Change in Indian Society.
       Ed. Milton Singer and Bernard S. Cohn. Chicago:

Aldine Publishing Co., 1968, pp. 423-52.
Uses family histories of outstanding industrial leaders
in Madras City to examine the relationship of the Indian
joint family to urbanization and industrialization.

1247. STERNBACK, Ludwik. Forms of Marriage in Ancient India
       and Their Development. Bombay: n.p., 1951.

1248. WILKINSON, Hiram Parkes. The Family in Classical China.
       London: Macmillan, 1926.
       Examines Chinese family life, land tenure, mother-right,
       infanticide, family nomenclature, and the social origins
       of the Chinese family.

1249. WOLF, Margery. The House of Lim: A Study of a Chinese
       Farm Family. New York: Appleton-Century-Crofts,
       1968.
       Analyzes the emergence and disintegration of a prosperous
       Chinese joint family, and describes the interrelations of
       family members.

FAMILY COMPOSITION AND STRUCTURE

1250. HAYAMI, Akira, and Nobuka UCHIDA. "Size of Household in
       a Japanese County Throughout the Tokugawa Era."
       Household and Family in Past Time. Ed. Peter Laslett
       and Richard Wall. Cambridge: Cambridge Univ. Press,
       1972, pp. 473-516.
       Examines the structure and size of preindustrial Japanese
       households, and concludes that small households were pre-
       dominant.

1251. NAKANE, Chie. "An Interpretation of the Size and Struc-
       ture of the Household in Japan Over Three Centuries."
       Household and Family in Past Time. Ed. Peter Laslett
       and Richard Wall. Cambridge: Cambridge Univ. Press,
       1972, pp. 517-43.
       Argues that mean household size in Japan has changed
       very little from the early 17th century to 1955.

1252. SMITH, Robert J. "Small Families, Small Households,
       and Residential Instability: Town and City in Pre-
       Modern Japan." Household and Family in Past Time.
       Ed. Peter Laslett and Richard Wall. Cambridge:
       Cambridge Univ. Press, 1972, pp. 429-72.
       Finds that small households were prevalent in preindus-
       trial Japan and that the small family made mobility
       easier.

1253. YIH-FU, Ruey. "Changing Structure of the Chinese Family."
       Bulletin of the Department of Archaelogy and Anthro-
       pology, 17-18 (1961), 1-14.
       Examines the changing structure of the Chinese family
       from the feudal period of clan-domination through the
       imperial period of family-domination where family

structure shifted from stem to lineal.

1254. ZARCO, Ricardo M. "The Chinese Family Structures in the Philippines." The Chinese in the Philippines, 1570-1770. Ed. Alfonso Felix. Manila: Solidaridad Publishing House, 1966, I, pp. 211-22.
Discusses the differences between the Chinese and Filipino families and the uniqueness of Chinese-Filipino marriages before the 17th century. Notes that in rural areas the Chinese family approximated the Filipino bilateral family (nuclear) while in urban areas it approximated the classical Chinese form (extended).

FAMILY LAW AND INHERITANCE

1255. CHIU, Vermier Y. "Marriage Laws of the Ch'ing Dynasty, the Republic of China, and Communist China." Contemporary China, 2 (1956), 64-72.
Discusses and compares the marriage laws of China in an historical perspective, stressing the problems of marriage in Communist China.

1256. DERRETT, J. Duncan M. "The History of the Juridical Framework of the Joint Hindu Family." Contributions to Indian Sociology, 6 (1962), 17-47.
Uses dharmashastra texts to examine the joint family as a legal institution, including its membership, acquisition and management of property, and changing functions of the joint family over time.

1257. GOODY, Jack R. "Inheritance, Property and Marriage in Africa and Eurasia." Sociology, 3 (1969), 55-76.
Compares the Eurasian system of inheritance where property is distributed directly from parent to child with African systems where property devolves between persons of the same sex, laterally and lineally.

1258. GOODY, Jack R. "Marriage, Prestations, Inheritance and Descent in Pre-Industrial Societies." Journal of Comparative Family Studies, 1 (1970), 37-54.
Shows the relationships between marriage prestation, inheritance systems, and kinship. Contends that the dowry system and bridewealth are not antithetical

1259. GOODY, Jack R. "Strategies of Heirship." Comparative Studies in Society and History, 15 (1973), 3-20.
Reviews the various strategies by which major African and Eurasian societies deal with the problem of heirship--especially its material aspects--in an historical perspective.

1260. MEIJER, M. J. "Early Communist Marriage Legislation in China." Contemporary China, 6 (1962), 84-102.
Examines marriage regulations implemented by the Chinese Communists from 1931 to 1950 and their impact on the

family, divorce, children, and spouse relationships.

1261. NAKAGAWA, Zennosuke. "A Century of Marriage Law."
Japan Quarterly, 10 (1963), 182-92.
Examines the changes in marriage law in Japan since
WWII and the ways in which the old system broke
down.

KINSHIP

1262. PASTERNAK, Burton. "Atrophy of Patrilineal Bonds in
a Chinese Village in Historical Perspective." Ethno-
history, 15 (1968), 293-327.
Argues that the role of kin bonds decreased over time
despite the lack of urbanization and industrialization
in a Chinese community because of the social and ecological necessity for extensive and continuous cooperation among non-kin.

1263. WILSON, Monica. "Changes in Social Structure in Southern Africa: The Relevance of Kinship Studies to the
Historian." African Societies in Southern Africa:
Historical Studies. Ed. Leonard Monteath Thompson.
New York: Praeger, 1969, pp. 71-85.
Argues that kinship is relevant to the African historian
since kinship structure affects the strength of certain
lineages, the spread of language, and the growth of
kingdoms.

SEXUALITY

1264. CHAKRABERTY, Chandra. Sex Life in Ancient India: An
Explanatory and Comparative Study. Calcutta: K.L.
Mukhopadhyay, 1963.
Discusses tribal migrations, comparative Indo-European
etymology, health and youth, and sex life in ancient
India.

1265. GULIK, Robert Han van. Sexual Life in Ancient China:
A Preliminary Survey of Chinese Sex and Society from
ca. 1500 B.C. till 1644 A.D. Leiden: E.J. Brill,
1961.
Focuses on various aspects of ancient Chinese sexual
life, including sex manuals, family life, prostitution,
medical and erotic literature, and sex customs..

1266. HU, Chi-hsi. "The Sexual Revolution in the Kiangsi
Soviet." Chinese Quarterly, 59 (1974), 477-90.
Shows that beginning in the 1930s, Chinese communists
wished to free marriage from its Confucian traditions
and began experimentation in new, more liberal sexual
patterns.

1267. MEYER, Johann Jakob. Sexual Life in Ancient India:
A Study in the Comparative History of Indian Culture.

2 vols. London: Routledge & Kegan Paul, 1930.
Discusses maidenhood, marriage ceremonies, family life,
sexual relations, concepts of love, and the role of
women in ancient India.

1268. SUGIYAMA, Sadao, and William J. SCHULL. "Consanguineous
Marriages in Feudal Japan." Monumenta Nipponica,
October 1959-January 1960, pp. 126-41.
Examines the frequency of marriages involving biological-
ly related individuals, and finds that in feudal Japan
these marries varied considerably among families, ranging from a few to twenty percent.

WOMEN

1269. KAPUR, Promilla. Marriage and the Working Woman in
India. New Delhi: Vikas Publications, 1970.
Examines marital adjustment of educated working women
in India, and concludes that the woman's happiness in
marriage is largely determined by what she was prior
to marriage.

1270. MEER, Fatima. "Women and the Family in the Indian En-
clave in South Africa." Feminist Studies, 1 (1972),
33-47.
Discusses the oppression of women in a sub-culture and
the conservative effect of the dominant South African
culture on the Indian family's treatment of women.

1271. WOLF, Margery. Women and the Family in Rural Taiwan.
Stanford: Stanford Univ. Press, 1972.
Studies the life cycle of Taiwanese country women, their
relationship to the kinship system, and the interrelationships among women in the community.

CHAPTER V:

FAMILY HISTORY PROJECTS

GENERAL

1272. ANGLIN, Jay P. "The Fundamentals of Genealogy: A
      Neglected but Fertile New Field for Professional
      Historians." Southern Quarterly, 13 (1975), 145-
      50.
      Concludes that recognition by historians of genealogy
      and a closer rapport between professionals in both
      fields will prove mutually beneficial. Proposes his-
      tory courses utilizing genealogical techniques.

1273. COHEN, Lizabeth. "How to Teach Family History by Using
      an Historic House." Social Education, 39 (1975),
      466-9.
      Discusses the educational potential in the historic
      house in terms of family history, notably familial
      roles and economic status.

1274. DONNE, John, and P. M. TAYLER. "Conferences on Family
      History at Bristol University." Genealogists'
      Magazine, March 1972, pp. 16-20.
      Reports on the family history short courses given by
      the University of Bristol, the topics discussed, and
      organization of the courses.

1275. HAYS, Samuel P. "History and Genealogy: Patterns of
      Change and Prospects for Cooperation." Prologue,
      7 (1975), 39-43, 81-4, 187-91.
      Argues that closer cooperation between genealogy and
      history would be mutually beneficial, particularly
      with regard to a standard approach of preserving and
      organizing those sources used by family and social
      historians.

1276. KYVIG, David E. "Family History: New Opportunities
      for Archivists." American Archivist, 38 (1975),
      509-19.
      Discusses the approaches taken by family historians
      and the necessity of archivists to be aware of both
      these approaches and the materials used in family
      history and biography.

FAMILY BIOGRAPHIES

1277. AMERICA THE BEAUTIFUL FUND. Old Glory: A Pictorial
      Report on the Grass Roots History Movement and
      The First Hometown History Primer. New York: War-
      ner Books, 1973.
      An excellent manual for family and community studies
      containing suggestions and guidelines for self-histories,

185

family histories, and community histories.

1278. BROWN, Richard, and Tamara K. HAREVEN. "Writing the
Social History of One's Family..." Worcester:
Clark Univ., 1973.
An excellent guide to writing a family history, with
detailed instructions on format, interviewing techniques,
interview questions, and source materials--primary and
secondary.

1279. CULBERT, David H. "Family History Projects: The Scholarly Value of an Informal Sample." American Archivist, 38 (1975), 533-41.
Explain what kinds of information come from family history projects, and suggests the scholarly value of such
an informal sampling of the changes in American society
as reflected in the family and the local community.

1280. CULBERT, David H. "Undergraduates as Historians: Family
History Projects Add Meaning to an Introductory Survey."
History Teacher, 7 (1973), 441-51.
Contains guidelines for family history projects, with detailed explanations of data collection, interviewing, organization and style as well as problems and advantages
in using such projects as a teaching strategy.

1281. HAREVEN, Tamara K., and Richard D. BROWN. "Student as
a Social Historian: Writing the Social History of
One's Own Family as a Teaching Device." Paper delivered at the Organization of American Historians,
Washington, D.C., April 1972.
Discusses the use of family history projects as a teaching strategy.

1282. JEFFREY, Kirk. "Write a History of Your Own Family:
Further Observations and Suggestions for Instructors."
History Teacher, 7 (1974), 365-73.
Contains a good discussion of the conceptual, inter-
pretative, and analytical problems confronted in family
history projects when used as a teaching device.

1283. MURPHY, Brendan J. "History Through the Family: I."
Teaching History, 2 (1971), 1-8.
Argues that family history projects as a teaching device
allow students to deal with primary materials and confront methodological problems faced by professional historians. Stresses the need for faculty guidance and
direction.

1284. STEEL, Donald John, and Lawrence TAYLOR. Family History
in Schools. Sussex: Phillimore & Co., 1973.
Argues that family history projects provide an excellent
educational tool and have much potential for interdisciplinary work. Includes examples, project reports, and
suggestions for organizing a project.

1285. STEEL, Donald John, and Lawrence TAYLOR. "History Through
       the Family: II." Teaching History, 2 (1971), 9-14.
       Discusses interviewing and material access problems in-
       volved in student family history projects and offers
       solutions and suggestions for writing family biographies.

1286. WATTS, Jim, and Allen F. DAVIS. Generations: Your Fam-
       ily in Modern American History. New York: Alfred A.
       Knopf, 1974.
       A textbook aimed at helping students understand them-
       selves and their family, and how their families have
       been influenced by historical forces and events, es-
       pecially movement and change. Contains good suggestions
       and guidelines for writing a family history.

GENEALOGICAL SOURCES

1287. BESTERMAN, Theodore. Family History: A Bibliography
       of Bibliographies. Totowa, N.J.: Rowman and Little-
       field, 1971.
       Contains entries on genealogy appearing in Besterman's
       World Bibliography, organized by periodicals, general,
       and countries.

1288. COLKET, Meredith Bright, and Frank E. BRIDGES. A Guide
       to Genealogical Records in the National Archives.
       Washington: GPO, 1964.
       Describes federal records at the National Archives, in-
       cluding census, land, and military records useful to
       family historians.

1289. DOANE, Gilbert Harry. Searching for Your Ancestors.
       Minneapolis: Univ. of Minnesota Press, 1974.
       Discusses the techniques of genealogical searching with
       discussions on family papers, local records, cemeteries,
       and reference books and materials.

1290. EVERTON, George B., and Gunnar RASMUSON. The Handy
       Book for Genealogists. Logan, Utah: Everton, 1971.
       Discusses how to do genealogical research in a straight
       forward manner, and includes data on state and county
       records.

1291. FILBY, P. William, comp. American & British Genealogy
       & Heraldry: A List of Selected Books. Chicago:
       ALA, 1970.
       An excellent, annotated bibliography of 1800 titles on
       family history and genealogy organized by general refer-
       ence, areas, individual states, and countries.

1292. GARDNER, David F., and Frank SMITH. Genealogical Research
       in England and Wales. 3 vol. Salt Lake City: Book-
       craft, 1956-65.
       Discusses in detail virtually all records needed for
       genealogical research, methods of research, and problems

of source materials from 1538 to the present.

1293. GREENWOOD, Val D. The Researcher's Guide to American
      Genealogy. Baltimore: Genealogical Society, 1973.
      Examines American records and their background, methods
      of research, and is an excellent guidebook to genea-
      logical research in the United States.

1294. KIRKHAM, E. Kay. Simplified Genealogy for Americans.
      Salt Lake City: Desert Book Co., 1968.
      Examines the problems, techniques, and sources of genea-
      logy and is a good introductory how-to-do-it manual.

1295. PHILLIMORE, W. P. W. How to Write the History of a
      Family: A Guide for the Genealogist. 1887; rpt.
      Detroit: Gale, 1972.
      Discusses records and methods of genealogical research,
      especially in Britain. Remains a good guide to tracing
      family histories, despite its early publication date.

1296. PINE, Leslie Gilbert. The Genealogist's Encyclopedia.
      New York: Weybright & Talley, 1969.
      Reviews the basic records in European genealogical re-
      search, and discusses heraldry, titles, peerage law,
      and orders of chivalry.

1297. RUBINCAM, Milton, ed. Genealogical Research Methods
      and Sources. Washington: n.p., 1960.
      Includes articles on genealogical materials and methods
      written for beginning and advanced students.

1298. SCHREINER-YANTIS, Netti. Genealogical Books in Print.
      Springfield, Va.: n.p., 1975.
      Includes over 5,000 in-print titles of books dealing with
      genealogical materials, methods, and research. An excel-
      lent bibliographical guide.

1299. SOCIETY OF GENEALOGISTS. Genealogists' Handbook. London:
      Society of Genealogists, 1969.
      Discusses genealogical sources for the beginner, including
      reference works, census and parish registers, wills, pro-
      fessional and educational records, and local and national
      record offices.

1300. SPUFFORD, Peter. "Recent Developments in Genealogy."
      Amateur Historian, 7 (1967), 178-81.
      Discusses research techniques and materials in genealogy,
      including family papers, Bibles, vital statistics, census
      and tax returns, and local records.

1301. STEVENSON, Noel C. Search and Research: The Researcher's
      Handbook. Salt Lake City: Desert Book Co., 1959.
      Examines primarily American genealogical sources and mat-
      erials, and explains basic genealogical research techniques.

1302. WRIGHT, Norman Edgar. <u>Building an American Pedigree</u>:
      <u>A Study in Genealogy</u>. Provo, Utah: Brigham Young
      Univ., 1974.
      Surveys the research methods and procedures in genealogy
      and provides extensive reference material as well as
      examples and illustrations.

Hiner, N., 708
Hinton, J., 938
Hirsh, J., 1020
Hoeber, D., 1107
Hole, C., 398, 449
Hollingsworth, T., 76, 77, 536
Holman, J., 336
Holmes, U., 246
Holmsen, A., 582
Homans, G., 260
Hopkins, K., 175, 178
Horn, P., 583
Hoskins, W., 367
Howard, G., 49, 463
Howard, R., 125
Howell, C., 430
Howington, N., 464
Howse, M., 465
Hu, C., 1266
Hufton, O., 450
Hughes, D., 261, 262, 272
Hunt, D., 337
Hurstfield, J., 431, 432
Hurvitz, N., 584
Hyman, H., 1171

Ilieva, N., 610
Illick, J., 709
Inden, R., 1235
Indiana University Library, 1129
Inkeles, A., 163
Ironside, C., 755
Israel, S., 50

Jackson, D., 368
Jackson, J., 1181
Jadin, L., 413
Jaffe, A., 880
Jaffe, F., 1086
James, E., 466
Jeffrey, K., 20, 939, 940, 1282
Jeger, L., 488
Jensen, R., 21, 22, 1060
Jester, A., 756
Johansen, H., 78
Johnson, C., 1132
Johnson, G., 941
Johnson, J., 319, 320, 321
Johnson, R., 813
Johnson, W., 640
Jones, B., 1151
Jones, J., 1021, 1124
Jones, R., 369

Kanter, R., 942

Kantrow, L., 94
Kapadia, K., 1236
Kapur, P., 1269
Kardiner, A., 107
Karpis, M., 585
Katrak, J., 1237
Katz, J., 399
Katz, M., 835, 943, 983
Kaufman, M., 308
Keim, C., 777
Keller, S., 1108
Kellum, B., 247
Kelly, H., 284
Keniston, K., 108
Kennedy, A., 814
Kennedy, D., 815
Kennedy, R., 881, 882
Kent, F., 433
Kephart, W., 944
Kermack, W., 370
Kern, S., 641, 642
Kett, J., 836
Keyssar, A., 793
Khatri, A., 1238
Kiefer, O., 226
Kimball, S., 575
Kirkham, E., 1294
Kish, L., 147
Kitchin, S., 568
Kittel, M., 285, 286
Klapisch, C., 414
Kleinberg, S., 1061, 1062
Knights, P., 79
Knodel, J., 503, 537, 538, 539,
    540, 541
Kobrin, F., 1063, 1097
Komarovsky, M., 945, 1109
Koomen, W., 586
Kovalevskii, M., 467
Krause, J., 80, 273, 542
Krier, D., 371, 375
Ktorides, I., 757
Kuchenman, C., 372
Kuhn, A., 838
Kyvig, D., 1276

Labinjoh, J., 1152
Lacey, W., 193
Lader, L., 816
Laing, R., 109
Lammermeier, P., 1172
Landes, D., 627
Langer, W., 489, 504, 543
Lansing, J., 147
Lantz, H., 758, 759, 760

195